New Directions in
Remedial Education

New Directions in Remedial Education

Edited and introduced by

Colin J. Smith

University of Birmingham

in conjunction with the
National Association for Remedial Education

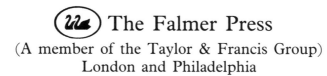 The Falmer Press

(A member of the Taylor & Francis Group)
London and Philadelphia

UK   The Falmer Press, Falmer House, Barcombe, Lewes, East Sussex, BN8 5DL

USA   The Falmer Press, Taylor & Francis Inc., 242 Cherry Street, Philadelphia, PA 19106-1906

First published 1985

Library of Congress Cataloging in Publication Data

Main entry under title:

New directions in remedial education.

(New directions series)
Includes index.
1. Remedial teaching—Addresses, essays, lectures.
2. Learning disabilities—Great Britain—Addresses, essays, lectures. 3. Educational tests and measurements —Great Britain—Addresses, essays, lectures.
4. Curriculum planning—Great Britain—Addresses, essays, lectures. I. Smith, Colin, 1938–   . II. National Association for Remedial Education (Great Britain).
III. Series: New directions series (Falmer Press).
LB1029.R4N445 1985 371.9 85-6757
ISBN 1-85000-064-6
ISBN 1-85000-065-4 (pbk.)

Jacket design by Leonard Williams

Typeset in 10½/12 Plantin by
Imago Publishing Ltd, Thame, Oxon.

Printed in Great Britain by Taylor & Francis (Printers) Ltd, Basingstoke

Contents

General Editor's Preface
Philip H. Taylor   vii

Acknowledgement   viii

Glossary   ix

Introduction: New Directions in Remedial Education
Colin J. Smith   1

1   Assumptions About the Nature of Remedial Education

Introduction   4

Whose Remedies, Whose Ills? A Critical Review of Remedial
Education
Michael Golby and John R Gulliver   7

The Teacher's Own Resources
Ronald Gulliford   20

Remedial Education Post-Warnock: Interment or Revival?
J.B. Edwards   30

The Changing Role of the Remedial Teacher
Mike Laskier   39

Remedial Education: The Challenge for Trainers
Charles W. Gains   50

2   School Organization and Classroom Management

Introduction   60

Slow Learner Provision in Secondary Schools: A Review of the
NFER Research Project
Louise Clunies-Ross   63

Learning Difficulties in the Primary School: An In-service Training Initiative
Mel Ainscow and Jim Muncey   77

Assessing the Advantages of Team Teaching in Remedial Education: The Remedial Teacher's Role
Neil Ferguson and Muriel Adams   92

Adopting a Resources Approach
Elizabeth Jones and Sandra Berrick   103

Helping Colleagues Cope: A Consultant Role for the Remedial Teacher
Colin J. Smith   112

3   **Pupil Assessment and Curriculum Development**

Introduction   120

Some Trends in Pupil Evaluation: The Growing Importance of the Teacher's Role
K.F. Cornwall   123

Teaching with Precision
Ted Raybould and John Solity   132

Recent Influences on the Assessment of Reading Difficulties and the Concept of Specific Difficulties
Robin C. Richmond   145

Towards Success in Mathematics
Alec A. Williams   161

Teachers' Involvement in Curriculum Change
Mike Hinson   177

Beyond the Sabre-toothed Curriculum
Paul Widlake   190

Contributors   203

Index   205

General Editor's Preface

Remedial education represents a long tradition of care and concern for those youngsters in our schools less able to learn than their fellows. It is a concern on which the *Warnock Report*, and what is to follow from it by way of integrating children with special needs, depends in good measure for its success. This is but one of the points made very clearly through this reader on remedial education.

Colin Smith's collection of papers, many original, shows just how much remedial education does in our schools; just how much a part of the educational scene it has become. But he also shows how in changing times the taken-for-granted assumptions of special education have to be examined, and, if necessary, be realigned with new realities.

This reader is both a guide to remedial education at the latter part of the twentieth century and a mine for students from which to quarry what they need (and ought) to know about those youngsters who, for one reason or another, find learning in our schools difficult, and how best to alleviate their problems.

Philip H. Taylor
Birmingham
April 1985

Acknowledgement

The National Association for Remedial Education has provided, for many years, the main forum for the dissemination of knowledge about the theory and practice of remedial education.

Any discussion of new directions in this area must inevitably draw extensively from the pages of *Remedial Education* and grateful thanks are due to NARE not only for their permission to publish so many extracts from their journal but also for their support and active participation in the production of this book.

Colin J. Smith
Birmingham
April 1985

Glossary

At a time when terminology in special education is undergoing a considerable change as a result of the 1981 Education Act, it may be useful, particularly for overseas readers, to have an explanation of some of the terms and abbreviations familiar to those well versed in the current debate on remedial and special education but perhaps less known to other readers.

Children with learning difficulties Descriptive term which the Warnock Report (1978) recommended 'should be used in future to describe both those children who are currently categorized as educationally subnormal and those with educational difficulties who are often at present the concern of remedial services.' Learning difficulties might be described as "mild", "moderate" or "severe". The Education Act 1981 uses the term 'learning difficulty' in a broader way. According to this Act a child has a 'learning difficulty' if he has a significantly greater difficulty in learning than the majority of children of his age or he has a disability which prevents or hinders the use of educational facilities generally provided within the area of his local education authority.

Education Act 1981 An Act to make provision with respect to children with special educational needs (Eliz.II c.60 30 October 1981). DES Circular 8/81 explains the effect of the provisions of the Act. DES Circular 1/83 considers the implications of the Act and offers advice to local education authorities on its implementation.

Special educational needs Defined by the Education Act 1981 in terms of a child having a learning difficulty which calls for special educational provision to be made.

Special educational provision Defined by the Education Act 1981 in relation to educational provision 'additional to, or otherwise different from' provision generally made for children of a given age by the local education authority concerned.

Statement of special educational needs Formal written statement which is maintained by a local education authority showing a child's special educational needs as assessed by the authority, the special educational provision which the authority deems necessary and the school or other arrangements considered appropriate to meet those needs.

Glossary

Warnock Report   Special Educational Needs. Report of the Committee of
  Enquiry into the Education of Handicapped Children and Young People.
  Cmnd 7212, HMSO, 1978.

ESN(M)   Educationally subnormal (moderate)
ESN(S)   Educationally subnormal (severe)
EWO   Educational Welfare Officer
INSET   In-service education and training for teachers
NARE   National Association for Remedial Education
NATFHE   National Association of Teachers in Further and Higher
           Education
NCSE   National Council for Special Education
NFER   National Foundation for Educational Research
ROSLA   Raising of the School Leaving Age
SNAP   Special Needs Action Programme
SPS   Schools Psychological Service

Introduction: New Directions in Remedial Education

Colin J. Smith

Difficulties in learning can be seen as merely one example of the variety of abilities, aptitudes and interests which a teacher should expect to encounter in any classroom. It can be argued that in a genuinely comprehensive system all teachers should be willing and able to adapt methods and materials to meet a wide range of educational needs, welcoming intellectual as well as cultural diversity.

This attractive ideal will be difficult to translate into everyday practice until there is a considerable adjustment of priorities in teacher training at both initial and in-service stages. However, progress is being made towards its achievement by sharing more widely the skills and experience of those teachers currently responsible for helping less able children whether in ordinary or special schools.

In 1978 the *Warnock Report* suggested that it was not possible to make a meaningful distinction between remedial and special education. In so far as this statement acknowledged a common concern with helping children whose difficulties in learning hindered their educational progress, it was wholly unexceptionable. However, there was a distinction in many teachers' minds and in many local authorities' practice, between special education, which was largely provided in separate special schools, and remedial education which took place in classes or groups within an ordinary school. That distinction too has been blurred in recent years.

The 1981 Education Act and the departmental circulars, which have advised on its implementation, have emphasized the point that an assessment of special educational needs should lead to a 'statement' of what additional help needs to be given. Only then should consideration be given to where this provision should be made. The presumption is that whenever possible extra teaching and resources should be made available within the ordinary school. A variety of initiatives has shown the possibilities for integrating pupils with quite severe mental, physical and sensory disabilities within ordinary schools.

Colin J. Smith

This approach has been generally welcomed by remedial teachers and indeed the National Association for Remedial Education is considering changing its title to reflect its involvement in this wider concept of special education.

Nonetheless the term 'remedial education' maintains its utility as the most common description for the work of teachers in ordinary schools working with children, whose difficulties in learning relate to a specific area of the curriculum or whose general delay in development is mild rather than severe.

In the past remedial teaching has often been associated with the teaching of reading almost to the exclusion of other activities. Remedial teachers have long sought to move away from this traditional image, as little more than patient coaches of poor readers. Whilst improving literacy remains a vital interest, there has been a growing involvement with issues related to school organization, classroom management, pupil assessment and curriculum development. It is with these new directions in remedial education that this book is concerned.

It is also concerned to show that the existence of a remedial service need not perpetuate a divisive and outmoded system, which labels and needlessly segregates a particular category of pupils as 'slow learners', if teachers are aware of recent developments in remedial education.

1
Assumptions About the Nature
of Remedial Education

Introduction

Many teachers hoped and expected that the recommendations of the *Warnock Report* would lead to an expansion of advisory and support services, with teachers from special schools and remedial departments taking on a wider role in helping colleagues in mainstream education. Whilst the 1981 Education Act has little in the way of legislative power to promote such innovation or ensure a national standard of advisory provision, it has certainly stimulated an examination by local education authorities of the ways in which they help children with special needs. As far as remedial education is concerned this has sharpened the debate about its function and purpose which has been a constant issue at the conferences of the National Association for Remedial Education and in the columns of that body's journal *Remedial Education*.

That debate about the assumptions underpinning the nature of remedial education is traced through the articles in the first section of this book. They reflect a change of emphasis from concern with a curative role with individual pupils towards a wider role in preventing educational failure.

Golby and Gulliver's article examines the historical and social genesis of remedial education and its role as an 'ambulance service' for the casualties of our educational system rendered accident-prone by a curriculum based on rigid streaming. They suggest that curricular and organizational changes in schools should oblige all teachers to tailor their material for pupils with a wide range of abilities.

As Gulliford shows, this is not a new idea, though one which has gained increased currency in recent years. He reviews the progress that has been made in helping teachers cope with the problems presented by slow learners and to develop their own resources for providing for low achievers.

Edwards considers past usage of the term remedial education, outlines the variety of analogies which have been used to attempt a definition of remedial education and questions such basic issues as the relationships between remedial and special education, the nature of remedial treatment and whether the aims and purposes of remedial education are sufficiently clear.

Laskier looks at the ways in which the role of the remedial teacher has changed over the years, assesses the possibilities for change and indicates some of the constraints on suggested innovation.

Gains examines the challenge for teacher trainers embodied in broadening the responsibilities of the remedial specialist. He outlines some guiding principles for in-service education and discusses a school based alternative to traditional approaches to teacher education.

Whose Remedies, Whose Ills?
A Critical Review of Remedial Education

Michael Golby
Senior Lecturer in Education, University of Exeter
and
John R. Gulliver
Adviser for Primary English, Devon Local Education
Authority

Context

While there is an accelerating trend towards integration, most children in England and Wales who have gross physical or psychological handicaps are educated in special schools or units. A greater number, however, with less marked or even no clearly definable impediments, but for whom learning is for one reason or another difficult, disrupted, or delayed, are catered for in ordinary schools. The role of local rather than national authorities as the direct providers of education, and the delegation of much of the power of organization and direction to schools themselves, is reflected in a variety of provision for these children. This provision is commonly referred to as 'remedial education'.

No one who looks at remedial education systematically can fail to notice the diversity of organization, staffing and function which exists both between and within local authorities. Some authorities, for instance, have remedial advisory services, which guide and support the work of schools; others have none. Where they do exist, they may have a measure of autonomy, or they may be subservient to educational psychology services. Within schools, remedial education may be given in full- or part-time units, or to groups of children extracted regularly from normal classes. In full-time units, a whole curriculum package is normally offered; in extraction groups the focus is commonly on 'the basics', with reading in particular to the fore.

This article originally appeared in *Journal of Curriculum Studies*, 11, pp. 137–47

Michael Golby and John R. Gulliver

Whether pupils receive remedial attention may depend upon attainments in
basic skills alone, on assumed potential, or on a marked discrepancy
between the two. Work content may stem directly from the rest of the
curriculum, or bear no relationship to it whatever, except in so far as it is
assumed that a general reading competence underlies other curricular
activities. Children may cease to receive remedial education once they reach
a certain level of proficiency in reading, or simply because there is no
provision beyond a certain age. They may be taught by teachers who have
recognized advanced qualifications in remedial education, or by others who
have none.

The Concept of Remedial Education

The range of practices suggested above should be more than enough to point
up the diversity of conceptual assumptions at work under the label of
remedial education. A question which now must be faced is whether such
varied practices can meaningfully be included under one label.

It is suggested that there is a fundamental difference between the
provision made in full-time special classes for pupils of low intellectual
ability, and that made for other pupils whose difficulties are seen to lie in
certain basic skills. Only thirteen of the 158 schools investigated by Her
Majesty's Inspectorate in 1971 referred to pupils being transferred frequently from full-time to ordinary classes.[1] If the aim of the special classes is to
return pupils to the ordinary, then it would appear that they are singularly
unsuccessful. What is more likely is that placement in such classes is seen to
be a once-and-for-all measure. The intellectual condition of children thus
placed is largely seen as permanent; even where it is not, the differences
between the curricula of the special and the normal classes ensure that
transfer is unlikely. In consequence, the question of remediation does not
arise; the concern is to provide suitable long-term general education. Given
this lack of transfer, it should be noted that the application of the term
'remedial' involves a departure from common usage, where it usually means
'putting things right, correcting, rectifying'. The use of the term to refer to
such classes can therefore be regarded at best as euphemistic, and always as
misleading. It might be better abandoned.

The exclusion of the term 'remedial' from special classes would leave it
free for use in a way more consistent with everyday usage. We suggest that
such usage is largely appropriate to remedial education as provided in
withdrawal groups. For in common usage, rectifying implies firstly that
there is a state of rightness, and secondly that something falls short of that
state. Central to remedial education is a notion of discrepancy, for instance,
between apparent mental ability and attainment. The implication is that the
difficulties which many pupils have with basic skills stem from some kind of
individual failure in their learning process.

Underlying this central concept, however, is an ideology, which, although never stated, is nevertheless implicit and is held by both remedial teachers and those who teach 'normal' children. It is that there is a level of functioning which may be regarded as 'normal'; and, distinct from this, there are others which are in different ways 'abnormal'. The condition ascribed to those children receiving remedial education is regarded essentially as pathological.

The Ideology of Pathology

The outward evidence for this 'ideology of pathology' is the use by teachers involved in remedial education of quasi-medical terms like 'diagnosis' and 'treatment'. But we would not regard such usage as crucial to the argument: 'diagnosis', for instance, is now a term with wide usage — a Volkswagen, for example, is said to be designed for 'diagnostic maintenance'. And the Bullock Committee has suggested that all of us who work in primary schools should be diagnosticians now.

The clue to the underlying ideology of remedial education is to be found not so much in its terminology as in the forms of organization and methods it employs. A common type of remedial provision is some form of temporary withdrawal of the pupil from the 'normal' situation. The purpose of the withdrawal is to enable the pupil to undergo therapy; this almost always involves attention being directed towards weaknesses in basic skills. The object of the attention is to return the pupil as soon as possible to what is regarded as normal functioning. The remedial teacher's success is theoretically measured in terms of the number of pupils he returns to normal classes. As for the school counsellor, the ultimate accolade is to work himself out of a job, the improbability of which enables him to continue his struggle for professional status without fear that eventual victory will be Pyrrhic.

The effect of this pathological approach to remedial education has been two-fold. On the one hand, teachers directly engaged in remedial education have come to see themselves as therapists. There can be little doubt that many of them have acquired a considerable expertise in the application of diagnostic approaches to the teaching of reading, drawing in particular upon the discipline of psychology, and in some cases, too, upon neurology.[2] On the other hand, the far greater number of teachers who are not specifically involved in remedial work have come to assume that children with reading difficulties are not their concern. Their concept of normality involves, amongst other things, being able to meet the literacy demands of their fields of interest *as they stand at present*. That is to say, participation in a subject, such as history, requires a certain level of literacy, a level determined by the subject itself and the media through which it is taught. Neither content nor media are regarded as open to change. Those pupils who cannot meet this criterion are deemed in need of special help, and the improvement of their condition is to be achieved by remedial techniques which are not part of the normal teacher's function.

Criteria for Selection

Here one finds a paradox. The subject teacher's exclusion of certain pupils on the grounds that they do not meet the entry criteria suggests that those criteria should play some part in the selection of pupils for remedial education. But generally they do not. Pupils are picked for remedial work on the basis of their intelligence, or their basic attainments, or by some notion which relates the one to the other. Few notions have achieved such respectability as the psychologist's assumption that intelligence tests measure educational potential, and that any shortfall between a child's mental age and his attainments in a particular area must be regarded as a remediable discrepancy. Certainly it is a respectability which has scarcely been shaken by the failure of remedial education to produce returns consistent with the discrepancies thus discovered.

The central feature of the selection criteria is that they are either psychometric or chronological, or both. No consistent attempt is made to define the standards of literacy and numeracy which are required for participation in the normal curriculum, and the provision and withdrawal of remedial education is not directly related to the attainment of such standards. If curricular rather than psychometric criteria were used, it is possible that far more pupils would be identified as in need of remedial education than at present. At secondary level, for instance, the reading demands posed by both printed texts and teacher-produced worksheets may effectively exclude from full participation in the curriculum far more pupils than are customarily picked out by psychometric measures. It is at least arguable that the continued emphasis on psychometrics, far from operating to the advantage of pupils who have difficulties, makes their situation worse by encouraging teachers to regard them as individual failures in an educational system which is basically sound.

Policy Issues

Just as psychometric criteria for selection for remedial education focus on the individual and his failings, so the policies for remedial intervention are aimed at individual cures, a point which finds its most recent statement in Bullock: 'We see no advantage in mass testing and centrally stored data unless the outcome is special and individualized help directed precisely at the children who need it.'[3]

Here we have a call for positive discrimination, a policy remedial work shares with compensatory education, together with selectivity of focus, which it does not. At the same time, there is a failure to recognize that the data collected through such mass testing could be used to question at least one of the assumptions upon which mass education beyond the infant school rests.

The post-infant curriculum in British schools is based amongst other things on an assumption that most children have made at least a good start to reading by the time they enter the junior school. In consequence, there is little provision in schools beyond the infant stage for the initial teaching of reading except that which is provided through remedial education. Whereas the beginning reader in the infant school is surrounded by aids to the achievement of initial literacy, in the junior school and beyond he is commonly faced with reading matter most of which is quite beyond his capabilities. Unlike the able reader, he cannot use reading to learn. It may be argued that the exclusion of this possibility is a major factor in his common subsequent failure to learn to read. The props which were available to the more able child when he passed through the same stage some years earlier are denied to the pupil who comes to reading late. His condition is regarded as one of learning difficulty rather than mere lateness. The crucial point, though, is that the mass education approach confirms him in his abnormality. It is more than possible that the need for the remedial teacher as an ambulance-man is created and sustained by a system which by its design is accident-prone.

Historical and Social Genesis

That such a position has been reached calls for explanation. In order to understand what exists, we must see remedial education firstly in its historical context, and secondly as a manifestation of ideologies obtaining not only within education but also having co-relative applications within wider social policy.

What is striking about remedial provision, as it developed in the 1940s, is its congruence with other aspects of contemporary social policy. Education, like health, was primarily regarded as an individual and not a communal matter. Hawthorn and Carter's point that the structure of society and, thus, ecological conditions of health were not regarded as relevant either as causes or as cures was as applicable to the contemporary framework of education as it was to the early development of the National Health Service.[4] But this similarity should not be a cause for surprise, for the ideology which informed educational policy also informed social planning. Basically, society (including the educational system) was functioning properly; so long as care was taken of the less fortunate on an individual basis, there was no need to look to the system itself for the causes of their distress. It was only much later that one began to see the development of policies based on a recognition of 'the complex forces in school and community which determine the meaning and effectiveness of educational experience . . .'.[5] Given the reluctance of successive governments to implement to the full the measures for Educational Priority Areas recommended by Plowden, there is room for doubt that what Halsey regarded as the complementary nature of policies directed at individual needs and area approaches (*ibid.*, p. 45) has achieved much more than academic recognition. In the meantime, we retain in education a policy towards children who for one reason or another find learning difficult which has its roots not in the latter 1970s but in the early years of the Second World War.

It is our contention that the 'ideology of pathology' outlined above has arisen largely because it was the psychologists who first showed an interest in individual differences. We are not trying to argue that the sole responsibility for this ideology can be laid at the psychologists' door. Neither do we seek to denigrate the very considerable benefits which have ensued from the work done on individual differences in the first half of this century. It is rather that, in the climate which prevailed at the time of the foundation of the first remedial services in the 1940s, psychological notions gave respectability and rationale to existing educational practices. Far from ensuring the development of a flexible system of education, the normative approach to psychological measurement had the effect of buttressing a mass education approach which had as its corollary a view of weakness as abnormality. Normality was represented by the abilities and attainments of the average child; abnormality by the statistically less common pupils whose achievements were markedly lower. It only needed the idea to be floated that weakness was not merely statistically rare, but also sometimes deviant, to ensure that abnormality would be seen as pathological. A hitherto unacknowledged achievement of early workers in the field of backwardness is that they supplied this idea.

Two books exercised a seminal influence — Burt's *The Backward Child*, and Schonell's *Backwardness in the Basic Subjects*. Burt distinguished between the innately dull and those whose backwardness was accidental or acquired. For the latter 'Individual attention . . . should result in progress being so speeded up that all who are not dull as well as backward should, after one or two terms, be fit for retransference to the ordinary class'.[6] Thus the child was to be rehabilitated to fit a given curriculum rather than the curriculum altered to fit the child. Schonell accepted Burt's distinction, refining it to produce a notion of 'improvable scholastic deficiency (which) . . . may characterize dull, normal, or supernormal pupils'.[7] Typically such deficiency was confined to a single school subject, and treatment for the condition was through individual or small group short coaching sessions arranged at frequent intervals rather than in full-time backward classes.

Here then we have two notions central to the early tradition of remedial education: a distinction between the retarded and the innately dull, and a system of coaching in the basic subjects. The crucial point is that these two factors were identified by people whose concern was psychology, and who looked at schools and children from outside, and often from a clinical experience. Moreover, their ideas were offered to the world at the very time when those educational notions which culminated in the 1944 Act were being formed. An idea of retardation which was based on psychometrics fitted well with education which would be given in accordance with 'the age, ability, and aptitude of the pupil'. It buttressed the idea that ability was measurable, that children could therefore be grouped and taught in homogeneous units, and that the curriculum for each of these units was distinct. Moreover, even though the primary section of the earlier Hadow Report had called for a curriculum conceived in terms of 'activity and experience rather than knowledge to be acquired or facts to be stored',[8] Burt and Schonell's focus upon reading and number confirmed teachers in the epistemic divisions which were still believed to be necessary by many educational practitioners.

Thus, when in the late 1940s the first remedial centres were set up, they were received with open arms by teachers, many of whom were newly trained, or had recently come back from the War to find the education system in relative disarray. At a time when reading standards were adversely affected by the aftermath of war, the establishment of remedial services by local authorities all over the country, and of remedial provision within individual schools, was seen to be a positive step towards the elimination of what were regarded as individual learning problems. The very fact that this development was seen to be positive step, however, diverted attention from the 'normal' curriculum itself. So long as remedial provision was made — an ambulance service in a system which was prone to accident — the curriculum could remain a static entity.

We now want to argue that even if wider social issues are disregarded, ideological and curricular changes in schools are forcing remedial education to adopt a new role.

A Changing Curriculum

A curriculum of the kind which existed when the first remedial services were set up needed an ambulance service. Literacy and numeracy were regarded as service skills which made participation in the whole curriculum possible. But the subject-oriented curriculum which was offered to pupils in rigorously streamed secondary schools (and many primary too) is now less prevalent than it was when the remedial movement developed in the 1940s and 1950s. One must therefore ask whether the perpetuation of a system which was partly the product of a particular education situation, and partly a determinant of its underlying ideology, is relevant in a changed educational world. We want in this section to look at some of the changes which have taken place, and at how they impinge on the work of the remedial teacher. Some of the changes are more of a hope than a reality, and we shall, in passing, try to distinguish them.

We think that the important changes relevant to remedial education are four in number: the gradual move away from grouping children by ability; the breaking down of subject boundaries; the move towards a common curriculum; and new ideas about the nature and acquisition of reading. We shall look at each in turn.

The move from grouping by ability

A major ideological shift in British education since the War has been the retreat from elitism and the espousal, first of equality of opportunity and then of equality of desert. The abolition of the 11+ selection test, which has been an outward sign, has been accompanied internally by the abandonment of streaming, first at primary level, and now at secondary. Special classes, which were part of the apparatus of streaming, have largely been abandoned; some schools have eschewed all forms of segregation, including the temporary kind involved in withdrawal systems.

It may be argued that the move from grouping by ability in schools is organizational rather than curricular. For two reasons we think this view is inadequate. Firstly, being selected for a particular ability grouping was part of the planned experience undergone by most pupils in schools until recently, and as such affected each pupil's image of himself and his relationship to society as a whole. It was thus part of his learning experience. Secondly, any form of grouping has pedagogical implications; alter the grouping principle and, in the long run, even if not in the short, you make it more likely that the teaching will change, if only because previous practices become unworkable.

The most frequent pedagogical response to the new situation has been the development of individualized approaches to teaching. Commonly this has meant presenting particular subjects at a variety of conceptual levels. But it has also entailed many teachers paying much greater attention to the demands they make on their pupils' literacy. Teachers increasingly accept that they must adapt the curriculum, not only for pupils of different cognitive levels, but also for pupils of varying degrees of literacy. The change represents a fundamental shift in their conception of normality.

In some schools structural change has been accompanied by curricular reform, but not in all. We would argue that where no attention has been paid to the curriculum, the retention of a conventional withdrawal remedial system has been essential. But where the curricular implications of the change have been thought through, the dependence on the 'ambulance service' has become much less marked.

The breaking-down of subject boundaries

In many schools where traditional subjects like history and geography have disappeared from the timetable, a particular notion of what it is to be a teacher has disappeared along with the subjects themselves. As Barnes has pointed out, part of teachers' conceptions of themselves and their subjects is bound up with the media through which they teach them.[9] Where they have relied heavily on textbooks, there has almost inevitably been an entry criterion involving a certain level of literacy. A feature of many of the new approaches, however, is their deliberate use of speech rather than writing as the main medium of communication. One could point to the Schools Council Humanities Curriculum Project as an example. Aimed at 'the average and below average' pupils, its emphasis is on small-group discussion. While pupils in need of remedial reading are supposed to be excluded (Introduction; p. 6), Gulliford and Widlake have noted that many schools are succesfully using the materials with these children, either by concentrating on those parts which are not dependent upon reading, or by supplementing the published material with matter of their own choosing.[10] Thus they bypass the demand for literacy in some instances, and in others enable pupils to use reading as a medium for learning by tailoring the reading levels to their abilities. The important point here is that weakness in reading is not seen to be a disqualification; it is rather that the teachers are accepting the obligation to adapt their material to the pupils.

A common curriculum

In an increasingly pluralist society, calls for the development of curricular as well as organizational measures which aid social cohesion have become increasingly important. The implementation of common curricula in schools poses special problems for remedial education. Withdrawal is a temporal as well as a structural step, and time spent on the remediation of deficiencies in basic skills in the traditional way is time not spent on other aspects of the curriculum. Moreover, it is often time lost by pupils who can least cope with the attendant disruption.

The crucial problem is, what does the pupil drop in order to fit in enough remedial sessions? An essential feature of the notion of a common curriculum is that every pupil should reach a minimum level of understanding and experience in the areas it covers.[11] The implication here is clearly that there are certain parts of the curriculum from which the pupil ought not to be withdrawn. Much therefore depends upon whether one thinks that the whole or just a part of the curriculum should be compulsory.

Many writers have conceived of the curriculum in two parts, one obligatory, and the other optional. The existence of an optional element in the curriculum enables the planners to allocate time to remedial work without encroaching upon the pupil's exposure to the compulsory common part of the curriculum. Lawton, for instance, has envisaged a week made of ninety twenty-minute modules, a proportion of which could be used for compulsory studies, and the rest of which would be discretionary. Up to ten of the discretionary modules could be used for remedial work, to enable the child, for instance, to catch up on work missed through illness.[12]

We want to make several comments on Lawton's proposals. Firstly, the conception of remedial work is wide. Missing work, for instance, is not the sole prerogative of weak readers, even though they may be more prone than most to absence. The implication of Lawton's conception is that *all* pupils might need remedial work at some stage, and that their needs would not necessarily be confined to basic skills. Whether a single teacher could meet so varied a demand is open to doubt, and it might well be necessary to seek some other solution, such as setting some part of each day apart in which subject specialists would be free to fulfil this role. Given the breadth of this conception, we would prefer to find some other name for it, and retain the term 'remedial' in connection with problems of literacy and numeracy.

Secondly, the practice of remedial work (however defined) in the optional part of the curriculum does ensure that only those pupils who *ask* for help will get it. One feature of remedial provision at all levels is that it seldom works unless the customers want it to.

One worry, however, relates to the fact that there is any remedial provision at all. We argue later that there must be *some* provision, although on a smaller scale than is sometimes the case. Where the provision is lavish, however, there may be a tendency to institutionalize a situation in which teachers do not regard it as part of their function to adapt their material to the abilities of the weaker pupils. An impossible burden may be placed upon the remedial teachers, who may be required to produce a literacy competence in their pupils which might better be achieved by work within the subject areas themselves. In consequence remedial teaching gets a bad name, and a too-high literacy criterion effectively excludes many pupils from full participation in the common curriculum.

Changing assumptions about the nature and acquisition of literacy

A view of reading which has gained much ground in recent years, and which has been endorsed by Bullock, is that it is best acquired incrementally and in conjunction with writing, talking, and listening, and in the course of meaningful activities.[13] Alongside this view of how it is acquired has come the rejection of the idea of reading as a single skill (at least beyond the earliest levels) which can be applied to a range of different materials. Instead we have a conception of reading competence as a repertoire of linked processes which differ according to the purpose of the reader and the nature of the text.

If these views on reading are valid, then one must ask just how much can be expected of an approach to remedial provision which concentrates upon work away from the situation in which reading is to be used. The consequence for the remedial teacher must be that the location of much of his activity should be in the classrooms and work-areas alongside the subject teachers, and the materials with which he works must derive from the subjects themselves. A major part of his work will entail helping the subject teachers to adapt their material to the literacy and conceptual levels of their pupils. In this sense his activity will be supportive rather than remedial. By making it possible for pupils to use reading to learn, however, he may well help to develop those conditions in which they will learn to read.

A Role for the Remedial Teacher

It has been our contention in this essay that the traditional role of remedial education has reflected particular notions of normality and therefore abnormality. Curricular and organizational changes in schools have pushed out the boundaries of what we mean by 'normal'. Teachers at all levels increasingly accept an obligation to tailor their material to children of very different abilities. In consequence many pupils now have the opportunity to acquire through participation in the normal curriculum skills which at one time they would only have attained through some form of segregation. This raises the question of the role of the remedial teacher in a much changed situation. We want to make a number of points.

(a)   For those who advocate that reading should be learned through the normal curriculum, there are at least two pedagogical, as opposed to ideological, problems. Firstly, the amount by which the readability demands of textual matter can be reduced is limited. Secondly, there are a number of children, who for a variety of reasons reach even these reduced levels only with the greatest difficulty. It would be unreasonable to expect every teacher to find the time or possess the necessary knowledge to give these children the kind of help they need. It is for them that the remedial teacher's traditional diagnostic and prescriptive skills remain relevant. Thus, we would expect the remedial teacher to retain his 'ambulance-man' role. But since many of the children who at present depend upon remedial assistance would be helped by the modification in the normal curriculum as described above, and the accompanying changes in the ordinary teachers' conception of their role, *the 'ambulance service' would be on a much reduced scale.*

(b)   While in some schools teachers have already gone far towards a change in outlook, in others they have hardly begun. In these more traditional schools, we would expect an intensive 'ambulance service' to be retained for some time. But a major obligation of the remedial teacher would be to combine with other departments, of which English would perhaps be the most important, to modify the prevailing climate. In these schools the remedial teacher would be an *agent of curricular and institutional change*.

(c) Modifying the media and the content of learning so that weaker pupils can profit from them is a task which requires both time and understanding. Given that neither would be abundantly at the disposal of many subject teachers, a major role for the remedial teacher would be to give support to the subject specialists in modifying their curricula to suit less able pupils. In order to fulfil this role adequately, it is likely that, in addition to his traditional concern with the psychology of teaching and learning, the remedial teacher would have to have a much greater understanding of linguistics and curriculum planning than he has at the moment. The role of the person providing this service would be *supportive to the subject teacher* rather than remedial in the 'putting things right' sense.

(d) The difficulties many pupils have in subject areas are both reading and cognitive problems. An extremely important aspect of the remedial teacher's work would be to help pupils cope with these aspects of their curriculum. The function of the remedial teacher here would be *supportive to the pupil*. Improvements to the pupil's literacy would be an accompanying but secondary concern.

(e) A variety of screening and monitoring techniques is now available which make it possible to identify those children who are likely to have difficulties with school work, and to watch their progress. The remedial teacher with his knowledge of psychometrics would have a vital role to play in using these techniques and making the information produced known to other members of staff. The role of the remedial teacher here would be *preventive*: he would ensure that appropriate measures were taken to help a pupil before he was put in a position in which he was bound to fail. He would thus maintain close links with compensatory education.

The role we envisage for the remedial teacher is therefore much altered from the traditional. It is one that cannot be adopted by the remedial teacher alone, for it depends on a different view of normality on the part of all teachers. The traditional remedial function would be much reduced, and alongside it a new emphasis on curricular change, support, and prevention developed. Whether the old name of 'remedial teacher' would still be appropriate is another matter. Certainly the ambulance-man would have in addition to become a consultant on road-safety.

Notes

1 DEPARTMENT OF EDUCATION AND SCIENCE (1971) *Education Survey 15, Slow Learners in Secondary Schools*, London, HMSO.
2 TANSLEY, A. (1967) *Reading and Remedial Reading*, London, Routledge and Kegan Paul.
3 DEPARTMENT OF EDUCATION AND SCIENCE (1975) *A Language for Life: Report of the Committee of Inquiry* (Bullock Report), London, HMSO, para. 17.13.
4 HAWTHORN, H. and CARTER, G. The concept of deprivation (unpublished paper for DHSS/SSRC Working Party on Transmitted Deprivation, quoted in Open University course: *E361 Education and the Urban Environment*, Unit 14, p. 31).
5 DEPARTMENT OF EDUCATION AND SCIENCE (1972) *Educational Priority, Volume 1*, London, HMSO, p. 45.
6 BURT, C. (1937) *The Backward Child*, London, University of London Press, p. 606.
7 SCHONELL, F. (1942) *Backwardness in the Basic Subjects*, London, Oliver and Boyd, p. 61.
8 BOARD OF EDUCATION (1931) *Report of the Consultative Committee on the Primary School (Hadow Report)*, London, HMSO.
9 BARNES, D., BRITTON, J. and ROSEN, H. (1969) *Language, the Learner and the School*, London, Penguin Books.
10 GULLIFORD, R. and WIDLAKE, P. (1975) *Teaching Materials for Disadvantaged Children*, Schools Council Curriculum Bulletin 5, London, Evans/Methuen Educational, p. 72.
11 LAWTON, D. (1973) *Social Change, Educational Theory and Curriculum Planning*, London, University of London Press.
12 *Ibid.*, p. 151.
13 DES, *A Language for Life, op. cit.*, para. 1.10.

The Teacher's Own Resources

Ronald Gulliford
Professor of Special Education
University of Birmingham

A few local education authorities have appointed teachers with special qualifications to visit a group of schools . . . to help with and advise upon the treatment of backward children. As an interim measure, until teachers in general have gained a greater knowledge of the educational needs of backward children, this practice has its value, but the creation of a new class of specialist peripatetic teachers as a permanency would be as likely to hinder as to help the spread of knowledge and skill in handling backward children, because of the temptation that would beset the teachers in the schools to depend on such outside help rather than upon their own resources.

That passage from the Board of Education's pamphlet *The Education of Backward Children*, published in 1937, was written at a time when the idea of remedial teaching was no more than embryonic. It was not until ten years later that the first diploma course for training remedial teachers was set up by Schonell at Birmingham University and the first remedial teachers began to be appointed by a few local education authorities. One is inclined therefore to view the opinion about the prospective introduction of peripatetic remedial teachers as showing a premature and cautiously conservative response to a new and unknown specialism, which seems strange in view of the limited provision at that time. The main resource was the special class and in a few places there were central remedial or adjustment classes drawing from several schools. As the Scottish Education Department's progress report in 1978 reminds us, the principal solution in the 1920s and 1930s was the practice of retaining retarded pupils in the same class to repeat a stage until a satisfactory standard had been reached; in the mid-thirties as many as 12 per cent of all pupils in the final year of primary schools in

This article originally appeared in *Remedial Education* (1983), 18, 4

Scotland were aged thirteen or more. Moreover, perusal of pre-war education reports shows that the theory available to teachers — both in the conception of learning difficulties and of curriculum and teaching methods — was rather circumscribed, as our present ones will surely seem in forty years' time! Moreover, there were few special resources — not even reading books for backward children.

On the other hand, it would be more just to view the comment about the importance of teachers relying on their own resources as a shrewd recognition of a valid principle — one which we are returning to with renewed emphasis. It has never of course really been lost sight of. While it may have been the case that the first remedial teachers and services saw themselves as a Task Force whose knowledge, skills and resources would win the battle against educational failure, remedial services soon developed an advisory and in-service training role. In the development and dissemination of knowledge and expertise, remedial teachers have made a significant contribution. Nevertheless, the tendency for separation of remedial tuition from the class teacher's role and from the child's experience of the curriculum was sufficient to evoke echoes of the 1937 comment in post-war education reports. *The Plowden Report* (DES, 1967) recognized the value of a remedial or opportunity class but warns of the danger of a remedial class 'becoming a place from which none can escape' and confidently asserted that 'slow learning children in ordinary schools are best served by the approach which characterizes the most progressive primary schools of today' and refers to the fact that many teachers develop a particular interest in handicapped children and become successful practitioners. The need for teachers to receive more preparation for this work was clearly identified but the remedy in initial training was weakly prescribed as being through the medium of a knowledge of the different rates of children's intellectual, social and emotional growth. It was suggested that 'this might be extended possibly by the provision of an optional course during the final year so as to give young teachers more help in dealing with the difficulties of slow learning and other handicapped children in ordinary schools'. Does one detect a lack of enthusiasm and conviction in the words 'possibly' and 'optional'?

For the secondary level, the *Newsom Report* (1962) examined the issues in the education of average and below average achievers and set in train lines of thinking that were developed during the era of Schools Council Projects and the run up to ROSLA. The *Survey of Slow Learners in Secondary Schools* (DES, 1971) revealed however the confusion and uncertainties about strategies for providing for the large number of low achievers, some of it partly due to the term remedial education being applied in a narrow sense. It presented a depressing picture which reflected the effects of a period of rapid educational change in which 'the needs of the slowest pupils seem to have received less than their share of consideration'.

It was in the *Bullock Report* (1975) that the 1937 comment reverberates most strongly. After stressing the fundamental importance of the creation of warm and sympathetic relationships with pupils, encouraging them to learn through the stimulus of success, the Report suggests that 'it is not a question of devising special remedial methods but of applying good teaching in such a way that failure is replaced by a sense of achievement' and recognizes that this requires a high level of teaching skill. Moreover, 'there is no mystique about remedial education nor are its methods intrinsically different from those employed by successful teachers anywhere'. Concern was expressed about a prolonged emphasis on basic skills where this is at the expense of other parts of the curriculum: 'remedial help in learning to read should wherever possible be closely related to the rest of a child's learning'.

Three years later, the Scottish Education Department's progress report, *The Education of Pupils with Learning Difficulties* (SED, 1978) comes out firmly and unequivocally with views in line with the reservations of the 1937 pamphlet. 'Because the range of learning difficulties is so wide and their nature so complex, it is too much to ask that they be tackled by the provision of remedial teachers alone.' 'Thus remedial education is a responsiblitiy of the whole school, whether remedial staff are employed or not.' 'Pupils with learning difficulties should be taught as far as possible, by class and subject teachers. If they are unable to give the proper kind of help, then the pupils involved should be given the additional support of a remedial teacher. That fact, however, does not reduce the class or subject teacher's responsibility for the pupils or absolve him from continuing his own endeavours.'

Finally, it scarcely needs to be said that the responsibility of every teacher for children with special needs was underlined by the Warnock Committee: 'It is imperative that every teacher should appreciate that up to one child in five is likely to require some form of special educational help and that this may be provided not only in special schools and classes but also with suitable support in the regular classes of ordinary schools.' The fact that the Committee felt the need to emphasize this and the fact that schools and teachers have shown some apprehension about it (albeit perhaps rather more in respect of pupils with severe disabilities) provides some confirmation of the 1937 Report's prediction that the new speciality of remedial teaching could lead to teachers doubting their own competence and resources.

A historical perspective tends to make one wise after the event. Why, for example, did the awareness of the class teacher's and subject teacher's responsibility for pupils with learning difficulties not lead to more attention to this area in courses of initial teacher training? The *McNair Report* (1942) in fact suggested optimistically but to little effect that 'what is learnt from experience with both normal and abnormal children will be available in the training of teachers generally'. The *Plowden Report* referred to 'an optional course' and recommended that 'Teachers in training should be equipped to help handicapped children so far as they can'. The *Warnock Report* attached much importance to a special educational component in all teacher training. The answer to why more was not done in the past could be sought in the present; five years after Warnock we cannot be complacent about the extent and quality of provision for a special education element in initial and in-service training although some useful new approaches have been initiated which could well serve as models.

The study of developments in B Ed courses (DES, 1979) commented that 'the compulsory elements of most courses did not ... bring students towards much awareness of the special needs of certain categories of children, in particular those with a cultural background different from that of the majority or those whose learning was otherwise handicapped'. The report adds that colleges usually had expertise among the staff but that it was made available chiefly in optional courses. That study was started in 1977. The recent discussion document on the new teacher in school (DES, 1982) gives slightly more encouraging findings. It records probationary teachers' views about aspects of their preparation: three-quarters considered themselves at least adequately prepared for teaching able pupils, two-thirds for the less able, a half for teaching the socially deprived and less than half for children with different cultural backgrounds. Some young teachers referred to the fact that some of these topics were only available as optional courses. Given the demands on time in initial training courses, particularly the PGCE, it is perhaps understandable that this should be so. However, some institutions have made progress in integrating content about children with special needs and about the teaching of low achievers into education and professional studies. With regard to preparation for mixed ability teaching, it is encouraging that three-quarters of the probationers felt themselves adequately prepared. It is not surprising that HMIs who observed probationers in their teaching should have judged a smaller proportion to be actually catering satisfactorily for the ability range; it is, after all, a problem even for experienced teachers. At least they felt they had a preparation for it and how far they build upon that must surely depend on the support and advice of senior staff in their school or department.

Finally, in view of the frequent complaint in the past that teachers were not sufficiently trained for teaching basic skills, it is interesting to read that three-quarters of primary teachers felt adequately prepared for teaching mathematics and only slightly fewer for teaching reading. That any should feel inadequately prepared might be considered less than satisfactory. It is interesting to note that 32 per cent of secondary probationers thought they had been adequately prepared to teach reading. The report appears not to regard this finding of sufficient importance even for a brief comment but I thought this was a sign of change. For all that my generation of secondary trained teachers heard about the matter, we could have been forgiven if we had assumed that children arrived in their cradles as fully fledged readers.

The information obtained suggests that progress has been made in developing skills relevant to teaching a wide ability range though the evidence, being based on teachers' own impressions of the training and short periods of observation of their teaching, is not very firm.

The aspects of teaching competence referred to do not of course cover the range of content proposed in the *Warnock Report* for a special educational element in initial training. This proposal was generally welcomed at the time and has certainly continued to be a live issue in discussions of initial and in-service training in relation to special needs even if there has been varied commitment and success in putting it into practice. Perhaps it is time to look again at the proposals after a lapse of five years to appraise how far they match current conceptions of what is required and also how far they reflect the importance of developing teachers' own resources.

If teacher training requires a balance between, on the one hand, knowledge, awareness and understanding and, on the other hand, skills, techniques and strategies, the balance of the proposals in paragraphs 12.7 and 12.8 of the *Warnock Report* might be thought to be tipped too much towards the former. The seven statements of aim in 12.7 refer to awareness, acquaintance, understanding and knowledge (three times). These words should of course be read in relation to the recommendation that the special educational element should be taught within the context of child development. However, a rewriting of the aims at the present time would surely include an aim which referred specifically to the acquisition of skills which enable the teacher to relate his own assessment of learning and adjustment to the practical measures which can be taken in the organization of the next steps in learning and in the management of behaviour. These are aspects of teaching competence which are common to the range of children with special needs whether these arise in the majority who have learning and adjustment difficulties or the minority with disabilities requiring other special procedures.

Although one aim refers to enabling teachers to recognize early signs of special need, the next one aims 'to give teachers knowledge of the part they can play in the assessment of a child's educational needs and in the execution of any measures prescribed'. The committee no doubt had in mind here that the teacher would be cooperating with a visiting specialist teacher or with the psychologist. This would be the case with only a small proportion of the one in five children likely to have special educational needs and therefore the aim might be stated in a way which would emphasize the teacher's own resources for assessment of learning needs and for planning teaching programmes ⁓ rather than just playing a part 'in the execution of special measures prescribed'.

The final aim stated in paragraph 12.7: 'to give teachers knowledge in general terms of when and where to refer for help' is obviously valid and important but the fact that it is prefaced by the words 'ABOVE ALL' might now be regarded as a questionable priority since 'ABOVE ALL' should surely apply, if to any aim, to the need to develop certain teaching skills which enable the class or subject teacher to adapt and provide for any child in the short term even if specialist help and advice is desirable or, as in the case of children with sensory handicaps, essential.

The following paragraph (12.8) refers to the skills, understanding and appreciation which must be developed if the aims are to be achieved, section iii referring particularly to skills. I believe that we would now wish to firm up the recommendations: not 'understanding of the practical steps' but training in those which are serviceable in the teaching of any child who has learning or adjustment difficulties irrespective of any specialized help he may need; not simply 'to appreciate the need' for modifications to school or classroom organization, curriculum and teaching techniques but able to formulate and carry out such modifications at least in respect of those children who, for whatever reason, are low achieving or not happily adjusted to school or class.

The suggestions in the *Warnock Report* for a special educational element were a valuable attempt to go further than merely re-stating the 'long felt need' for greater attention in initial teacher training to children with special needs. In particular, it broadened the issue beyond merely emphasizing the importance of preparation for teaching reading and other basic educational skills. In essentials, it was on the right lines and has had a beneficial effect in focusing attention on the issues. Although at first glance, it seems a lot to accommodate within a course of teacher training, this should not be the case if, as was recommended, it is taught within 'the general context of child development'. This phrase is reminiscent of the *Plowden Report's* reference in paragraph 855 to 'knowledge of differing rates of children's intellectual, social and emotional growth'. Desirable though this is, the reference to 'the general context of child development' could lead to teacher trainers seeing the responsibility for special needs as lying in a particular department — in education studies or special education — rather than as a responsibility for everyone contributing to a training course.

To be specific, all tutors should be able to refer to the essential features of teaching their subject to slow learners, to indicate what adaptations need to be made to content and method and to published sources of further help. We can assume — or we should be able to assume — that this is normal practice in the training of primary teachers since primary schools have now had a long experience of providing for a wide range of ability and attainment in non-streamed settings. The trend in primary schools to emphasize conventional subject areas such as science, geography and history creates a need, comparable to the much greater one in secondary schools, to examine how low achievers may be helped to benefit from these fields of study. In several respects the primary teacher has an advantage in providing for the slow learner: primary methods with their emphasis on environmental topics, activity, enquiry, language and other forms of expression (pictorial, practical, etc.) can more readily be suited to the low achiever; there is a good range of information books suited to different ages and reading levels upon which to draw for pupils of lower attainment. Nor is there the pressure of curricula geared towards examination requirements.

The problems are admittedly greater in relation to the training of secondary teachers in subject methods, not simply because of pupils' difficulties but because the expertise is only now being developed. In the 1950s the problem was 'solved' by streaming; in the 1960s the solution was seen as 'remedial' with the confusion and uncertainty reported in the DES Survey published in 1971; in the 1970s mixed ability teaching increased and latterly the trends to minimize separate treatment for low achievers and to develop a consultative role for the remedial specialist are still in process. Early in the 1970s a survey of the use of Schools Council Projects with slow learners (Gulliford and Widlake, 1975) commented that there was a tendency to assume that SC Curriculum Project materials were not intended or suitable for slow learners. One well-known project did specifically exclude remedial pupils. The teacher's guide to another included two pages of suggestions for work with slow learners. A number of others, for example, Geography for the Young School Leaver, the Moral Education Project and several of the Science Projects were certainly seen by the Project teams as appropriate for slow learners. Gulliford and Widlake suggested that Curriculum Project Teams should always include a remedial specialist in order to ensure that the needs of low achievers were given due consideration. The survey of curricular needs of slow learners (Brennan, 1979) reported some successful work in science, environmental studies and integrated studies but little in geography and least in history.

That the situation is changing is shown by the increased number of publications on the methods of subject teaching with slow learners. During the 1970s it was possible to point to only a few articles which referred to this, several of them about science teaching. Recently there have been booklets on the teaching of slow learners in history (Cowie, 1979) and geography (Boardman, 1982). Many more articles have appeared in subject teaching journals, in *Remedial Education* and *Special Education: Forward Trends*. The recent book by Hinson and Hughes (1982) based on papers at a NARE conference is a useful source for references to the growing discussion of practice in 'the planning and implementation of curricula suited to the needs of children with learning difficulties'.

Clearly more subject teachers and method tutors on training courses are responding to this obvious area of needed development. It is perhaps understandable that some may feel that they have no special knowledge of the problems of pupils with learning difficulties and no relevant training. They may, confirming the prediction of the 1937 pamphlet on the *Education of Backward Children*, feel that this is the speciality of the remedial or special needs department. Remedial teachers' knowledge and experience of learning difficulties is of course an important resource now being used in more varied ways than withdrawal teaching, but they themselves have come to focus more on what has to be learnt rather than the causes of failure. An understanding of why children fail and the nature of their difficulties in learning is of course important but equally, or even more important, is an understanding of the subject. A vast amount of research and practice has been given to study of the causes and nature of learning difficulties, particularly with regard to the major problem of reading. The publications fill the library shelves. Some of the real advances, however, have come from examination of the concepts and skills to be learnt and how they are learnt. Better understanding of the processes of learning to read have significantly influenced teaching. Failure in mathematics at one time was seen simply as failure to learn number facts and processes, the remedy for which was simply to diagnose weaknesses and to give interesting practice and drills. A better understanding of the primary mathematics curriculum and how children's mathematical thinking develops has created a firmer basis for appreciating the needs of the slow learner. Likewise the old view that the verbal limitations of slow learners implied the need to concentrate on practical activities rather than verbal has been transformed by the study of language in education with the result that it is easier to encompass the needs of slow learners.

The first step is to be convinced of the values of purposes of teaching a subject to slow learners and to be able to accept that while the goal of academic achievement is important for *all* learners, the significance of a subject's content and methods of study for the personal, social and intellectual development of young people growing into and through adolescence is the main *educational* justification for teaching it and relatively more important in the case of slow learners.

A second step is to be aware of the difficulties in teaching the subject. Apart from the major difficulties presented by reading and writing problems — which is where the remedial department can assist and advise — the difficulties of slow learners in subject areas are on the same continuum as other pupils. In her book on teaching history to slow learners, Cowie remarks that 'much careful and exact classroom observation of language in history is needed' and goes on to emphasize that most pupils have language difficulties in history and that slow learners may serve to reveal the nature of those difficulties more exactly. She refers to the fact that history requires the full range of past tenses and the *majority* of pupils do not use these in their informal speech until the later years of the secondary school. Until late adolescence *most* pupils find the true conditional difficult and learn only a precarious use of such conjunctions as *but, if, although, nevertheless*. Similar comments are made about the language required for understanding and expression in other subjects (for example, science). Boardman (1982) usefully identifies some of the difficult concepts in geography such as the concept of scale as consistent proportional representation and points to the need to time the learning of certain concepts across subject areas. In stressing the importance of concrete experience in teaching concepts, he gives the illustration of developing the idea of contours by means of a plasticene island in a tank, the contours being marked on the island as appropriate amounts of water are poured in to reach the levels indicated by the height scale. As with many other concepts, a practical or pictorial experience of this kind is good teaching with average pupils. In a similar vein, Kemp (1979) proposes five teaching strategies which, in essence, stress that abstract ideas should be based on concrete examples and supplementary visual material; written text should not be overused and should be linked with visual material; the work should be divided into limited objectives and should have a well defined structure; imaginative practical tasks create involvement and satisfaction as well as contributing to overcoming weaknesses in understanding. These strategies do not seem inapplicable to average pupils except perhaps in the extent to which they need to be acted upon.

In conclusion: the issue raised in the introductory quotation of this chapter has remained incompletely resolved for a long time and, as in the case of many other educational matters, the reasons why are not too difficult to see. However, it is clear that in recent years, progress has been made both in teaching training and in the practice of schools which will assist in the development of the teachers' own resources for providing for low achievers. This in turn will facilitate the trend for remedial specialists and services to develop and extend their advisory and consultative role in addition to the teaching of children whose severe educational retardation and personal difficulties continue to require remedial help on a withdrawal basis. The problem remains of training a sufficient number of able remedial/special teachers to develop the peripatetic and in-school roles which were not anticipated in 1937 and are now required in the implementation of the 1981 Act.

References

BOARDMAN, D. (1982) *Geography with Slow Learners*, Sheffield, The Geographical Association.

BOARD OF EDUCATION (1937) *The Education of Backward Children*, London, HMSO.

BOARD OF EDUCATION (1942) *Report of the McNair Committee on the Training and Recruitment of Teachers and Youth Leaders*, London, HMSO.

BRENNAN, W.K. (1979) *Curricular Needs of Slow Learners*, London, Evans/Methuen.

COWIE, E.E. (1979) *History and the Slow Learning Child*, London, The Historical Association.

DEPARTMENT OF EDUCATION AND SCIENCE (1962) *Half our Future* (Newsom Report) London, HMSO.

DEPARTMENT OF EDUCATION AND SCIENCE (1967) *Children and their Primary Schools*, London, HMSO.

DEPARTMENT OF EDUCATION AND SCIENCE (1971) *Slow Learners in Secondary Schools*, London, HMSO.

DEPARTMENT OF EDUCATION AND SCIENCE (1975) *A Language for Life: Report of the Committee of Inquiry* (Bullock Report), London, HMSO.

DEPARTMENT OF EDUCATION AND SCIENCE (1978) *Special Educational Needs* (Warnock

Report) London, HMSO.

DEPARTMENT OF EDUCATION AND SCIENCE (1979) *Developments in the BEd Degree*, London, HMSO.

DEPARTMENT OF EDUCATION AND SCIENCE (1982) *The New Teacher in School*, London, HMSO.

GULLIFORD, R. and WIDLAKE, P. (1975) *Teaching Materials for Disadvantaged Pupils*, Evans/Methuen.

HINSON, M. and HUGHES, M. (Eds) (1982) *Planning Effective Progress*, Hulton/NARE.

KEMP, R. (1979) 'Teaching strategies for the less able.' *Teaching Geography*, 5, 2.

SCOTTISH EDUCATION DEPARTMENT (1978) *The education of pupils with learning difficulties in primary and secondary schools in Scotland*, a progress report. Edinburgh, HMSO.

Remedial Education Post-Warnock: Interment or Revival?

J.B. Edwards
Educational Psychologist, Wales

There have been many articles about the aims of 'remedial education' and the way this term is used. Like so many other educational terms, though frequently used, we are unclear as to its precise meaning — if it has one. The habit has grown, in recent years, of placing 'education' after a variety of other terms as though this accords a seal of approval, respectability and clarity on these preceding terms. For example, health training becomes health education, religious instruction becomes religious education and remedial teaching becomes remedial education. It is possible that the addition of 'education' instead of clarifying, actually confuses, as we are vague and unsure about how to define this slippery term. Is it possible we are, even now, unaware of such a basic distinction as that between 'training' and 'education'? With respect to 'remedial education', if one looks at what is written in the *Warnock Report* (1978), is the term largely out of date or does it provide a meaningful concept for the eighties?

Remedial Education — Past Usage and Difficulties

Many changes have taken place since the earlier work of Burt (1937) and Schonell (1942). Their use of such concepts as 'backward' and 'retarded' has been much discussed and criticized. Problems arose with children who were described as 'under-functioning'; but more came with those pupils who were claimed to be 'over-functioning'. For example, were remedial teachers to teach only pupils who were deemed retarded? Moseley (1975) sums up these issues and concludes that to assume that a child's performance on an intelligence test indicates his capacity for learning to read is to make more than one mistake: 'The fact is that IQ is not a measure of capacity at all: it is a measure of achievement'. Sampson (1975) gives an account of both early

This article originally appeared in *Remedial Education* (1983) 18, 1

history and later developments in the area of remedial education and analyzes many of the main problems.

Some of these problems will now be grouped in the form of statements about the aims and use of the term remedial education (RE).

1.   a: RE — *the all things to all persons analogy*

Some writers have commented on the imprecise nature of the term remedial education, for example:

Tansley (1967) — 'term remedial often questioned by teachers': suggests 're-education'.
Sampson (1975) — 'in the remedial sphere an initial difficulty is the lack of any agreed definition of what term remedial implies ... RE — Special teaching? Therapy? Euphemism? Hoax?'
Ablewhite (1977) — 'loose term means nothing at all'.
Brennan (1977) — 'an unsatisfactory term'.
Gains (1980) — 'there seem to be as many definitions of the term as there are practitioners'.

1.   b: RE — *its aims* — 'we might hit the target if we knew where it was' analogy

Many writers describe conflicting aims, or targets, for remedial education, differ as to whether these aims can be achieved by all pupils, and whether these aims should be limited, even to individual schools:

Leach and Raybould (1977) — 'aim of RE to enable the child to take up his position as a full-time member of his normal group as soon as possible'.
McNicholas (1979) — 'Aims of remedial education reveal a confusing picture ... The goal of raising everyone's standards to a norm is incapable of achievement'.
Clark (1979) — 'Each stage in remedial education ... important to set long term and shorter term goals which are realistic'.
Gains (1980) — 'A pre-requisite of change must lie in a clearer definition of remedial education and its aims ... up till now most remedial work has ... had little impact on alleviating the majority of learning difficulties'.

2.   a: RE — *the para-medical analogy*

Other writers have stressed the aspect of remedial education being a remedy, putting right what is wrong:

Leach and Raybould (1977) — 'desired primary objective an acceleration of progress in basic educational attainments'.

Ablewhite (1977) — 'Put right what is wrong'.

NARE Guidelines (1977) — 'Prevention, investigation and treatment of learning difficulties'.

McNicholas (1979) — 'RE has traditionally concerned itself with the under achievement of children in the basic subjects . . . teachers have to raise standards to the level of normality'.

2. b: Disagreements are discerned about the use of the term remedial education: is it similar to treatment or rather educational?

(i) Writers such as Moseley (1975) and Brennan (1977) stress educational aspects: Moseley is against a medical model and advocates 'learning' aspects in place of a comparison to medicine.

Brennan affirms: 'Remedial education is postulated as an educational service'.

(ii) Tansley (1967), on the other hand, suggests medical or even pathological associations but still prefers to use term remedial (if he is forced to) because it implies a scientific diagnosis of reading disability.

3. RE — we should do ourselves out of a job — the redundancy analogy. A number of writers believe prevention to be vital:

McNicholas (1979) — 'Teachers should be striving for the cessation of remedial education as presently constituted — ensuring that the situation does not arise — one of its ultimate aims the eventual phasing-out of remediation in schools'.

Gains (1980) — 'There is no doubt that dramatic results have been achieved by intelligent early intervention ⁓ word 'prevention' opens up a whole new dimensions'.

4. RE — special education or not? — 'who are our clients' analogy

Authors have questioned the relationship between remedial and special education (i.e. that carried out in special schools for pupils with marked learning difficulties).

Westwood (1975) — 'Special education may be sub-divided into four categories: one of which is remedial education'.

Brennan (1977) — 'Remedial education is that part of special education concerned with children with learning difficulties which takes place outside the special schools'.

Clark (1979) — 'If not another name for special education then what ways are they different forms of intervention? . . . Is RE different or just slower than normal education?'

McNicholas (1979) — 'RE teachers should thus play a part in guiding the courses of all the children in the school'.

5. *RE — the expertise analogy*

Most writers agree on the complex nature of remedial education:

(i)   Tansley, Brennan and Ablewhite believe neurological aspects are relevant.

Tansley (1967) — 'We have stressed neurophysiological and psychoneurological processes involved in learning to read'.

(ii)   Other writers believe emotional and motivational aspects are relevant with many failing pupils, for example Lawrence (1973).

Schonell (1942) — 'Methods must have therapeutic as well as pedagogical value'.

Sampson (1975) — 'Claims that RE involves or should involve a form of psychotherapy are in line with the general concept of remediation'.

Clark (1979) — 'crucial contribution of RE is a therapeutic role'.

Gains (1980) — 'There has long been recognized a high correlation between learning failure and emotional or social disturbance'.

On at least five issues, therefore, there is uncertainty and confusion. In looking at the definition of remedial education, it might be expected that no 'real' definition (i.e. about the nature of the thing itself) could be agreed upon: there is the danger of circularity and only adding what is already implied in the term remedial education. An example of this is Gains' (1980) support for the NARE Guidelines' definition. He does not question certain terms used, for example, 'remedial education is part of education' and 'investigation' and 'treatment' of 'learning difficulties' are tautologous; they are already implied in the terms 'education' and 'remedial' and add nothing new. Furthermore, Gains does not query the nebulous phrase 'normal development of the student'. An examination of the literature, i.e. a lexical definition — as we have seen — does not really help as various authors use the term 'remedial education' in different, almost contradictory ways, so no real consensus is apparent. The third possibility of using 'operational-type' definitions again displays a striking lack of agreement; but some contributors seem to favour operational-type or stipulative definitions: in the latter the author states how it is proposed to use the term. In perusing the literature, nevertheless, it is valuable to understand which definition is being used.

Most writers on remedial education, in fact, describe what remedial education does and not what it *is*, although the NARE definition, quoted by

Brennan (1977), is more concerned with where remedial education takes place. One is not even sure who should receive this remedial education or whether it is of a para-medical nature. Then there is the inevitable slide from remedial 'education' to remedial 'training' or 'teaching', with an emphasis on basic educational skills, more often with an over-emphasis on reading and the effectiveness, or otherwise, of sustained remedial teaching. This slide from 'education' to 'teaching' can be illustrated by two examples, first by Clark (1979): 'If remedial education is seen as a specialized kind of teaching'; and, secondly, by Moseley (1975): 'Remedial education is ... in practice, remedial teaching is normally offered'. It is difficult to gauge how this teaching/training links with education. Making a similar point, Clark (1979) seeks a broadening of the conception of remedial education to ensure that a child is not deprived of many of the valuable aspects of education (not defined).

The Message from Warnock

If we can assume — always a dangerous practice — that there is some measure of agreement about issues 3 and 5 previously listed — that we should try to make ourselves redundant and the complex nature of remedial education — three crucial issues remain:

1 Is remedial education synonymous with special education or not?
2 Is it similar to medical treatment?
3 Are the aims of remedial education muddled?

Does the *Warnock Report* (1978) in its discussion of remedial education shed any light on these basic issues?

1. Is remedial education synonymous with special education or not?

This issue relates back to discussions about the earlier work of Burt and Schonell: with which pupils should 'remedial education' be concerned?

The *Warnock Report* groups together pupils with learning difficulties: this includes both the present ESN category and those remedial pupils with more specific learning problems. A conclusion made by Warnock was: 'meaningful distinction between remedial and special education should no longer be maintained'. It would seem that remedial teachers are to lose their identities and to be absorbed under the amorphous blanket of special education. Clark (1979) foresees this danger when she writes: 'Unless remedial specialists are alert to the implications for them of new developments ... they may awake to discover that integration ... has imperceptibly changed the type of children for whom they are responsible ...!' This is a major issue for those involved in remedial work. Warnock's recommendation surely opposes what Gulliford (1974), Sampson (1975) and Westwood (1975) — representing many other writers — have advocated over the years. This group would claim that special and remedial education are different, though interconnected. Gulliford has argued that remedial education is something additional to instead of something different from normal education; but that many slow learners require education specially planned to take account of learning characteristics and future needs. Westwood also asserts that 'the highly intelligent child with specific learning problems will need remedial education'. On the other hand, Warnock gains support from the viewpoints first, of Leach and Raybould (1977) who comment that 'the idea that more intelligent "underfunctioning" or "retarded" children can be expected necessarily to be more promising . . . is a very shaky assumption', and second, of Moseley (1975) who questioned the distinction between backward and retarded readers. Gains (1980) also approves of Warnock's conclusion and the opportunity to draw wide boundary lines in remedial education. However, he does not help his case through stating that 'the remedial teacher must now accept that children of all abilities can think effectively': this borders on being a self-contradiction.

Does then Warnock blur the distinction between pupils who might be aided in the shorter term and those who require a more generalized sustained form of special education? Does the introduction by Warnock of terms such as mild, moderate and severe learning difficulties break down distinctions previously made, or give new labels for these distinctions? It is in the interests of remedial teachers for this debate to continue, as it bears directly on the nature and focus of their distinctive contribution to pupils with learning problems.

2. Is remedial education like treatment?

It seems unfortunate that Warnock (following the 1977 NARE definition) in discussing remedial education, uses the analogy of treatment, i.e. a medical model, which is not an accurate comparison.

Such a model suggests that these pupils have something wrong with them that can be cured; yet they are not sick or ill, and to think otherwise misleads. There is a dictionary definition of remedial which includes 'intended to remedy disease' and a 'cure for disease'; but is this what educators have in mind? The other more likely dictionary definition is that of 'to rectify, make good, put right, correct'. But to what extent can this be achieved in the context of remedial education? Obviously a sine qua non of education is that a teacher should always aid pupils to the best of their 'ability'. One can compare some recent approaches to the teaching of ESN(S) and physically handicapped pupils. Even the most severely handicapped can be helped to make some progress.

In reality, however, for example in the area of reading, can all 'reading retardation' be rectified? Again, much depends on what we mean by reading; it is certainly for many a complicated process. It might be possible to rectify mechanical reading, for example by a course in phonics, through establishing a basic sight vocabulary, etc. This is what Tansley might describe as 're-education' and Brennan as 'adaptive' or 'corrective' work. But what about more advanced reading skills, for example, comprehension and 'cloze' procedure? Can we merely 'train' pupils in these advanced skills? McNicholas (1979) agrees that teaching reading makes possible other activities which are valuable in themselves. So if you could train reading skills successfully — and rectify weaknesses — have you then educated a pupil? We are referring to remedial 'education' and not remedial 'training'. Training in reading, number, or spelling skills is a necessary but not sufficient condition for a pupil to be educated. Obviously, to remedy or rectify a weakness is a prerequisite for a pupil to be educated. But much more is required. Sampson (1975) mentions the teaching of reading as being a means to an end. Moreover, Moseley (1975) accepts that 'in general remedial teachers are concerned to develop fluent decoding skills rather than the more advanced comprehension and study skills'.

One must thus question the 'treatment' aspect of providing a remedy for, or rectifying some educational 'illness' or 'disease'. A remedy seems inappropriate in a strictly educational, although it may be apt in a medical, context. It is unfortunate that Warnock is imprecise in its discussion of remedial education. It follows the vague and questionable use of 'needs' and 'maladjusted' in this report, where as many questions are raised, as are answered.

3   Are aims of remedial education muddled?

What 'meaning', therefore, does education have in linking it with the word 'remedial'? Education, however it is defined, is a difficult concept: (see discussions by, for example, Peters (1975), Dearden, Hirst and Peters (1975), and McNicholas (1979). McNicholas (1979) and Gains (1980) both stress that remedial education can only be viewed in the context of the general aims of education. In recent years, philosophers such as Peters have analyzed what it means to be an 'educated person'. An educated person would, at least, be able to deal with principles, be aware and be able to understand, seek something worthwhile, and be constructively critical. How can we reconcile 'rectifying' reading or number skills with this carefully reasoned viewpoint? Is it possible the word 'education' is being debased and used too loosely? If we assume that, in reading, 'comprehension' comes nearest to Peters' concept of 'understanding' in an educated person, how can a lack of ability to comprehend or criticize in a constructive and rational manner be rectified? McNicholas has argued that the remedial teacher should broaden his objectives to include the 'best' aspects of education which are open to all children. He does not clarify the 'best aspects of education' and seems optimistic in his contention. Yet one must cast doubt on such a claim when he includes 'all children' in an unrealistic manner. Is it stretching the concept of an educated person to an extreme if this can incorporate many pupils with learning difficulties? Is there the inherent danger of hypocrisy, insincerity or double-talk? Can educational aims, unless defined in a very restricted and meaningless way, ever be attained by a certain proportion of pupils? One option would be to follow McNicholas (1979) and introduce a 'relative' or operational definition with each school providing its own aims: this would be an extreme course to take. Clark (1979) and Moseley (1975) concede that even certain limited objectives are beyond the capabilities of some children, for example a child achieving a reading age of 10 or 11. Thus adding 'education' to remedial is a mixed blessing: remedial gains prestige but is blighted by a clutter of equivocal aims.

Following the comments in the *Warnock Report* about remedial education and the challenges which remedial teachers will face in the eighties, is it not time to reconsider the meaning and application of such key terms as remedial education? Leach and Raybould (1977) stress that 'a re-think of the objectives, implications and efficiency' of remedial provision is required. Are we justified in coasting along as in the past, believing that as the term remedial education was 'good enough' for the 1960s and 1970s, it will be 'good enough' for the present decade? Some will contend that it is not abstract semantic distinctions which are important, but how we teach children in a practical situation. Yet can one ignore such distinctions? The Oxford moral philosopher, Hare, defending his interest and work in analyzing moral concepts has argued: 'I was always interested in the practical problems. But I thought it was essential that we get our concepts straight before we tried to discuss anything else'. Can therefore vagueness in our thinking about basic terms be justified? How can we evaluate the effectiveness of our practice, if we are not clear what it is that we are doing?

Instead of using remedial education, perhaps our thoughts should be concentrated on devising a new, and more accurate, term for use during the remainder of this century. This new term should denote that the work done by remedial teachers is a necessary prerequisite for a child to be educated: it has a high instrumental value. And it should direct attention to such fundamental issues as 'realistic aims', 'our clients' and to stress that it is not a para-medical 'flying-teacher' service. Much hard thinking is required, as any attempt to define this term is fraught with difficulties. Yet it must be made clear what this term implies so that subsequently our practice will be more effective. To know what we should be doing can lead to further advancements in our knowledge of relevant techniques (for example, precision teaching, micro-computers, etc.) and lead to more fruitful research into this important area.

J.B. Edwards

References

ABLEWHITE, R.C. (1977) 'What is remedial education' in WIDLAKE, P. (Ed.). *Remedial Education: Programmes and Progress*, London, Longman.

BRENNAN, W.K. (1977) 'A policy for remedial education', in WIDLAKE, P. (Ed.). *Remedial Education: Programmes and Progress*, London, Longman.

BURT, C. (1937) *The Backward Child*, London, Hodder and Stoughton.

CLARK, M.M. (1979) 'Why remedial? Implications of using the concept of remedial education' in GAINS, C.W. and MCNICHOLAS, J.A. (Eds.) *Remedial Education: Guidelines for the Future*. London, Longman.

DEARDEN, R.F., HIRST, P.H. and PETERS, R.S. (Eds.) (1975) *A Critique of Current Educational Aims*, London, Routledge and Kegan Paul.

DEPARTMENT OF EDUCATION AND SCIENCE (1978) *Special Educational Needs*, (Warnock Report), London, HMSO.

GAINS, C.W. (1980) 'Remedial education in the 1980s', *Remedial Education*, 15, 1, pp. 5–9.

GULLIFORD, R. (1974) 'Advances in remedial education', in PRINGLE, M.K. and VARMA, V.P. (Eds.) *Advances in Educational Psychology* 2. London, University of London Press.

LAWRENCE, D. (1973) *Learning Through Counselling*, London, Ward Lock Educational.

LEACH, D.J. and RAYBOULD, E.C. (1977) *Learning and Behaviour Difficulties in School*, London, Open Books.

MCNICHOLAS, J.A. (1979) 'Aims of remedial education: a critique' in GAINS, C.W. and MCNICHOLAS, J.A. (Eds.), *Remedial Education: Guidelines for the Future*. London, Longman.

MOSELEY, D. (1975) *Special Provision for Reading*. Slough. NFER.

NATIONAL ASSOCIATION FOR REMEDIAL EDUCATION (1977) *Guidelines No. 1 Report on In-service Training*.

PETERS, R.S. (Ed.) (1975) *The Philosophy of Education*. London, Oxford University Press.

SAMPSON, O.C. (1975) *Remedial Education*, London, Routledge and Kegan Paul.

SCHONELL, F.J. (1942) *Backwardness in the Basic Subjects*, Edinburgh, Oliver and Boyd.

TANSLEY, A.E. (1967) *Reading and Remedial Reading*. London, Routledge and Kegan Paul.

WESTWOOD, P. (1975) *The Remedial Teacher's Handbook*, Edinburgh, Oliver and Boyd.

The Changing Role of the Remedial Teacher

Mike Laskier
Peripatetic Remedial Teacher, Liverpool

'Whatever is remedial education?' enquired Olive Sampson (1975). The recent history of the remedial service records that many practitioners, as well as academics, are raising similar questions. Pirandello (1921) entitled his play, 'Six Characters in Search of an Author'. The remedial service is similarly in search of a role and seems to be spending an inordinate amount of effort in the quest. Sometimes it must seem to an outsider that the attempt to discover an identity and a purpose diverts energy which, in these difficult times for the education service, would be better expended in seeking improved methods of attaining a generally agreed goal.

To take an analogy: suppose that, as obesity is perceived as a major health hazard in the developed world, official agencies were set up to remedy the problem. Imagine the initial arguments over the definition of the target client:

'Can we help long-term fatties?'
'How much above average weight is the obese?'
'Perhaps the entire developed world is too fat and even to be average is to be at risk.'
'Would our efforts be better spent on anorexics?'

Consider too, the wonder diets: the claims for weight-loss; the excitement of a new breakthrough. 'Sawdust and water give fantastic results during a strict four-week regime.' Then the disappointment when longer-term results show that the short-term improvements are not maintained.

Later, perhaps, might come the realization that the concept of 'obesity' is a matter of relativity and that the proportion of the population who may be said to be obese is not meaningfully quantifiable. Similarly, gimmicky short-term remedies might be seen to be chimerical. Perhaps, too, the solution might seem to be connected with the inculcation of healthy eating habits for all: clinics which deal with the effects of poor diet would give way to agencies which promoted healthy dietary practice for all.

There are indications that remedial education has entered this latter stage and it might be of interest to show why it has taken so long and proved so difficult.

In considering the search for an identity for the remedial service, it is important to stress that it is a comparatively novel institution. In many respects remedial education in England and Wales may be thought of as a product of the 1960s, although a service did exist before then. Various dates are given, from the 1920s (Sewell, 1982), 1930s or 1940s (Gulliford, 1979 and 1983) and the 1950s (Sampson, 1969b). However, Bushell (1974) in his history of the first ten years of the National Association for Remedial Education (NARE) expressed the view that the national provision of remedial education may be considered to be coeval with NARE, the foundation of which was the result of a meeting held early in 1962. At that time, the fledgling remedial service, as would any new organization, needed to establish defensible role boundaries.

> In any institution workers must struggle to align broad goals and realistic demands of their work. By responding to role expectations projected by workers holding different organizational ranks and by meeting the technical challenges of day to day work, professional workers in organizations create roles for themselves.
> (Milofsky, 1976, p. 118)

By the end of the 1960s, when 65 per cent of boroughs and 71 per cent of counties maintained a remedial service (Sampson 1969a), NARE was working on a definition which claimed remedial education to be 'that part of special education concerned with children with learning difficulties which is provided outside the special schools' (Bushell, 1974, p. 7). It defined the following settings:

(a) in special classes within ordinary schools,
(b) in special remedial centres which children attend on a part-time basis,
(c) withdrawal groups taken either by members of staff or a visiting peripatetic remedial teacher.

It must be stressed that the definition leant heavily towards small group teaching. Only at the end, almost as an afterthought, was there a reference to a 'wider' role: 'it also includes the work of the specialist advisory remedial teachers who may guide and support other teachers or schools'.

That there was a wider role can be seen from the results of the enquiry into the remedial service (Sampson, 1969b). Questions in this enquiry elicited claims of a range of roles which embraced out-of-school activities, parental involvement, attainment and diagnostic testing and advisory work (Sampson, 1969a). Similarly an article in *Remedial Education* entitled 'The Extension of Peripatetic Remedial Teachers' Professional Expertise' listed ten 'widening' roles (Pumfrey, 1971). However, 'real' remedial education —

the bread-and-butter role — remained as Gulliford (1979) has described it as being in the 1940s: group withdrawal. Collins (1974) coined the telling phrase, 'emergency educational first aid'. Attempts to fulfil this role through providing separate remedial centres often produced an inconsistent approach because of the lack of continuity between work at the centre and the school (Cuthbert, 1971; Widlake, 1974). Within schools remedial departments provided locational rather than functional integration.

> Far too often we do find that remedial departments are separated both physically and spiritually from the main corpus of the school, with neither body fully aware of what is going on in the other. These departments are not infrequently looked upon as entities in their own right with little or no liaison with the rest of the school.
> (McNicholas, 1979a p. 31).

Blackburn (1972) wrote 'for approximately half their week the children live in the close confines of the department'. Garnett (1976) described her remedial unit as being 'to all intents and purposes . . . a separate entity with its own way of life but obtaining "pay and rations" from the parent school'.

Lihou described how 'remedial readers' were extracted daily in groups for thirty-minute sessions:

> cloak room, staffroom, corridor and finally a curtained-off section of the dining room were all tried . . . a . . . hut became available for conversion into a reading centre and it is in the peace and quiet of this room, away from the main school, that most of the remedial work is now done.
> (Lihou, 1974).

But it was not only this separation from the mainstream of a school which made untenable the main role as expert 'educational first-aiders', chosen by the new service. As this role was being constructed, research was undermining its rationale (Carroll, 1972, DES, 1975, 18, 10). Wolfendale (1979, p. 70) wrote of the 'conspicuous lack of sustained success with traditional remedial methods' and Gains (1980) claimed that there was evidence to suggest that some children were actually being handicapped by the efforts which were meant to help them.

Other factors adversely affected the credibility of traditional remedial teaching. Lawrence (1972 and 1973) suggested that *better* results could be obtained through the use of non-professional counsellors. In the USA, Headstart, a compensatory pre-school education programme was widely held to have been a failure: 'the adverse publicity generated by the Ohio-Westinghouse study left politicians and public with the impression not only that Headstart itself had failed but also that early intervention programmes in general were pointless' (Cookson, 1981).

The economic expansionism of the sixties had by then given way to the austerity of the seventies (Lacey and Lawton, 1981). During a period when rolls were falling, remedial teaching was increasingly perceived as a luxury. It was felt that 'the falling birthrate (and economic factors) may result in ordinary schools retaining more children with disabilities than in the past' (Green, 1976, p. 108). There was uncertainty and confusion over key issues in remedial education, such as:

(a) The extent to which it is synonymous with special education.
(b) confusion over aims: are we really trying to raise every child to some norm? (Edwards, 1983).

The problem was further aggravated by the lack of agreement as to what constituted a target-client. Originally, following the theories of Burt and Schonell, the client was thought to be backward and in need of a period of intensive coaching to enable him to rejoin his peers (Sampson, 1975). Later the definition was widened to allow a more heterogeneous grouping. O'Hagan (1977) wrote of the remedial service,

> For instance, children with many different problems are their immediate concern. This spectrum of pupils can include the slow learner, the physically handicapped pupils, the child from a deprived area, the autistic child, the emotionally and socially disturbed pupil and the school drop-out to name but a few. Each child may require a different kind of assistance and guidance and this will call for a knowledge of specialist skills.

This blurring of the boundary, whilst making it easier to claim a need for the service, made the task of justifying its approach more difficult. Worse, standards of provision differed considerably.

Clark (1976) claimed that whether a child received remedial help depended not on a given level of difficulty in some area of the curriculum but on factors such as home area, school attended, age, intelligence, score on a particular screening test or whether there was a diagnosis of dyslexia, brain dysfunction or similar condition.

Making a Choice

Faced with these problems of face validity in its chosen role, the remedial service had to decide its next move. The three main choices which were then available were:

1 To continue the same approach, arguing that there will always be a need for someone to give extra coaching to those who fail in or are failed by the system. Further, it might be that new research would uncover hitherto undetected long-term gains by remedial pupils.
2 To become specialized in less vulnerable fields such as dyslexia.
3 To expand its role.

This last was the choice of the NARE establishment. In 1982 the president of NARE claimed that his organization had been 'extending its brief beyond the rather narrow sphere of basic subject teaching' for the best part of a decade (McNicholas, 1982). Certainly by 1977 NARE had produced a new definition of remedial education:

> Remedial education is regarded as that part of education which is concerned with the prevention, investigation and treatment of learning difficulties from whatever source they may emanate and which hinder the normal education development of the student. (NARE 1977 p. 2).

This definition had, they claimed, several advantages over its predecessors. It suggested that remedial teachers should be skilled at dealing with learning failure across the curriculum rather than exclusively concerned with basic subjects; it brought adults within their remit, and, finally, it included effective and social, as well as cognitive dimensions within remedial education.

By 1979 NARE had developed and refined the new role definition to include: assessment, prescription, teaching and therapy, support for colleagues, liaison with support services, parents and the community at large (NARE, 1979, pp. 3 and 4). Across the country, remedial teachers were adopting this wider role. However, a survey of peripatetic remedial teachers in Liverpool (Owen, 1979) showed a preference for the traditional roles of surveying, withdrawal-teaching and advice to teachers and heads.

Recent Developments

Mao Tse Tung argued that progress in the arts and sciences would be promoted by 'letting a hundred flowers blossom and a hundred schools of thought contend' (Cohen and Cohen, 1980). In the mid-seventies, the remedial teachers were busily propagating their hundred flowers and roles proliferated. They related to children, teachers, schools and the big world outside. In relation to the individual child O'Hagan (1977) defined roles for the remedial teacher as, guide and counsellor, therapist, evaluator, manager of the learning environment and curriculum developer.

With regard to teachers NARE (1979) suggested that the remedial teachers should support and advise colleagues on grouping techniques for the whole range of special educational needs on materials and apparatus and on remedial work across the curriculum. The argument is that, as rolls fall, remedial teachers will increasingly be called upon to work with the class teachers (Kent and O'Brien, 1984) and as more handicapped children are, as a result of the 1981 Education Act, being taught in the ordinary school, remedial teachers will increasingly be called upon to exercise a consultant role in helping colleagues to cope (Smith, 1982). Remedial teachers will also need to help class teachers to cope with 'the additional burden presented by comprehensive developmental record keeping' (Evans, 1979).

As far as schools were concerned models were constructed which would have the effect of ensuring that the remedial department in schools made input to all significant decisions: curriculum content and methodology, resources and organization, careers education, work experience, counselling, computer-aided learning and in-service education of teachers (Bailey, 1980; Gains and McNicholas, 1981; Cant, 1982).

Other roles were suggested requiring greater involvement with outside agencies, parents and the community at large. McNicholas (1983) suggests that the 'named person' under the 1981 Education Act should be a remedial specialist and Sewell (1982) suggested Warnock Action Research Groups drawn from Co-ordinators of Special Education for a number of schools.

It can be seen that following the demolition of the empirical basis for its earlier 'narrow' role, the remedial service has tried to broaden its scope so as to inform virtually all areas of education. This has had the admirable effect of changing other teachers' and administrators' role expectations of remedial teachers, thus allowing the service a much more central role than it formerly occupied. There is, however, another side to this coin. The massive expansion has led to a loss of clarity and focus. There is a well-known description of Chinese rice-fields: they cover acres of land but are only a couple of inches deep. There is a possibility that this description may come to apply to the remedial service. There is also the danger that, having emerged from his broom closet, the remedial teacher may now be thought to be barging into everyone else's classroom trying to find a place for himself.

Meanwhile personnel in other areas of special education have also examined their role boundaries within the post-Warnock context of increasing provision for children with special needs in ordinary schools. Educational psychologists and teachers in special schools, for example, have sought not only to justify their traditional role but also to extend their activities into areas previously considered the province of the remedial service.

The tendency to maintain their role is well-documented by Potts (1983). She examined some of the pronouncements and decisions made since the publication of the *Warnock Report*, by local education authorities, teachers' unions and other bodies. Potts questions whether, for instance, a mushrooming of courses on special educational needs is a positive response to integration or whether it is one of the methods being used to maintain special education as a separate discipline needing a boost in status. She draws attention to a tendency to use resources intended for the implementation of the 1981 Act, not for any of the *Warnock Report*'s three priority areas but for:

> additional psychologists and administrators, ranks of middle-management advisers rather than school or classroom based practitioners. This raises the status of special education, but in doing so confirms an identity separate from the mainstream.

The latter, colonizing, impetus is also on record. On publication of the *Warnock Report*, the editor of *Special Education: Forward Trends* the National Council for Special Education (NCSE) journal, counselled her readers not to see the recommendations as a source of anxiety, but as an opportunity to contribute their knowledge and experience in new roles such as advisory work, teacher training and operating special schools as resource centres:

> It is essential to realize that the report is recommending not a contraction of special education but an expansion to provide an organized system of special help for the considerable number of pupils with special needs in the ordinary school.
> (Peter, 1978).

Marra (1981) suggested that special schools might respond to falling rolls by developing 'a new product market' which could be sold to mainstream schools. As an example he described a system of part-time attendance at a special school supplemented by 'a remedial programme ... offered to the parent school for each child to be implemented during the remaining weekdays'.

Petrie in the 1978 presidential address to NCSE, quoted that organization as suggesting that in a broadly-based special education service the special school could provide services over and above that of providing education for the more severely handicapped. He suggested the title for these establishments: 'Special Education Centre'.

Ainscow and his colleagues (1978) had made a similar proposal in anticipation of the *Warnock Report*. They piloted a scheme to use a special school as:

> a melting pot for testing hypotheses about the development of appropriate curricula and teaching methods ... we might develop the role of the special school as an area resource of advice and ideas for teachers in ordinary schools.

However, they noted that special school teachers, while 'skilful classroom operators' did not necessarily have the skills and techniques needed to pass on this expertise to other teachers. It is in just this area that remedial teachers have most experience.

The Future Role of the Remedial Teacher

The Warnock Committee recommended a service which would combine the strengths of special *and* remedial teachers. They saw the formation of a special education advice and support service as an 'indispensable condition for effective special educational provision in ordinary schools' (13.2). In establishing this joint enterprise the term 'remedial' might, with advantage, disappear.

To return to the analogy with dietary matters, which was made at the beginning of this article. Picture the dieticians moving away from the short-term crash diets, towards health education for all and towards providing a healthy diet for all. Suppose, however, that the clinic has a fluorescent sign above the door which still proclaims 'The Weight Watchers' Slim-Fast Crash Diet Centre'. Wouldn't that discourage new custom?

Galletley (1976) wrote an article with the self-explanatory title, 'How to do away with yourself'. In this, he explained his concept of the role of 'Head of opportunities faculty'. The title 'remedial' has associations and connotations which hinder change. Lewis (1984) has addressed the problem of the negative and distancing effect of the title, 'remedial'. He suggests 'support service' as a title. Many authorities have appointed heads of support services. Sheffield decided in 1977 to set up a support teacher service (Hannon and Mullins, 1980). Certainly a new unified service needs to be as long on support as on advice, if it is to gain credibility with teachers in ordinary schools.

Care would need to be taken to ensure that advice was not substituted for support. As Lord Chesterfield wrote to his son in 1748:

> Advice is seldom welcome; and those who want it the most always want it the least.

Sir Edward Britton, a member of the Warnock Committee, said upon publication of the report that LEAs should develop its special education advisory report but:

> I do not mean you should be swamped by the hit-and-run brigade who turn up for twenty minutes, tell the teacher what he is doing wrong and then disappear back to county hall (quoted in *The Times* 14 July 1978).

Teachers in this country are no different from those in California who were observed by Milofsky (1976):

> One way teachers defined an outsider who was not to be talked to was as a person who only spends one or two hours at infrequent intervals at a school. This is a common pattern among supervisory personnel from the central offices of school districts. They view such persons as basically untrustworthy and not necessarily interested in children (p. xxii).

The main contribution to the new service from the present Remedial Service will be in the areas of assessment, in-school support and in-service education for teachers.

According to Peter (1984), the 1981 Education Act concentrates upon 'time-consuming and costly procedures of assessing and making statements for the estimated 2 per cent of children with severe or complex learning difficulties'. She argues that at a time when the government is cutting-back,

LEAs foresee a dimunition of funds for children with moderate learning difficulties unless they double the number who are statemented. The remedial service has shared in this role with the school psychological service, and to the extent that manpower resources are being stretched to the limits by the exigencies of 'statementing' under the 1981 Education Act, will need to increase its involvement. In most areas, remedial teachers are well used to screening and assessment procedures.

The type of support which the ordinary school will require is altering. Expertise in reading and writing will no longer suffice. Support will need to be of two main types: 'ecological', that is, supporting the school as a system and 'individual', helping a school to serve an individual with special needs. The remedial service is ideally placed to act as an interface between the special school and the ordinary school.

Despite the failure of government to provide proper funding for local initiatives, INSET will have to expand. Again the present remedial service is well prepared for organizing such courses and arranging the necessary specialist input to them.

The Hargreaves report on under-achievement in London comprehensive schools (ILEA, 1984) recommends closer liaison between subject and special needs departments to ensure that pupils receiving extra help with basic skills do not thereby lose touch with the mainstream curriculum.

HMI in Scotland suggested a twin approach of curriculum development and team-teaching between remedial class and subject teachers. This was coupled with an extension of mixed ability teaching, thus reducing 'withdrawal' teaching. At the same time, the status of remedial teachers was enhanced (Booth, 1983).

Developments such as these emphasize the need for school based in-service training, in which skills gained from extensive experience with pupils with difficulties in learning will be shared with colleagues.

As class teachers in primary schools and subject teachers in secondary schools are expected to take more responsibility for the direct teaching of children with special needs, the future for remedial staff looks likely to be in the role of consultant advisers rather than emergency first aiders.

References

AINSCOW, M., BOND, J., GARDNER, J. & TWEDDLE, D. (1978) 'A new role for the special, school?'. *Special Education: Forward Trends*, 5, 1, pp. 15–16.

BAILEY, T.J. (1980) 'Role change' *Times Educational Supplement*, 26 September, pp. 31 and 34.

BLACKBURN, S. (1972) 'Westfield school: the slow learner department,' *Remedial Education*, 7, 3, pp. 11–14.

BOOTH, A. (1983) 'A teaching approach to learning difficulties,' *Times Educational Supplement*, 9 September p. 44.

BRENNAN, W.K. (1971) 'A policy for remedial education.' *Remedial Education* 6, 1, pp. 7–11.

BUSHELL, R. (1974) 'NARE The first ten years' *Remedial Education*, 9, 1, pp. 5–7.

CANT, M. (1982) 'Educational learning difficulties format for school policy,' in PURDY, F. (Ed.) *NARE Newsletter*, autumn, pp. 7–10.

CARROLL, H. (1972) 'The remedial teaching of reading: an evaluation,' *Remedial Education*, 7, 1, pp. 10–15.

CHESTERFIELD, Earl of (1748) Letter to his son dated 29 January 1748.

CLARK, M.M. (1976) 'Why remedial? Implications of using the concept of remedial education' *Remedial Education*, 11, 1.

COHEN, J.M. and COHEN, M.J. (1980) *The Penguin Dictionary of Modern Quotations*, 2nd Ed, Harmondsworth, Penguin.

COLLINS, J. (1974) 'The remedial teacher's banner with a new device,' *Remedial Education*, 9, 3, pp. 121–4.

COOKSON, C. (1981) 'Safe future for Head Start,' *Times Educational Supplement*, 13 February.

CUTHBERT, T. (1971) 'The NARE national survey of remedial centres for retarded pupils,' *Remedial Education*, 6, 2, pp. 34–6.

DEPARTMENT OF EDUCATION AND SCIENCE (1975) *A Language for Life*. (Bullock Report), HMSO.

DEPARTMENT OF EDUCATION AND SCIENCE (1978) *Special Educational Needs* (Warnock Report) London, HMSO.

EDWARDS, J.B. (1983) 'Remedial education post-Warnock: interment or revival?' *Remedial Education*, 18, 1, reprinted in this volume.

EVANS, R. (1979) 'Identification and intervention' in GAINS, C. and MCNICHOLAS, J.A. (Eds.) *Remedial Education: guidelines for the future*, London, Longman, pp. 39–69.

GAINS, C. (1980) 'Remedial Education across the basic curriculum,' *Times Educational Supplement*, 26 September.

GAINS, C. and MCNICHOLAS, J. (1981) 'Broader remedies', *Times Educational Supplement*, 11 September.

GALLETLEY, I. (1976) 'How to do away with yourself.' *Remedial Education*, 11, 3.

GARNETT, J. (1976) 'Special children in a comprehensive' *Special Education: Forward Trends*, 3, 1, pp. 8–11.

GREEN, L. (1976) 'Developments in special education: implications for children in ordinary schools,' *Remedial Education*, 11, 3, pp. 107–11.

GULLIFORD, R. (1979) 'Remedial work across the curriculum.' in GAINS, C. and MCNICHOLAS, J. (Eds.) *Remedial Education: guidelines for the future*, London, Longman, pp. 143–9.

GULLIFORD, R. (1983) 'The teacher's own resources,' *Remedial Education*, 18, 4, pp. 150–5, reprinted in this volume.

HANNON, P. and MULLINS, S. (1980) 'Support teachers in Sheffield', *Special Education: Forward Trends*, 7, 4, December.

ILEA (1984) '*Improving secondary schools*' ILEA Learning Resource, Kennington Lane, London.

KENT, M. and O'BRIEN, T. (1984) 'Separate development,' *Times Educational Supplement*, 20 January, p. 21.

LACEY, C. and LAWTON, D. (1981), (Eds.) *Issues in Evaluation and Accountability*, London, Methuen.

LAWRENCE, D. (1972) 'Counselling of retarded readers, by non-professionals.' *Educational Research* 15, 1, pp. 48–51.

LAWRENCE, D. (1973) *Learning through Counselling*, London, Ward Lock Educational.

LEWIS, G. (1984) 'A supportive role at secondary level,' *Remedial Education*, 19, 1.

LIHOU, H.A. (1974) 'A school-based reading centre,' *Remedial Education* 9, 2, pp. 75–6.

MCNICHOLAS, J.A. (1979) 'Aims of remedial education: a critique,' in GAINS, C. and

McNICHOLAS, J.A. (Eds.) *Remedial Education: guidelines for the future*, London, Longman, pp. 27–36.

McNICHOLAS, J. (1982) *Towards Quality Education*, Presidential address given to NARE conference, August, reprinted in PURDY, F. (ed.), *NARE Newsletter*, autumn.

McNICHOLAS, J. (1983) 'Deviation from Warnock', *Times Educational Supplement*, 9 September 1983, p. 43.

MARRA, A. (1981) 'A helping hand', *Remedial Education*, 16, 3 pp. 115–9.

MILOFSKY, C. (1976) *Special Education: a sociological study of California programs*, New York, Praeger.

NATIONAL ASSOCIATION FOR REMEDIAL EDUCATION (1977) *NARE guidelines No. 1: report on in-service training*, Stafford, NARE.

NATIONAL ASSOCIATION FOR REMEDIAL EDUCATION (1979) *NARE guidelines No. 2: the role of remedial teachers*, Stafford, NARE.

O'HAGAN, F. (1977) 'The role of the remedial teacher: problems and perspectives,' *Remedial Education*, 12, 2, pp. 56–9.

OWEN, S.H. (1979) *The development of the remedial service in Liverpool with special reference to the Everton Remedial Team*, unpublished special study for Diploma in Special Education, University of Liverpool.

PETER, M. (1978) Editorial 'Warnock Reports', *Special Education: Forward Trends* 5, 2, June, p. 7.

PETER, M. (1984) 'A hard act to follow,' *Times Educational Supplement*, 30 March p. 2.

PETRIE, I. (1978) Presidential address in *Facing the future: roles and responsibilities*, report of the sixth National Conference of the National Council for Special Education, Stratford-on-Avon, National Council for Special Education.

PIRANDELLO, L. (1921) *Six Characters in Search of an Author*, (trans Linstrum, J.), London, Methuen, 1979 edition.

POTTS, P. (1983) *Role-call: providing teachers for children with special needs*, Liverpool, University of Liverpool, School of Education occasional paper.

PUMFREY, P.D. (1971) 'The extension of peripatetic remedial teachers' professional expertise.' *Remedial Education*, 6, 2, June.

SAMPSON, O. (1969a) 'Remedial education services. Report on an enquiry,' *Remedial Education*, 4, 1, Part 1 (Facts and figures) pp. 3–8, Part 2 (Views and methods) pp. 61–5.

SAMPSON, O. (1969b) 'A real need for rescrutiny,' *Special Education*, 58, 1, pp. 6–9.

SAMPSON, O. (1975) *Remedial Education*, London, Routledge and Kegan Paul.

SEWELL, G. (1982) *Reshaping Remedial Education*, Croom Helm.

SMITH, C.J. (1982) 'Helping colleagues cope: a consultant role for the remedial teacher,' *Remedial Education*, 17, 2, pp. 75–8.

TRICKEY, G. and KOSKY, R. (1983) 'The Barking Project: organising for diversity,' *Remedial Education*, 18, 2, pp. 53–8.

WIDLAKE, P. (1974) 'Editorial', *Remedial Education*, 9, 1, pp. 3–4.

WOLFENDALE, S. (1979) 'Early identification screening systems (with reference to the Croydon Screening Technique)' in GAINS, C. and McNICHOLAS, J.A. (Eds.), *Remedial Education: Guidelines for the future*, London, Longman, pp. 69–82.

Remedial Education: The Challenge for Trainers

Charles W. Gains
Principal Lecturer in Special Educational Needs,
Edge Hill College of Higher Education

> We are living in the time of the parenthesis, the time between eras.
> It is as though we have bracketed off the present from both the past
> and the future, for we are neither here nor there ... Although the
> time between eras is uncertain, it is a great and yeasty time, filled
> with opportunity. (Naisbitt, 1984)

In this time of bewildering social and economic change the teaching
profession is understandably on the defensive. Higher expectations are
coupled with fewer resources, accountability with diminished status. It is
claimed that at no time has morale been lower. A recent report on London's
secondary schools (ILEA, 1984) devotes some time to this problem and
among its recommendations the need for staff development is stressed. This
follows a long line of other reports that belatedly have come to recognize the
crucial role of the teacher as a mediator. This article is concerned with those
designated 'remedial teachers' who inevitably find themselves at the sharp
end of educational problems. The debate is examined, some recent developments outlined, several principles given for the training and re-training of
such personnel, and finally a model examined for improving schools.

Defining Remedial Education

For many years the term 'remedial education' was accepted almost without
question. It was generally thought of as a simple rescue operation. The small
band of beleaguered children were seen as awaiting the arrival of the
remedial cavalry who would quickly rout their learning difficulties and
would escort them on their way to the promised land. Such a vision was
never really the case but was fostered in the fifties and sixties by the child

deficit model which led to the proliferation of such expressions as 'culturally deprived', 'restricted code', 'compensatory education' and so on. In short, nothing was seen as being wrong with the system, the fault lay in environmental factors beyond the control of teachers. The research into the effects of teacher attitudes and expectations led by the famous Rosenthal and Jacobsen (1968) study altered this, as did more recent work on effective schools (Rutter *et al*, 1979). Now there is a growing acceptance that the school itself can contribute as much, if not more, to learning failure as supposed low intelligence or unfortunate background. The rapid growth in remedial provision which has taken place in the last two decades has coincided with this shift in attitude and opinion.

Initially, despite poor career prospects, the quality of recruit to the new profession was very high. The early editions of the journal *Remedial Education* were filled with articles describing new materials, techniques and interesting strategies. But here and there a few voices were raised querying the whole basis of the operation. Collins (1973), for example, described remedial education as a 'hoax' based on his earlier research. During the somewhat heady days of expansion this was to find few friends but gradually remedial education was subjected to an increasing amount of intellectual rigour (Clark, 1976; McNicholas, 1976; Golby and Gulliver, 1979; Gains, 1980; Edwards, 1983). Early definitions of remedial education based on the concept of retardation, the gap between performance on intelligence tests and tests of attainment in basic subjects, was found wanting. Eventually the National Association for Remedial Education arrived at the following:

Remedial education is that part of education which is concerned with the prevention, investigation and treatment of learning difficulties from whatever source they may emanate and which hinder the normal educational development of the student.' (NARE Guidelines No. 1, 1977)

This broke new ground in two principal ways. First it had resisted the temptation to categorize pupils i.e. it did not use terms such as 'backward', 'slow learner', 'retarded' etc. In this sense it pre-empted the *Warnock Report* which appeared the following year. Second, it recognized a new element in remedial work, namely that of prevention. Prevention implies, of course, that the base of the operation should be in the mainstream and not confined to the largely withdrawal group technique. Remedial teachers had been urged for some time to come out of the 'broom cupboard' and a further NARE publication (Guidelines No 2, 1979) went on to suggest the clearest definition of role then available.

The argument continues to generate heat. Edwards (1983) reviews succinctly the attempts at defining remedial education without coming to any particular conclusion other than to stress the need for a more accurate term than remedial education 'for use during the remainder of the century'.

Charles W. Gains

The *Warnock Report* had concluded that '... a meaningful distinction between remedial and special education can no longer be maintained' and it is becoming increasingly popular to use that Committee's expression 'special educational needs' to describe the wide variety of activity in the area of the treatment of learning difficulties. The question is no longer simply a matter of semantics and is even forcing NARE to reconsider its own title. Remedial education has clearly worked through its infancy and is now experiencing the pangs of adolescence.

Contemporary Developments

A wide variety of developments is affecting remedial teachers, indeed is affecting education in general. Some of these can be grouped under the heading of institutional change and response. In secondary schools, for example, remedial work has been organized pretty much along the same pattern as subject teaching. Similar staff hierarchies exist, discrete areas of the school are set aside for the activity, there are often internal examinations conducted on the same lines as elsewhere in the school. Remedial education may be difficult to define but the one thing it is *not* is a subject. Rather it is part of a general strategy for alleviating learning failure. It is encouraging in this respect to hear of team teaching approaches and a whole variety of ingenious intervention strategies. Much of this has been prompted by Warnock and the implications of the 1981 Education Act for integrating handicapped pupils into mainstream activity.

Similarly curriculum innovations abound. These range from mastery learning (Gains, 1976) to precision teaching (Raybould and Solity, 1982) to the exciting area of thinking skills (Weber, 1978; Feuerstein, 1980). To this we can add the concept of remedial work across the curriculum (Gulliford, 1979) and the extension of remedial work into the 14–19 curriculum (McNicholas, 1979; Lofthouse, 1983). The impact of the new technology has not been lost on the profession either and remedial teachers are actively involved in transferring much of their traditional work on to the computer (Clamp, 1983). As if this were not enough, encouraging results from parental involvement activities (Bush, 1983) have added yet another important dimension to the work.

A decade ago little of the above existed. Most of the teaching activity was firmly grounded in what Weber (1978) unkindly termed 'repetitious remedial exercises'. The current explosion of knowledge and technique has certainly caught some teachers unaware and it would be wrong to assume that all the innovations have been greeted with universal acclaim. Nevertheless, they remain a challenge and demonstrate that we do indeed live in ' a great and yeasty time'.

52

In-Service Training: Some Guiding Principles

In the face of the above, in-service provision has yet to respond effectively. It is proving difficult to get out of the para-medical groove i.e. assessment, then diagnosis followed by prescription. There is clearly still room for traditional approaches but the amount of time and enormous detail spent on the sub-skills of reading and associated areas is increasingly hard to justify. The challenge posed by the wider curriculum, parental involvement, computers and developments in the area of problem solving is yet to make a major impact on the training and retraining of teachers. Teacher training institutions remain the major suppliers of substantial courses in the area of special educational needs and the following thoughts are directed largely in that direction. There have, of course, been critics of this near monopoly. Anning (1982) for example states: 'One gets the feeling that courses have been hastily cobbled together in a desperate attempt to justify the two evenings per week statutory in-service provision and so resist staff redundancies, rather than to serve the training needs of teachers.' Anning is keen to see a reversal of the approach that teaches theory before practice and urges teachers to shop around for more relevant courses. There is no doubt that the evidence regarding the effectiveness of full-time courses is not particularly encouraging. Some of these courses have developed in a random fashion and been built around a particular personality who having garnered some experience and expertise many years before can proceed to live off the residue until retirement. A decade or so ago such a model could be sustained; research, techniques and materials were limited and capable of mastery. This is not the case today. A more rational approach would start with market research, identifying the needs of teachers, schools and local authorities. It would proceed to examine whether the institution can actually meet those needs from its own resources or whether these need supplementing in some way. Almost certainly this would require a collaborative or collegial approach to the problem. The end product would be a dynamic and flexible course initially and continuously negotiable.

In view of this it seems apt to consider some general principles which might govern our more substantial courses.

1 Personal Development

Courses should be firmly based on programmes of personal development. No two teachers have precisely the same needs. To force groups time after time through the same syllabus is crude to say the least. This take-it-or-leave-it pattern inevitably means that some students identify with the course content, some partially and some none at all. The latter soldier on making the qualification the goal and barely concealing their cynicism. It should be possible within course requirements for students to negotiate and design their own programmes of study and work.

2 Broad Based

Courses should be broad based in that they can be sensitive to contemporary issues and developments. For example it would be remiss of trainers nowadays not to include some knowledge and understanding of an emergent multi-cultural society. Broad based courses also provide opportunities for students to change career direction with the minimum of inconvenience.

3 School Focused and School Based

Teaching still remains a profession in which theory is regularly examined in isolation from practice and expects the student to make some connection at a future date. It is obviously more sensible to work the other way round to look at the operation and then raid the theory for solutions. To this end courses should not only be school focused but school based and have at their core problem-solving activities.

4 Multi-disciplinary Approaches

Courses should encourage multi-disciplinary thinking. The complexity of most problems is such that there is no real alternative to team approaches. This means not only to work in partnership with immediate colleagues but to encourage involvement with parents, the community and the range of voluntary and statutory agencies.

5 Local Authority Involvement

A major course should be viewed as an on-going activity involving the contributory authority, through its Advisory Service, at all stages. A much stronger triangle needs to be forged between LEAs, INSET providers and the teaching force and this needs to be more than just some nominal Consultative Committee.

6 Innovation

Advanced courses, indeed any sort of course, should encourage innovation. Assignments should be set so as to promote innovatory thinking rather than the turgid recapitulation of research findings or the small-scale investigations that merely confirm large-scale research. Faced with genuine tasks students generally show a surprising degree of flair and ingenuity.

The advanced course will still be a major route for the ambitious teacher but to survive will need to catch more accurately the prevailing mood and needs of the time. It will certainly be necessary to examine what really constitutes 'academic rigour'. This concept must have buried a good few ideas and innovations in its day.

A New Model for Staff Development

While we can no doubt improve existing methods of training teachers for remedial work present models may in the end still prove deficient in many aspects. One interesting innovation that may help us in our search for a more effective strategy is that being pioneered at Eastern Michigan University. Known as Staff Development for School Improvement (SDSI) it purports to be a unique experiment in school-university collaboration. It is based on the premise that class teachers best understand their own needs and can, with help, identify priorities and plan effective programmes. The emphasis here is not on individual professional growth, although this happens, but on staff development for school improvement. A six stage process has been formulated as described by Warnat (1983).

Step 1 — Awareness, Readiness and Commitment

The university facilitator and person operating as district co-ordinator meet with school staff to explore needs and to develop a readiness for involvement in some project. During this period the whole staff are committed and can actually vote on whether they should continue to be involved. A 75 per cent vote in favour is required before proceeding.

Step 2 — Interactive Needs Assessment

The outside consultant helps staff identify needs, establish priorities and set up planning groups. Interestingly it proposes that where appropriate a parent representative should be involved.

Step 3 — The Plan and Its Approval

A written strategy is produced by the planning group which needs again a consensus before proceeding. Changes and amendments are referred back until this is achieved.

Step 4 — Implementation

The plan is put into action. If the framework for the entire operation is a school year this fourth step might typically take between three and six months.

Step 5 — Reporting and Evaluation

Evaluation is seen as a continuous process. Quantitative and qualitative information is gathered and assessed under such headings as knowledge and skills acquired by the learner, changes in the behaviour and attitudes of the participants and impact on the community.

Step 6 — Adoption

The final step is the adoption of the innovation and its integration into normal school activity. This step usually leads to a further identification of need and the six stage process is repeated in respect of another dimension.

An interesting aspect of the above is the change in the role of the trainer from content expert to process consultant. Encouraging work is taking place here along these lines but we still have some way to go in institutionalizing it in the way it has been done in Eastern Michigan. The apparent dichotomy between individual professional growth and school improvement need not be as great as that envisaged at EMU and has indeed been overcome elsewhere (see Clark *et al*, 1983) not to mention the work of our own Open University. Altogether we have not been nearly as adventurous in this area as we might.

Summary and Conclusions

This article has looked at remedial education from the point of view of a teacher trainer. Briefly it reviews the debate surrounding the precise meaning of the term and describes some contemporary developments that are shaping its destiny. Six principles are then outlined which, in the opinion of the author, should govern the approaches to the training and retraining of remedial teachers. Further, the Staff Development for School Improvement Model pioneered at Eastern Michigan University is offered for the consideration of the reader as an alternative to traditional approaches. It is recognized that much of the above is not merely applicable to remedial educators but if as we are urged '. . . remedial education should not be divorced from the aims of education in general' (McNicholas, 1976) perhaps neither should be the sort of training required.

What emerges from this discussion is the following:
(a) A re-examination of what is 'remedial education' is now overdue.
(b) Courses purporting to train such personnel should review both their content and process in the light of contemporary thought and development.
(c) Trainers should begin to shift from the role of content giver to that of facilitator.
(d) A new partnership between training establishment, local authority and teaching force needs to be forged.
(e) A re-examination of what constitutes rigorous academic exercise in relation to award bearing courses should be undertaken.
(f) New models of staff development should be researched and pioneered.

In the past the National Association for Remedial Education has given the only clear sense of direction to remedial teachers in this country. Perhaps it is time for it to give such a lead to those who train?

References

ANNING, A. (1982) 'Casting a critical eye over INSET', *Child Education*, 59, 2, p. 9.
BUSH, A.M. (1983) 'Can pupil's reading be improved by involving parents?' *Remedial Education*, 18, 4, pp. 167–170.
CLAMP, S. (1983) 'Computer assisted learning and the less able,' *Remedial Education*, 18, 1, pp. 15–18.
CLARK, M. (1976) 'Why remedial? Implications of using the concept of remedial education', *Remedial Education*, 11, 1, pp. 5–8.
CLARK, R.J. *et al* (1983) 'An urban secondary school development collaborative', *Urban Educator*, (Wayne State University) 7, 1, pp. 8–14.
COLLINS, J.E. (1973) 'The remedial education hoax', *Remedial Education*, 7, 3, pp. 9–10.
DEPARTMENT OF EDUCATION AND SCIENCE (1978) *Special Educational Needs* (Warnock Report), London, HMSO.
EDWARDS, J.B. (1983) 'Remedial education post-Warnock: interment or revival?', *Remedial Education*, 18, 1, pp. 9–13, reprinted in this volume.
FEUERSTEIN, R. (1980) *Instrumental Enrichment*, University Park Press.
GAINS, C.W. (1976) 'Mastery learning and its implications for remedial teachers', *Remedial Education*, 11, 1, pp. 25–31.
GAINS, C.W. (1980) 'Remedial education in the 1980s', *Remedial Education*, 15, 1, pp. 5–9.
GOLBY M. and GULLIVER, J.R. (1979) 'Whose remedies, whose ills? A critical review of remedial education', *Journal of Curriculum Studies*, 11, 2, pp. 137–47, reprinted in this volume.
GULLIFORD, R. (1979) 'Remedial work across the curriculum', in GAINS, C.W. and McNICHOLAS, J.A. (Eds.) *Remedial Education: Guidelines for the Future*, Longman.
INNER LONDON EDUCATION AUTHORITY (1984) *Improving Secondary Schools*, ILEA Learning Resources.
LOFTHOUSE, A. (1983) 'Further Education provision for 16–19 year olds with special educational needs,' *Remedial Education* 18, 4, pp. 178–80.
McNICHOLAS, J.A. (1976) 'Aims of remedial education: a critique', *Remedial Education*,

Charles W. Gains

11, 3, pp. 113–6.

McNicholas, J.A. (1979) 'Life skills: a course for non-academic fourth and fifth year children in a comprehensive school', *Remedial Education*, 14, 3, pp. 125–9.

Naisbitt, J. (1984) *Megatrends*, Warner Books.

National Association for Remedial Education (1977) *Guidelines No. 1 Report on in-service training*, NARE.

National Association for Remedial Education (1979) *Guidelines No. 2 The Role of remedial teachers*, NARE.

Raybould, E. and Solity J. (1982) 'Teaching with precision', *Special Education*, 9, 2, pp. 9–13.

Rosenthal, R. and Jacobsen, L. (1968) *Pygmalion in the Classroom*, Holt, Rinehart and Winston.

Rutter, M., Maughan, B. Mortimore, P. and Ouston, J. (1979) *Fifteen Thousand Hours*, Open Books.

Warnat, W.I. (1983) 'The staff development for school improvement' in Edelfelt, R.A. (Ed.) *Staff Development for School Improvement: an illustration*, National Center on Learning and Teaching, Eastern Michigan University.

Weber, K. (1978) *Yes, They Can!*, Open University Press.

2
School Organization and
Classroom Management

Introduction

Changing assumptions about the nature of remedial education has many implications for school organization and classroom management and this second section of this book takes up the theme of how new ideas can be translated into actual practice and makes suggestions about greater integration of remedial work within the ordinary classroom and shows that these require careful consideration of how specialist knowledge, experience and advice can best be conveyed to teachers.

Clunies-Ross reviews the findings of a major research project which investigated current provision for slow learners in secondary schools and identifies key issues relating to the assessment of pupils, staff training and deployment, and curricular innovation.

Ainscow and Muncey describe one local education authority's initiative in helping teachers provide for children with special needs in the primary school. This article illustrates the problem in defining any border between remedial and special education in ordinary schools and it also provides an example of the behavioural objectives approach to teaching children with difficulties in learning.

Ferguson and Adams evaluate the effectiveness of a team teaching approach and demonstrate some of the problems encountered in implementing this apparently easy and attractive alternative to the stigmatizing consequences of a system of withdrawal for separate remedial teaching.

An alternative approach based on the flexible use of specialist facilities and equipment within a resources department is outlined by Jones and Berrick. With its concern for the integration of pupils with a wide range of mental and physical disabilities this article indicates the potential broadening of the responsibilities of remedial teachers.

Another possible role is that of consultant teacher, providing colleagues with advice and supporting them through sharing skills in classroom management. Smith recommends some ways in which remedial teachers can tackle this exacting task, demanding as it does a blend of interpersonal skills and professional experience.

Slow Learner Provision in Secondary Schools: A Review of the NFER Research Project

Louise Clunies-Ross
Deputy Education Officer,
Royal National Institute for the Blind

> The main question is whether we ought to segregate slow learners from their peers and thus emphasize their situation. This must be balanced against their educational need.

The words of this headteacher were representative of many who faced similar problems in planning and implementing an educational programme for slow learners which was appropriate for pupils' needs in terms of their cognitive, emotional and social development.

Some twelve years after HM Inspectorate explored the arrangements made for slow learning pupils in 158 secondary schools in England, the National Foundation for Educational Research (NFER) launched a major research project to investigate the way in which provision was made for slow learning pupils and to record the implications of contemporary practice for the pupil as well as for curriculum, staffing, teacher training and in-service education. For since the 'widespread uncertainty of aims, objectives and methods for slow learners' identified by HMI and published in *Education Survey 15* (1971), many changes had taken place in education, some of which had brought issues concerned with the less academically able into sharper focus.

Since the establishment of comprehensive schools following reorganization in the 1970s, an increasing number of headteachers were facing the question of how best to provide for the less able pupil in each new intake. Many decisions had to be made. For example, on what criteria should pupils be selected to receive special or supplementary teaching? How should provision for such pupils be organized? What form should the curriculum take? For how many years should special provision be made available? How could class teachers, without extra assistance, best provide for the needs of slow learners in the group? In what ways could special help be made available to slow learners in a mixed ability class? What resource materials and teaching techniques were most appropriate for less able pupils?

Confronting both heads and teachers were issues of school organization. Should slow learners be the responsibility of one special department or should this responsiblity be shared among several or all departments? Should slow learning pupils be taught in a remedial department or should they be integrated with the mainstream? How best could advice and guidance about pupils' specific learning difficulties be presented to staff? To what extent should the role of the remedial teacher be an advisory one? What lines of communication could be set up to strengthen links not only between staff but with service agencies beyond school?

The project aimed to address these questions and to explore the issues in detail, providing within the research report an information source on which staff seeking to establish or to review provision for slow learners might draw to aid their decision-making. By 1980, when the research was under way, a further change was affecting schools in the secondary sector, where falling pupil rolls and consequent reductions in the staffing establishment were resulting in a number of school closures and mergers. Combined with financial cutbacks, such changes were beginning to have an effect on some schools involved in the research. For example, changes in staffing and in school organization had led to a reduction in the amount of slow learner support given in several schools in the sample. The most economical ways of maintaining adequate levels of provision for slow learners were thus being sought in terms of staff deployment, resource production and in the allocation of teaching spaces and equipment.

Research Design and Methodology

One in five of all maintained secondary comprehensive, modern, bi-lateral, technical and middle deemed secondary schools was selected at random by computer to provide the sample for the first ever national survey of slow learner provision. The sample was structured to be representative in terms of size and type and by area of all such schools in England and Wales. A substantial two-part questionnaire was sent to the headteachers of these 931 schools. The first section focused on school policy and organization while the second sought details of school type, size, staffing, pupil grouping and the organizational structure of slow learner provision. The response rate of 85 per cent indicated the high degree of concern about provision for slow learners and the many comments received on teacher training and recruitment prompted the team to include in the research a brief survey of initial and in-service courses currently available for those wishing to teach slow learners in secondary schools. Follow-up questionnaires were completed during 1980 by teachers in charge of provision as well as by others who taught slow learners for a substantial part of their timetable. These questionnaires explored the structure of pupil groups, the nature of the teaching accommodation, testing procedures and teaching materials used, together with information about the training, subject background, teaching experience and in-service preparation of staff who were teaching slow learning pupils.

The schools in which case studies were carried out exemplified the different forms of slow learner provision identified from questionnaire data. The team made visits to these schools of at least four working days during which discussions, interviews and periods of classroom observation took place. The intake year group was selected for intensive study and one, or occasionally two, pupils deemed 'typical' of the slow learners catered for in the school and selected for us by the staff, were observed throughout one day. A record was kept of the work set and the pupil's responses to various tasks together with details of the time spent on different activities, the resources used and the pupil's interactions with peers and with the teacher. Observations were placed in context since information on teaching strategies was included and further background data gathered by means of an extended interview with the teacher(s) concerned. At the time of these observations a standardized reading test was administered to the intake year in all case study schools in order to establish a common baseline with regard to pupils identified by teachers as 'slow learners', and in view of the wide range of catchment areas represented by participating schools. Young's SPAR Reading Test was selected for this purpose, yielding both reading ages and quotients.

The Organization of Provision for Slow Learners

Six out of every seven headteachers combined several forms of pupil grouping to create a variety of different systems of slow learner provision within their schools. The most widely used way of providing extra or alternative tuition for slow learners was by withdrawing them from the mainstream for individual or small group teaching. Pupils identified as requiring support in basic skills or in specific subjects were withdrawn for this purpose in 85 per cent of secondary schools. Withdrawal took place in all year groups and from all kinds of classes. This, of course, has widespread implications for curriculum, teaching methods and teacher liaison as well as for the pupil, who might be rejoining a special class, a mixed ability group, a subject set or a streamed teaching unit. Pupils were withdrawn for remedial tuition slightly more often in the lower school, i.e. in years 1 to 3, than in the fourth and fifth years. Subject-specific sets for slow learning pupils were present in 73 per cent of schools, constituting the second most widely adopted form of organization. More schools provided slow learner sets in the upper school (years 4 and 5) as part of the whole school's setting and option system than in the lower school (years 1 to 3), where slow learner sets were often organized for literacy and/or numeracy skills only. Slow learner classes, the third most widely adopted form of slow learner provision, were present in 55 per cent of schools and were twice as common in the lower school as in the upper. Options designed specifically for slow learners were provided in 52 per cent of schools, and as expected were most usually available in the fourth and fifth years. However, it was found that one in seven of these schools offered a special slow learner option to younger pupils.

Thirteen per cent of schools employed other means of providing for slow learners in addition to those described above, for example parents or sixth formers would hear pupils read on a one-to-one basis, 'floating' teachers would assist in mainstream lessons and in some schools special groups for spelling or handwriting were established. In some schools provision was made available for pupils in the sixth form who were experiencing difficulties.

There is, understandably, considerable consensus over the benefits which accrue from certain modes of organization in the education of slow learners as well as the problems which can arise. Widely held beliefs about the stable, secure learning environment provided by a small, special class, taught for most of the time by one remedial teacher, have led to its adoption by many schools for pupils in the early years of their secondary education. A slow learner set was seen to offer an advantage additional to those cited above; namely of flexibility, as slow learners had the opportunity to move 'up' or 'down' within one subject area. The generally small size of slow learner sets in which specialist teaching was available was seen to provide a particularly helpful learning environment for slow pupils. Those schools in which special slow learner sets were organized from entry until the fifth year most commonly offered this facility in the curricular areas of English and maths.

Special options for slow learners were available in a wide range of subjects, reflecting teachers' concern to provide a preparation for adult life and to give slow learners the opportunity of mixing with age peers. Topics offered were diverse but the emphasis was clearly on situations which pupils were likely to experience on leaving school, since in most cases basic skills were offered alongside these options in small classes, sets or withdrawal groups. Options for slow learners gave some opportunity for choice and enabled all pupils in one school to participate in the same option system. Withdrawal groups, widely used to provide support for slow learners afforded the advantage of individual or small group tuition which could be tailored to pupils' needs. Pupils were withdrawn from mixed ability, banded, setted and streamed groups and although heads acknowledged that a few pupils experienced problems on rejoining the mainstream, the consensus of opinion was that the benefits of near full-time mainstream education outweighed the difficulties some pupils encountered on rejoining the class after a period of special teaching.

Headteachers were clearly sensitive to the changing needs of slow learners at different stages in their educational development and were aware of both shortcomings and benefits in the special provision made within their schools. The different ways in which classes, sets, options and withdrawal were combined were indicative of a widespread concern over the welfare of slow learners, as heads attempted, within the constraints of existing building space, staffing levels and timetabling arrangements, to make appropriate provision for their needs. The research also showed that the organization of the whole school often influenced but did not dictate the way in which slow learners were grouped for periods of special teaching.

Who Are the 'Slow Learners'?

Each autumn headteachers and their staff are faced with the task of providing continuity of educational experience for a new intake which includes pupils whose abilities and aptitudes range widely and who come from a variety of different educational backgrounds. The survey revealed that almost half of the schools in the sample typically received pupils from more than ten feeder schools, each of which provided a variety of test results, attainment grades and teachers' comments which were used to assist decision making regarding pupils' placement in tutor and teaching groups. It was common for both standardized and school-based tests to be used as a means of discovering those pupils who were in need of remedial help. A survey of teachers in charge of remedial education in 397 secondary and fifty middle schools indicated that a number of the same tests were used to identify slow learners, to diagnose the nature of their learning difficulties and to monitor progress.

The most commonly used series of tests were those compiled by Daniels and Diack. Test 12, the Graded Test of Reading Experience, which is inexpensive and easy to administer and to score, was used in many schools to 'identify' slow learning pupils after entry, and a selection of tests 1–12 were also those most commonly used to gain a profile of the individual capabilities of slow learning pupils. However, although designed to discriminate at the lower end of the ability range, the test was first published in the 1950s and is now somewhat dated. The Neale Analysis of Reading Ability was used by teachers in some schools to 'identify' slow learners but was more usually employed to construct an individual pupil profile. As this test takes twenty minutes per pupil to administer it is not really suitable for use with large numbers of pupils; however its assessment of accuracy, speed and comprehension in reading is most useful for individual studies.

The research revealed that there are few up-to-date tests which are designed for pupils of low ability in the 11+ age group, and which are at the same time inexpensive and relatively straightforward to administer. In some schools staff were attempting to construct their own test batteries by combining both published and school-based tests and viewing the results in profile form. A number of teachers who were in charge of slow learning pupils with behavioural and emotional problems, made use of instruments such as the Bristol Social Adjustment Guide in order to assist in the diagnosis of pupils' needs.

The report contains a detailed account of allocation procedures in three schools in which arrangements for slow learners differed considerably. In the first, information from feeder schools was used to structure a separate slow learner class; in the second all pupils were placed in mixed ability groups for practical subjects and in sets for English, maths, humanities and science, while in the third school all subjects were taught in mixed ability groups from which slow learners were withdrawn to receive help with literacy skills. In these contrasting situations, the teachers in charge of slow learner provision played very different roles. In the first school, for example, this teacher was not involved at all in initial allocation procedures and only took charge of, and taught, pupils in the special class. In the third school, however, the withdrawal system operated independently of the school's other grouping procedures and was organized entirely by the teacher in charge of slow learner provision.

Because of the wide variation in schools' catchment areas, it was necessary for the team to find a means whereby slow learning pupils in the different schools might be compared. A test was sought which was appropriate for pupils in the 11–14 age range, which discriminated at the lower ability levels, was straightforward to administer and which would fit readily into a lesson period. Young's SPAR Reading Test was finally chosen, consisting of fifteen pictorial and thirty written items. However, its reading age scores give only an indication of a pupil's ability to decode and by recognition to select the correct word to complete a sentence. Thus the results provided an indication of pupils' reading ability but not of other learning attainments and difficulties or of emotional problems. Scores from 2302 pupils in eleven of the participating schools showed that at the age of 11+, 17 per cent of the pupils had a reading age at least two years behind their chronological age and would undoubtedly have been experiencing reading difficulties. It was found that all pupils with a reading age of 7.5 years or less were receiving remedial help but only about half of those who scored between 9.6 and 10 years on the SPAR Reading Test. Constraining factors appeared to be the number of specialist remedial staff available and the school's policy regarding the organization of pupil groups. A flexible withdrawal system appeared to make it possible for a few specialist teachers to reach a larger number of pupils than where the same number of staff were assigned to teaching a small, special class. However, the question of whether to teach a small, special group or to help pupils individually is one which each school must resolve for itself. Decisions on the balancing of resources in terms of curriculum, time and staff can only be made by those most closely involved with slow learner provision.

Teachers in Charge of Slow Learner Provision

The different kinds of slow learner provision described above were mediated through remedial departments in 76 per cent of the schools surveyed. In 15 per cent of schools, provision was organized by a group of teachers who did not in themselves constitute a separate department, while in eight per cent, one member of staff was appointed with special responsibility for slow learning pupils and in the remaining one per cent of schools slow learners were catered for within one or more of the subject departments or by means of a remedial teacher from the local authority peripatetic team. Our survey revealed that the education of slow learning pupils between the ages of 11 and 18 was most commonly organized by the teacher or group of staff who provided the school's remedial teaching support. The terms 'slow learner' and 'remedial' were, in many cases, used synonymously.

The role of teachers in charge of remedial provision was examined in detail in case study schools, using a structure outlined by NARE in their 1979 publication entitled *The Role of Remedial Teachers*. In this booklet NARE presented a five-point model in which the assessment, prescriptive, teaching, supportive and liaison roles of the remedial teacher were outlined, and in addition those duties identified as specific to heads of department were also described.

Our research indicated that the assessment of pupils and the diagnosis of their learning difficulties was unquestionably central to the work of every teacher in charge of remedial education, but the placement of slow learners in teaching and registration groups was not. Indeed, involvement of any head of remedial education in allocation procedures for new entrants was found to be less frequent than might have been expected of staff holding scale 3 or 4 head of department appointments. In many schools, however, testing to establish the nature and extent of learning difficulties among pupils who had been allocated to particular teaching groups took place after entry, and these programmes were often organized and supervised by the teacher in charge of slow learner provision. A similar picture emerged from the wider sample, in which 82 per cent of the heads of department reported that they used tests in order to identify slow learning pupils in the new intake each autumn.

The prescriptive role was found to be well-developed at classroom level, where heads of department had drawn up syllabuses as well as individual learning programmes for pupils with literacy problems. These written syllabuses were usually prefaced by general aims and specific objectives, and some covered curricular areas other than basic skills, extending for example into the humanities. At management level, while several heads of department served on a variety of school committees, such as those concerned with curriculum, with guidance and with in-service training, and some were members of senior management teams, not all were involved with policy making at the level recommended by NARE. That is to say, not all were as closely involved with the organization, grouping and resourcing of slow learning pupils as NARE considered desirable. As regards teaching support, while it was common to find two remedial teachers working together with a special group of slow learning pupils, it was not common to find remedial staff supporting subject teachers in mainstream classes by assisting slow learners in this setting. Those schools in which support in the ordinary classroom took place all withdrew pupils for individual or small group teaching, and thus a tradition of informal liaison between remedial and subject teachers had built up.

A further factor which appeared to facilitate teacher liaison and thereby the establishment of a wider role for teachers in charge of slow learner education was a simple one — the name or title by which this member of staff was known. A 'head of remedial teaching' was expected by both staff and students to be responsible solely for the less academically able pupils, and traditionally to cater for their needs in a special teaching area or department. The role of a 'learning adviser' on the other hand, was less specifically defined, making it easier for the member of staff to work with subject teachers in planning alternative resources, designing special units of work or organizing supplementary teaching, and to help a wider range of pupils with learning difficulties. In some schools liaison was fostered by means of in-service training courses, when heads of department took the opportunity to draw the attention of subject teachers to the problems faced by slow learners in ordinary classrooms, following up these initial meetings by more detailed work in specific subject areas with individual members of staff.

The liaison role concerned contact with service agencies beyond school, with parents and with the local community. Most teachers in charge of slow learners called upon external support agencies directly, and only a few were required to make such requests through the school's senior management team. The advisory and schools' psychological services were most frequently contacted with regard to slow learners' education and progress, and heads of department commented that these appeared to be overstretched and as a consequence unable to meet all the requests made of them. Teachers encouraged parents to visit the school informally to discuss a pupil's progress, and some heads of department made home visits to parents who did not respond to invitations to call at the school and who did not attend parents' evenings. For older pupils, some teachers in charge of remedial education were able to arrange link courses in conjunction with local colleges as well as work experience schemes and community service, often drawing on contacts built up over a number of years.

Teachers in charge of slow learner provision thus supervised work in a variety of curricular areas, both within and outside the school. Several of these staff held other responsibilities in the school which brought them into contact with many other teachers: one, for example, was a deputy head, another ran induction courses for all new staff. The importance of liaison and co-operation was emphasized by several headteachers who were keenly aware of the problem of isolation faced by many teachers in charge of slow learner education, questioning whether a special department was indeed the best way of organizing provision for slow learners. As one head wrote 'perhaps a "good" school has no staff who specialize in teaching slow learners. Specialist teachers and departments encourage other teachers to shrug off the problem'.

The role of the teacher in charge of slow learner education can and should develop along each of the dimensions outlined by NARE. The assessment role of these teachers could, with advantage, be extended to include participation in allocation procedures for new entrants: with a knowledge of individual feeder schools and expertise in the interpretation of test results, many teachers could make very useful contributions in this area. Advice, guidance and prescription, all reasonably well developed in the classroom, were found to require strengthening at management level. Similarly, the support role, well established in special classes, needs development across the curriculum. The various facets of liaison within school could be facilitated by the provision of school-based in-service opportunities, as well as by individual subject-specific meetings between teachers of slow learners and subject staff, focusing on teaching strategies, resource production and curriculum planning. Bailey (1981) urged teachers to join curriculum development teams in different subject areas in order to advise on how the curriculum might be adapted for pupils with special needs; a suggestion which some heads of department might take as a useful starting point for establishing links with subject staff. The importance of liaison was stressed by McCall (1977), when, in exploring a withdrawal system he wrote that 'the teacher acting as the withdrawal agent must see the supportive nature of the role and make considerable efforts to gain acceptance as a consultative supporting teacher working as a team member with specialist colleagues.'

The Teachers

Information about 1467 members of staff who taught slow learners in survey schools was gathered by means of a brief questionnaire which elicited a response from more than 400 teachers in charge of provision and over 1000 other members of staff. Length of teaching experience among this large sample ranged from a few weeks to over twenty years and, as could be expected, the variety of teaching experience was considerable. The sample included staff who had taught in primary, middle and secondary schools, as well as those with experience in special schools, in the private sector and in overseas schools and colleges. About 40 per cent of the staff were graduates and many of the teachers, both graduate and non-graduate staff, held specialist diplomas and certificates in remedial or special education.

As expected, most staff had moved into remedial education from other areas of teaching. However, although four out of every five spent most of their time teaching the basic skills of language and number to slow learning pupils, only one in five was trained for English teaching and one in twelve for maths. Most of the staff in the survey had backgrounds in the humanities subjects. This situation highlights the vital importance of making in-service opportunities available to teachers: over half of the teachers in this survey had attended an in-service training course concerned with slow learners during the preceding five years and many had gained additional professional qualifications by this means.

In-service courses were deemed particularly valuable on a number of counts. Teachers appreciated the opportunity afforded for informal discussion, for the chance to see and to use new books and equipment and to learn about practical teaching strategies. Language, literacy and maths were the curricular areas most frequently mentioned as being particularly helpful. Most of these in-service courses had been arranged by local education authorities, whose role in the professional development of staff was found to be particularly important outside the major metropolitan and city areas, as the research showed that the majority of courses listed in the DES and NATFHE handbooks took place in the larger centres of population, leaving teachers who lived and worked elsewhere almost totally reliant on LEAs for in-service training.

With regard to initial training, the research showed that fewer than one in three of the staff who taught slow learners had received initial training specifically for this purpose although four out of five considered this to be an essential or very important prerequisite. Seven out of ten headteachers also considered initial training in the teaching of slow learners to be a very important asset to staff. However, since the mid-1970s a growing number of initial training courses have included a unit or units on the teaching of slow learners; for example it was found that over half of the staff who trained since 1975 had taken a course on slow learning pupils in contrast to one-fifth of those who trained ten years earlier. At present more of this training appears to be available in courses which prepare teachers for junior and/or middle school work than for secondary teaching. Our survey of initial courses listed in the DES and NATFHE handbooks indicated that all the major courses were oversubscribed and also revealed that their main focus appeared to be on assessment, testing, and on methods of identifying and making provision for slow learning pupils. The point was made by several teachers that *all* initial courses should contain a section of work on slow learners and, in view of the comments made by those currently teaching slow pupils, our findings suggest that units on the teaching of basic skills, on child development, psychology and curriculum design could usefully be included in all initial teacher training courses.

Issues of contemporary concern to teachers of slow learning pupils were wide in compass and included the balance of time staff spent with slow learners and with other pupils, and the importance of establishing and maintaining liaison with other members of staff as well as with parents, feeder schools and with outside agencies. A number of teachers felt that slow learner education offered little in the way of a career structure and that promotion opportunities were few; the survey, however, showed that three out of every four staff in charge of slow learner provision were on scale 3 appointments or above, suggesting that this perception of the status of slow learner education might be in need of some revision. A number of the teachers wanted the curriculum for slow learners to be planned as a whole, others wished the question of optimum group size to be considered together with that of group structure, and many were concerned that suitable procedures were adopted in schools in order to identify and make appropriate provision for pupils who were slow at learning. Other issues included the importance of discovering slow learners as early as possible, preferably in the primary sector; there was a call for an improved pupil/teacher ratio for remedial groups and a request that consideration be given to those pupils for whom no special provision was made but who required some extra support in order to maintain their progress in the mainstream. By far the most frequently mentioned issue, however, was teacher training and the preparation of staff to work with slow learning pupils: one in three of the staff felt that too few initial or in-service courses concerned with slow learners were currently available.

The Curriculum

Survey data and information obtained during the case study research showed that the curriculum provided for slow learners frequently differed from that provided for others in the same year group. Moreover, practices employed for pupils in the lower school, i.e. years 1 to 3, were often different from those in the upper school, and for this reason these two age groups were reported separately. In many cases, for pupils of any age, a modern language was replaced by English, slow learners spent more time on basic skills than did their peers and remedial teachers were frequently responsible for teaching more than one subject to them. Attempts were made to provide for individual needs in English/literacy skills and in maths, while in other subjects special courses were designed or the mainstream syllabus adapted and a variety of different methods and materials were used to cater for a variety of individual needs.

Years 1 to 3

Wide variations in school policy resulted in a range of different curricular practices. At one end of the spectrum was the policy of providing slow learners with a programme substantially different from that of their mainstream contemporaries. Remedial staff typically selected appropriate methods and materials and taught within a child-centred framework. Another variation implemented by many schools was that slow learners should be taught 'academic' subjects by remedial staff who had a specialist understanding of pupils' learning difficulties: it was considered that teaching strategies should differ but that the syllabus should be an adaptation of that followed by the mainstream, so that all pupils of the same age received similar kinds of learning experiences. Another variation was that slow learners should have a different syllabus for literacy and numeracy only. It was also found that different teaching methods and materials were often used to accommodate pupils with special needs in slow learner sets in a number of other subjects. For example, in one school, the remedial staff took responsibility for all English and maths teaching while humanities and science subject specialists liaised with the head of remedial education in order to ensure that the methods and materials used in the mainstream were appropriate for slow learners' needs.

At the other end of the spectrum there was the policy of providing slow learners with all the same opportunities as their peers and making remedial provision by withdrawing them for individual or small group tuition in literacy skills. In this case, slow learners were taught beside their mainstream contemporaries, frequently in mixed ability classes in which consideration was given to a wide range of individual needs and, ideally, where activities and tasks were planned so that all pupils could respond at their own level. In one such school, all subject teachers knew that each class contained a wide range of ability and lessons were planned so that all could participate fully. Close liaison between staff was maintained to ensure that all classes were taught from the same syllabus and that all pupils in a year group were given similar educational experiences and opportunities.

Although every school made some form of provision for pupils with learning difficulties it appeared that in some cases this had been planned without reference to other curricular components or to the nature of the resulting educational programmes. A different syllabus, for example, made the transfer of a pupil to another class or group difficult if not impossible to arrange. A slow learner taking extra English lessons could find that time spent on other subjects was reduced or that in some cases certain subjects were omitted altogether from the curriculum.

Differences in the balance of the curriculum followed by mainstream and by slow learning pupils were recorded in many schools. Commonly, slow learning pupils in the lower secondary years had a restricted curriculum in which certain subjects were not available to them. The most usual practice was to replace foreign language lessons by extra English language teaching. However, where English tuition was confined to basic skills, slow learners missed many other important aspects of the subject such as literature and drama. Similarly in maths, slow learners commonly focused on computational skills as it was felt that they could not cope with topic work until these had been mastered: a wider application of such skills could have proved helpful to the learning process. In other subjects, observation of special slow learner classes led us to the conclusion that some lessons were unnecessarily limited in content and in depth and failed to extend the pupils fully. In particular, repetitive exercises or drills proved unstimulating for many slow learners and led to inattention and time-wasting among many of the younger pupils observed.

A fundamental question raised by this research on curriculum is how best to structure a pupil's learning programme so that a balance is achieved in terms of curricular content, resource variety and teacher guidance, and opportunities are provided for independent learning and group discussion which are appropriate for the pupil at his or her particular stage of development.

Years 4 and 5

In over 95 per cent of schools all fourth and fifth year pupils took a common core of subjects which usually included English and maths, PE and religious education and often humanities or science. Practical subjects were usually part of the option system. However, the research revealed that the structure of the option system in some schools gave slow learners few, if any, real choices to make among the alternatives available; the effects of a restricted curriculum and the fact that certain subjects were only offered to potential GCE candidates combined to produce this situation.

In a few schools the staff provided slow learners with a complete specially designed course, and those who had spent all or the greater part of their time being taught by remedial staff in the lower school were routed into this programme. Some of the specially designed courses led to Mode 3 CSE examinations, others were not certificated, and the majority were either based entirely on continuous assessment or had a large coursework component. Many had been devised to prepare the pupil for adult life, for example consumer education, money management, first aid. Some schools organized link courses, many of which were vocational in nature, in collaboration with local technical or further education colleges.

A major issue to emerge was the question of whether slow learners should join classes preparing for public examinations. In some schools almost all courses led to CSE; in others slow learners could take both CSE and non-examination subjects. However where slow learners did not work towards any examination goal, a number of staff commented on the poor attendance rates of many of these pupils.

Schemes containing work experience and/or community education opportunities were rare, and so were link courses with local FE colleges. There is a need for both school and local authority based initiatives to link schools more closely with FE colleges, with industry and with the local community. Now is the time for a review of the existing educational programmes provided for pupils in their final years at school who are not following traditional academic courses, for an evaluation of present facilities and for the development of new, collaborative initiatives.

Which Way Now?

The survey documented the many different ways in which head teachers and their staff sought to make provision for slow learning pupils at a time of considerable educational change. It should also be remembered that slow learners were but one of a number of pupil groups who were making demands upon a finite supply of resources and that at the time of our survey some of these resources were reducing in line with the decline in the school population. The issues which the research set out to explore are those which confront any headteacher who is reviewing or restructuring provision for slow learners. However, teachers of slow learners have a crucial part to play in developing and implementing educational programmes for slow pupils and in planning appropriate curricular and resource provision.

To achieve the right balance is no easy task; it is to be hoped that some of the ideas and advice culled from current practice and contained in the report will assist those involved in planning and implementing provision for slow learning pupils and at the same time offer guidance to those in the process of reviewing such provision in the face of changing circumstances. The report has highlighted factors which are clearly crucial in such deliberations, but the implications for curriculum content, resource production, teaching strategies and the deployment of staff within the organization can only be fully realized by those already working there.

References

BAILEY, T.J. (1981) 'The secondary remedial teacher's role redefined', *Remedial Education*, 16, 3.
CLUNIES-ROSS, L. and WIMHURST, S. (1983) *The Right Balance: Provision for Slow Learners in Secondary Schools*, Windsor, NFER-Nelson.
DEPARTMENT OF EDUCATION AND SCIENCE (1971) *Slow Learners in Secondary Schools: Education Survey 15*, London, HMSO.
McCALL, C. (1977) 'Remedial strategies in secondary schools', *Forum*, 19, 2.
NATIONAL ASSOCIATION FOR REMEDIAL EDUCATION (1979) *Guidelines 2*. Stafford, NARE.
NATFHE (1978) *Handbook of Institutions providing both Teacher Training and other Full-time Advanced Courses.*
REID, M., CLUNIES-ROSS, L., GOACHER, B. and VILE, C., (1981) *Mixed Ability Teaching: Problems and Possibilities*, Windsor, NFER-Nelson.
YOUNG, D. (1976) *SPAR Reading Test*, London, Hodder and Stoughton Educational.

Learning Difficulties in the Primary School: An In-service Training Initiative

Mel Ainscow
Adviser for Special Education, Coventry
and
Jim Muncey
Senior Educational Psychologist, Coventry

The changes in thinking which have occurred both nationally and internationally, about children with special needs, necessitate a reappraisal of the procedures used for the identification, assessment and support of such children. In this country some important aspects of the *Warnock Report* have been embodied in recent legislation (DES, 1981) which require local education authorities to review and revise their existing procedures for supporting children with special educational needs. Thus, many authorities are seeking ways to assist teachers in meeting their responsibilities. This article describes the development of an in-service initiative which is concerned with these issues.

The main aims of the article are to describe:

the background to and the rationale for the development of a comprehensive in-service training programme;
the organization of the programme within one Local Education Authority;
the content and presentation of the first course within the programme; a course on teaching children with learning difficulties.

The Special Needs Action Programme

The course on learning difficulties is a self-contained multi-media package of the type sometimes referred to as a 'Minicourse' (Borg, 1972). It is part of a

This article originally appeared in *Remedial Education* (1983) 18, 3

much larger in-service initiative mounted in the Coventry Education Authority, known as the 'Special Needs Action Programme' (SNAP).

SNAP has grown out of a desire to utilize the heavy resource investment and expertise in special education facilities and services to support the large group of pupils with special needs in ordinary schools referred to in the *Warnock Report*. Specifically, the aims are:

1   to encourage headteachers of all schools to develop procedures for the identification of pupils with special needs;
2   to assist teachers in ordinary schools to provide an appropriate curriculum for such pupils; and
3   to co-ordinate the work of the various special education services and facilities in supporting teachers in ordinary schools.

At the moment, the focus of SNAP is on primary education on the assumption that extra support to children at this early stage may reduce the incidence of what Keogh (1975) refers to as 'self-perceived inadequacy' brought about as a result of long experience of classroom difficulty.

In order to achieve its aims, SNAP concentrates on four main areas:

1   Information is provided for headteachers and co-ordinators about the resources and services available within the Authority. To this end each primary school has been issued with a staffroom handbook which provides an explanation of the importance of meeting special needs in ordinary schools, suggestions as to how they might be identified and sources of help and information.
2   Courses are presented, initially to coordinators and subsequently as part of school-based staff development programmes. They aim to increase teachers' skills in developing, implementing and monitoring programmes for pupils with special needs and develop positive attitudes to these approaches. Courses deal with different aspects of special need (for example, learning difficulties, sensory disabilities).
3   Materials are disseminated which have been used and evaluated by experienced special education teachers. In addition, the contacts that are developed between colleagues in primary and special education provide opportunities for the sharing of ideas and exchange of resources.
4   Advice and help is given to schools by teams of peripatetic remedial teachers, educational psychologists and special school teachers, thus providing the type of co-ordinated special education support service recommended in the *Warnock Report*.

As can be seen from the aims for SNAP, the emphasis has been placed on schools taking responsibility for their children with special needs and, indeed, creating their own policy matched to the needs and organizational constraints of the individual establishment. To facilitate this, each primary school has been asked to nominate one member of staff to act as 'co-ordinator for special needs'. This teacher's role is:

to make colleagues in the school aware of their responsibilities to pupils with special needs;

to co-ordinate the development of school-based strategies for the identification and review of these pupils;

to assist teachers in the development of appropriate programmes for these pupils;

to provide information for colleagues about special education resources and services available in the authority.

Since this is such a key role, involving support to and liaison with colleagues, schools are encouraged to nominate a relatively senior member of staff and, indeed, in some cases Heads or Deputies have chosen to take personal responsibility for the task.

Theoretical Issues

The course 'Teaching Children with Learning Difficulties' is the first, and arguably the most important, of the SNAP courses. Co-ordinators are expected to complete it before attending other courses since it places particular emphasis on the creation and development of the role of the co-ordinator within each school. Furthermore, it makes sense for schools to establish a policy for dealing with learning difficulties first since this represents the largest group of pupils with special needs (Jones and Jones, 1981).

In designing this course, note was taken of experience and evidence from other initiatives aimed at overcoming learning difficulties at the primary stage. Of particular interest were the results of the various early screening projects introduced in many local authorities during the early 1970s (Makins, 1976; Marshall, 1976). The initial enthusiasm that existed for this type of approach has diminished as a result of a number of articles which have drawn attention to possible disadvantages (for example, Bookbinder, 1978; Wedell and Lindsay, 1980). These suggest that early screening procedures have been instigated in some areas without adequate evaluation being carried out; that the procedures used provide very little information that will be directly useful to a teacher wishing to develop a teaching programme; and are, therefore, of doubtful merit in the light of possible negative effects on teacher expectations.

The negative effects that may result from early intervention programmes has remained a major concern of the authors, particularly the fear of promoting labelling and segregation of groups of children within schools. These tend to be the features of initiatives in which the promoters' orientation is to interpret a child's learning difficulties in terms of causes centred within the child (Wedell, 1981). Recent thinking, however, sees pupils' special needs as being an outcome of the child's unique range of aptitudes and attitudes seen within the context of the environment in which he exists. Thus, the emphasis in special education is swinging away from the so-called 'medical model', with its search for child-centred causes as possible solutions to a child's difficulties, towards a greater concern for curriculum, teaching methods and classroom arrangements. In other words, teachers are being encouraged to concentrate on things they can do something about, rather than variables which are largely outside their control (Ainscow and Tweddle, 1979).

In a related way, the danger of pupils being offered a reduced, narrower educational diet needs to be avoided. Consequently, the emphasis within the course is placed on maintaining children with learning difficulties within the normal curriculum, whilst at the same time providing intensive and effective instruction in areas of specific weakness. Class teachers are taught how to design and implement their own procedures for assessing the entry behaviour of pupils to specific programmes. These are designed to provide curriculum experiences matched to the needs of each child (Bloom, 1976). This has the benefit that the child is assessed in terms of those competencies needed to progress effectively within a particular classroom (Eaves and McLaughlin, 1977), and in relation to a particular curriculum.

Course Design

Despite the investment in in-service training for teachers in recent years, the results in terms of improvements in children's learning have tended to be disappointing (Moss and Childs, 1981). Those involved in teacher education often feel that they have been successful in changing course participants' verbal behaviour but not so much in bringing about changes in classroom practice.

Clearly the relating of theory to practice is an age-old problem. The traditional in-service model, involving a series of lectures from which participants are required to interpret practical implications and then, most difficult of all, generalize these to the classroom, is increasingly being questioned. For example, Georgiades and Phillimore (1975) note that the model has been singularly unsuccessful probably because the capacity of individuals to instigate changes in practice is limited within complex organizations such as schools.

Recently, in special education there have been a number of interesting attempts to develop more sophisticated training models aimed at overcoming some of these difficulties. Becker and Engelmann (1977) describe how intensive training sessions involving modelling and practice of specialist techniques, followed by supervised classroom work, were used in the highly successful *Follow Through Project*, aimed at accelerating the learning of disadvantaged children. Hall *et al.* (1976) use what they call a 'Responsive Teaching Model' in which theoretical principles are applied to the problems of pupils within the classes of course participants. Both the Schools' Council Project *Education of Severely Educationally Subnormal Pupils* (Leeming *et al.*, 1979), and the Huddersfield Polytechnic *Teaching and the Severely Subnormal* (TASS) Project (Robson, 1979), have examined how classroom-based research can help teachers to define and achieve short-term objectives in specific language skills — the former by means of teacher workshops, the latter using micro-teaching self-instructional packages.

In addition, the *Education of the Developmentally Young* Project at the Hester Adrian Research Centre in Manchester has been offering intensive one-week, school-based behaviour modification workshops for one adviser or educational psychologist from each LEA in England and Wales (Farrell, 1982). They participate on the understanding that they, in turn, will run similar workshops for groups of teachers in schools in their own LEAs.

A common feature of each of these initiatives is that the in-service experience includes practical activities in which theoretical ideas are applied to problems arising in the teacher's own classroom. The SNAP course described below attempts to take advantage of this approach.

Organization

The course on teaching children with learning difficulties is presented to each primary school over a period of approximately two terms and consists of three phases. The initial phase is concerned with negotiating the management aspects. Once a school has agreed to take part and nominated a suitable member of staff to act as coordinator, the head attends an initial meeting during which the aims and methods of the course are explained using tape-slide presentations. The main purpose is to make heads aware of the crucial importance of their supporting the designated coordinator in establishing and carrying out his role in the school.

During the meeting the head is provided with a copy of the course manual, *Small Steps* (Ainscow and Muncey, 1981a), and asked to have a look through it before passing it on to the school's coordinator.

The second phase of the course is carried out at the Teachers' Centre and consists of six three-hour sessions. Prior to coming on the course each teacher must select a child in the school who has learning difficulties, and write a brief summary of this child's problems. This summary is used as a basis for discussion in the first unit of the course, as well as a means of evaluating change by comparing this description of the child's difficulties with a case study completed on the same child at the end of the course.

Participants in phase II of the course work in groups of approximately six, tutored by special school or remedial teachers and educational psychologists who have previously completed the course successfully. Prior to each session, students are required to read one unit from *Small Steps*. This contains ALL the necessary theoretical information required to complete the course. The sessions consist of group discussions focused on the pre-session reading material and practical assignments that each participant carries out with one pupil.

There are no lectures, and tutors are instructed not to become regarded as experts to whom group members can turn to have issues resolved and problems solved. In such situations tutors are required to direct attention back to the course materials and to encourage the group to search collectively for appropriate solutions. This is an attempt to demonstrate the value of group problem-solving strategies that should be nurtured within the staff-room by each co-ordinator.

Group tutors are provided with a *Tutors' Guide* (Ainscow and Muncey, 1981b), which explains how sessions should be run and what points are to be emphasized, as well as providing relevant background reading. During the period of the course, tutors meet on a weekly basis to review the previous session and plan for the next one.

The only additional input consists of a 15-minute video film at each session which shows teachers applying the course methods within their classrooms.

The emphasis placed on discussion and practical assignments is a central feature of the course. All participants become actively involved in analyzing the problems of a group of children and, in so doing, examine and apply the principles presented in the course materials.

At the end of the sixth session, participants are asked to write up the practical work they have carried out as a child study, using a standard format with which they are provided. Those who submit a satisfactory report are presented with a course certificate, and a selection are printed in booklet form. Gradually, a series of useful volumes of child studies is being developed and these are made available to students on subsequent courses.

The third phase of the course, which is undoubtedly the most important, is school-based. At this point, the aim is to provoke discussion amongst all members of staff as to the ways in which the school deals with children's learning difficulties.

Following the attendance of the coordinator at the six sessions held in the Teachers' Centre, a support team, led by the school adviser, including a specialist remedial teacher, an educational psychologist, and a special school teacher, negotiate with the head a plan for dissemination of the course materials within the school. At this stage, schools are encouraged to run the course on site for the whole staff, with the coordinator acting as tutor assisted by outside support personnel. The *Tutors' Guide* referred to above provides information as to how these school-based sessions should be organized and conducted.

In some cases, schools opt to go for a less formal follow-up initiative involving an awareness session for staff followed by the coordinator establishing his role by supporting class teachers in planning programmes for individual children.

To date, schools that have already embarked on part three of the course have shown a range of responses. Some have run a full course, with or without outside help. These courses have been run in the teachers' own time; for example, lunch breaks or in the evenings at the home of a teacher from the school. Other schools have started to develop on-site resource centres containing programmes and materials to be used by all staff. Some headteachers have released the coordinator from full-time class teaching, so that he/she can be more actively involved in supporting teachers directly in their classrooms in dealing with pupils with special educational needs.

During the course of phase three, the coordinators and headteachers are invited to visit their local school for children with moderate learning difficulties. All three of these day special schools in the city have teachers on their staff who have themselves successfully completed the course. It is hoped that such visits will be the first step in forging closer links between special and ordinary schools.

The end of this third and final session is marked by a meeting for heads of the primary schools that have taken part, at which they are asked to make a brief report of the policy the school has developed for dealing with learning difficulties. It is recognized, of course, that policies will vary in style depending on the nature and organization of the individual establishment.

Content

In designing the course, the need to make it completely self-sufficient was paramount, in order that it could be used independently within schools. A further important constraint was a desire to present theoretically reputable ideas in a form that would be easily read, meaningful and relevant to busy primary school teachers.

The content was influenced by recent thinking and research evidence regarding the most successful ways of accelerating the progress of pupils with learning difficulties (for example, Ainscow and Tweddle, 1979; Becker, 1977; Engelmann, 1977; Haring *et al.*, 1978; Howell and Kaplan, 1980; Lovitt, 1977; Rhine, 1981). In particular, the course materials recommend approaches based upon criterion-referenced assessment, precisely stated objectives and task analysis. These approaches have a number of practical advantages:

1 Assessment is classroom based and is the responsibility of the teacher, not an outside expert (Kratochwill and Green, 1978).
2 Information gained from assessment is specific and has direct implications for teaching (Larsen, 1977).

3 Programmes of objectives can facilitate continuous assessment and review (Bijou, 1977).
4 They are useful in terms of organization of resources, teaching groups and team teaching (Nussel *et al.*, 1976).
5 They provide a basis for individualized instruction with pupils progressing at their own rate (Charles, 1976).
6 The philosophy behind the approaches is essentially optimistic in the sense that where pupils do not learn, there is assumed to be a flaw in the instructional design, not the child (Hersch and Cohen, 1972).

The course manual, *Small Steps*, is divided into six units, one for each of the sessions. It explains, with examples, how teachers should establish teaching priorities for individual pupils within the general school curriculum. The assumption is made that once a child's short-term needs can be defined in a precise way it is more likely that a positive step forward will be determined.

The course uses a competency-based approach (Blackhurst, 1977) with clearly stated objectives for participants, which indicate the skills and knowledge they are to acquire. These objectives are used to guide and evaluate learning. This is perhaps best illustrated by an example. The objectives for Unit 4, 'Assessment and Record Keeping', are presented as follows:

At the end of this unit you will be able to:

1 state the reasons why the class teacher has a fundamental role in assessment;
2 state how tasks can be set at an appropriate level;
3 assess and place a pupil at the appropriate place within a programme;
4 record the child's progress through the programme; and
5 state the important features of record keeping.

During the early part of the course, use is made of the 'Basic Skills' Checklist' (BSC) which consists of a list of skills in six areas of development, i.e. arithmetic, language, reading, social competence, spelling and writing. A page from the checklist is shown in Figure 1. The items included in the BSC are based on 'market research' of those aspects of the curriculum that primary school teachers feel to be particular problems for their pupils. It is stressed, however, that the content is not seen as being comprehensive and that users are free to add further skills or, indeed, areas of concern. Emphasis is placed on the need to examine a child's attainments in a wide sense, since children may experience difficulties in areas other than reading and number.

It is important to note that the BSC is not a test but rather a means by which a teacher can clarify her ideas about what a child can and cannot do.

Figure 1

R4 Fluency and Comprehension	Can do
For the child's usual reading book: (state title) _____	
R4.1 Uses key words from the reading book in oral sentences.	
R4.2 Reads new words from the book when presented in a sentence.	
R4.3 Reads new words from book when presented in isolation.	
R4.4 Reads the book fluently.	
R4.5 Answers oral comprehension questions on sections of the book.	
R4.6 States the main idea of the book or part of the book.	

SOCIAL COMPETENCE

	Can do
SC.1 Fasten buttons and zips.	
SC.2 Puts on coat.	
SC.3 Dresses and undresses self in reasonable time.	
SC.4 Ties own shoe laces.	
SC.5 Cares for self at toilet.	
SC.6 Washes and dries own hands.	

SPELLING

	Can do
S.1 Writes own name correctly from memory.	
S.2 Writes letter sounds from dictation.	
S.3 Spells phonically simple two letter words, for example, at, up.	
S.4 Spells phonically irregular two letter words, for example, to, me.	
S.5 Spells phonically regular consonant-vowel-consonant words, for example, bag, bit.	

In completing it, teachers are invited to compare the child's performance with that of others in the same class with a view to defining areas of priority that need extra attention if he is to progress.

Once priorities have been determined, the teachers then learn how to

Figure 2
Special Needs Action Programme

PROGRAMME RECORDS

Pupil's name   Steven V

Code	Material	Instructions	Pupil behaviour	Criteria	Record		
					Working on	Mastered	Checked
A8	Large clock face. Work sheets containing clock faces	'What time is it?'	Tells the time (minutes past the hour)	Without error on three occasions			
STEP 7	Tells all the previously learnt times mixed up.				17.6.82	17.6.82	19.6.82 23.6.82 30.6.82
STEP 6	Tells the time 20 and 25 mins past the hour				16.6.82	16.6.82	17.6.82
STEP 5	Tells all the previously learnt times mixed up				14.6.82	14.6.82	15.6.82
STEP 4	Tells the time 5 minutes and 10 past the hour				11.6.82	11.6.82	14.6.82
STEP 3	Tells the time whole hour, half past, and quarter past mixed				10.6.82	10.6.82	11.6.82
STEP 2	Tells the time on whole hour and quarter past				9.6.82	9.6.82	10.6.82
STEP 1	Tells the time on the whole hour and half past				8.6.82	8.6.82	9.6.82

Notes/comments
Steven made very quick progress with telling the time — minutes past the hour.

write these as performance objectives and, if necessary, apply simple task analysis strategies to form more finely graded teaching steps. These programmes are used to conduct a more detailed assessment of the child's existing capabilities, for planning teaching methods and materials, and for monitoring progress using a simple checklist format which can be dated as the child proceeds. As an example, Figure 2 is a programme designed and implemented by a primary school teacher who attended the course recently.

Evaluation

To date, the evaluation of the course has been approached in different ways. In the first place, prior to the production of any materials, there was considerable discussion with different professional groups. These discussions enabled an assessment of the needs of schools to be made, as well as generating ideas about possible approaches and course content. In addition, as the course materials were developed, they were shared with appropriate colleagues to enable further ideas to be included, and modifications made.

Once the materials for the course had been assembled, it was run with members of the remedial team and school psychological service as well as selected teachers from special schools. This served a two-fold purpose it trained a number of professionals who could act as tutors and it provided further feedback on the course materials. This was aided by the completion of questionnaires which were produced for each unit.

Following this, a pilot course was held involving twelve selected primary schools in the city. The coordinators who attended this course all agreed to take part in a formal evaluation of the materials, which took the following form:

1   self-assessment at the beginning and end of the course on all the course objectives;
2   assessment at the end of each unit on the content of the unit;
3   assessment at the completion of the course of the method of delivery, course content and presentation, and satisfaction with the course.

The results of the evaluation have provided an internal evaluation of course content, rather than providing a means of assessing whether the method of in-service education developed for the Special Needs Action Programme is more effective than other methods of training. Nevertheless, the results obtained from the pilot study indicate that the course has been successful in enabling teachers to achieve the objectives set for the package.

In total, thirty-two questions were used to assess increase in skills, on the completion of each unit. Of these questions, only seven were answered incorrectly (by between 7 and 25 per cent of the course participants). Similarly, when asked to assess their own competence on eighteen course objectives 100 per cent felt they could 'definitely do' thirteen of the objectives and with the remaining five objectives no less than 80 per cent felt they could 'definitely do' them. Overall course evaluation indicated that all participants enjoyed the course and agreed with its method of presentation. The aspect which received the lowest rating was the video-tapes — an area of the course about which the authors are particularly concerned because of the comparatively poor quality of the films.

The most important aspect of the course is the final part — the follow-up — because unless participation in the course results in a change in practice in the schools, it cannot be regarded as a successful training programme. The effectiveness of the material in effecting change in this respect is currently being independently evaluated by Leicester University, and it is hoped the findings from this study will be available towards the end of the year.

Implications

The approaches introduced on the course are geared towards early intervention with a view to preventing difficulties of learning from developing. They will also have implications for the way in which help is provided for pupils who need special educational provision, possibly in a special school or unit.

The *Warnock Report* proposes a five-stage assessment hierarchy through which youngsters may move as necessary. The first three stages are school-based, with the head and staff attempting to meet the child's needs within normal school arrangements. During the third stage, assistance from support agencies will be incorporated.

In attempting to sharpen the awareness of school staff to their responsibility to identify pupils' special needs, and devise and monitor individualized educational programmes, the course attempts to help schools in establishing the type of responses recommended by Warnock. The coordinator for special needs in each school is seen as being the person who can support class teachers and co-ordinate provision for individual pupils assisted, when appropriate, by members of the various support services.

It is anticipated, therefore, that in future where pupils are being assessed with a view to the establishment of a 'statement' under the 1981 Education Act, the information gathered by class teachers as a result of their systematic teaching and observation, including the records that have been kept, will form an integral part of the decision-making process. This information should be particularly valuable since it will give a clear picture of the child's progress, or lack of it, over a period of time in the ordinary classroom. Furthermore, it will provide a valuable analysis of the child's existing attainments from which further teaching programmes can be devised.

Conclusion

The course described here is the first to be developed within the Special Needs Action Programme. The following courses are also being devised:

(a) Daily Measurement: This is an advanced course for coordinators who have successfully completed the learning difficulties course. It has been devised by three educational psychologists (Winteringham *et al.*, 1983), and will be piloted early this year. It is anticipated that the course will in turn lead to a further course on using daily assessment and teaching in the primary school curriculum (Akerman, T. *et al.*, 1983).

(b) Hearing Difficulties: A tape/slide presentation is nearing completion and will be released as a self-contained package which can be used in schools to alert teachers to the needs of children with impaired hearing.

(c) Visual Difficulties: A small working party is currently meeting to devise a self-contained package dealing with the educational needs of children with impaired vision.

(d) Behaviour and Emotional Difficulties: A working party is currently discussing the development of a course dealing with the needs of children with behaviour and emotional difficulties. This package is expected to be available in 1984.

It is hoped that others involved in similar initiatives will find the information in this article useful.

Readers wishing to purchase SNAP materials should write for details to: Elm Bank Teachers' Centre, Mile Lane, Coventry CV1 2LQ.

References

AINSCOW, M. and MUNCEY, J. (1981a) *Small Steps: A Workshop Guide About Teaching Children with Learning Difficulties*, Coventry LEA Publication.

AINSCOW, M. and MUNCEY, J. (1981b) *Tutors' Guide: SNAP Learning Difficulties Course*, Coventry LEA Publication.

AINSCOW, M. and TWEDDLE, D.A. (1979) *Preventing Classroom Failure: An Objectives Approach*, Wiley, Chichester.

AKERMAN, T., GILLETT, D., KENWOOD, P., LEADBETTER, P., MASON, L., MATTHEWS, C., TWEDDLE, D.A. and WINTERINGHAM, D. (1983) 'Daily teaching and assessment: primary aged children. A response to the 1981 Education Act', submitted to *Special Education: Forward Trends*.

BECKER, W.C. (1977) 'Teaching reading and language to the disadvantaged — what we have learned from field research', *Harvard Educational Review*, pp. 518–543.

BECKER, W.C. and ENGELMANN, S. (1977) *The Oregon Direct Instruction Model*, University of Oregon Follow-through Project, Eugene, Oregon.

BIJOU, S.W. (1977) 'Practical implications of an interactional model of child development', *Exceptional Children*, 44, 1, pp. 6–15.

BLACKHURST, A.E. (1977) 'Competency-based special educational personnel preparation', in KNEEDLER, R.D. and TARVER, S.G. (Eds.), *Changing Perspectives in Special Education*, Columbus, Merrill.

BLOOM, B.S. (1976) *Human Characteristics and School Learning*, New York, McGraw-Hill.

BOOKBINDER, G. (1978) 'Meddling with children?' *Times Educational Supplement*, 1 February.

BORG, W.R. (1972) 'The mini-course as a vehicle for changing teacher behaviour'. *Journal of Educational Psychology*, 63, pp. 572–9.

CHARLES, C.M. (1976) *Individualising Instruction*, Saint Louis, Mosby, C.V.

DEPARTMENT OF EDUCATION AND SCIENCE (1978) *Special Educational Needs (Warnock Report)*, London, HMSO.

DEPARTMENT OF EDUCATION AND SCIENCE (1981) *Education Act 1981*, London, HMSO.

EAVES, R.C. and McLAUGHLIN, P. (1977) 'A systems approach for the assessment of the child and his behaviour: getting back to basics', *Journal of Special Education*, 11, 1, pp. 99–111.

ENGELMANN, S.E. (1977) 'Sequencing cognitive and academic tasks', in KNEEDLER, R.D. and TARVER, S.G. (Eds.). *Changing Perspectives in Special Education*. Columbus, Merrill.

FARRELL, P.T. (1982) 'An evaluation of an EDY course in behaviour modification techniques for teachers and care staff in an ESN(S) school', *Special Education, Forward Trends*, 92, 2, pp. 21–5.

GEORGIADES, N.J. and PHILLIMORE, L. (1975) 'The myth of the hero innovator and alternative strategies for organisational change', in KIERNAN, C.C. and WOODFORD, F.P. (Eds.). *Behaviour Modification for the Severely Retarded*. Amsterdam, Association Scientific.

HALL, R.V., COPELAND, R. and CLARKE, M. (1976) 'Management strategies for teachers and parents: responsive teaching,' in HARING, N.G. and SCHIEFELBUSCH, R.L. (Eds.). *Teaching Special Children*. New York, McGraw-Hill.

HARING, N.G., LOVITT, T.C., EATON, M.D. and HANSEN, C.L. (Eds.) (1978) *The Fourth R: Research in the Classroom*, Columbus, Merrill.

HERSCH, R.H. and COHEN, S.J. (1972) 'Beyond behavioural objectives: individualising instruction', *The Elementary School Journal*, 73, pp. 101–6.

HOWELL, K.W. and KAPLAN, J.S. (1980) *Diagnosing Basic Skills: A Handbook for Deciding What to Teach*. Columbus, Merrill.

JONES, N. and JONES, E. (1981) 'Oxfordshire looks towards the future', *Special Education, Forward Trends*, 8, 2, pp. 23–5.

KEOGH, B.K. (1975) 'Social and ethical assumptions about special education', in WEDELL, K. (Ed.). *Orientations in Special Education*, London, Wiley.

KRATOCHWILL, T.R. and GREEN, L.M. (1978) 'Process assessment', *Academic Therapy*, 13, pp. 563–8.

LARSEN, S.C. (1977) 'The education evaluation of handicapped students'. in KNEEDLER, R.D. and TARVER, S.G. (Eds.). *Changing Perspectives in Special Education*, Colombus, Merrill.

LEEMING, K., SWANN, W., COUPE, J. and MITTLER, P. (1979) *Teaching Language and Communication to the Mentally Handicapped*. London, Evans/Methuen.

LOVITT, T.C. (1977) *In Spite of My Resistance, I've Learned from Children*, Columbus, Merrill.

MAKINS, V. (1976) 'Bullock plus one — with a bang or a whimper? Diagnosis and screening', *Times Educational Supplement*, 6 February.

MARSHALL, C.P. (1976) 'Screening for the early identification of children in need of help', *A.E.P. Journal*, 4, 2, pp. 2–12.

MOSS, G. and CHILDS, J. (1981) 'In-service training in behavioural psychology: problems of implementation' in WHELDALL, K. (Ed.). *The Behaviourist in the Classroom*,

Birmingham, Educational Review.

NUSSEL, E.J., INGLIS, J.D. and WIERSMAN, W. (1976) *The Teacher and Individually Guided Education*, Reading, Mass, Addison-Wesley.

RHINE, W.R. (1981) *Making Schools More Effective: New Directions from Follow Through*. New York, Academic.

ROBSON, C. (1979) 'A self-instructional course on language development through structured teaching', in INMAN, J. (Ed.). *Aspects of Curriculum Development: Teaching Language to the Mentally Handicapped*. Birmingham, Westhill College.

WEDELL, K. (1981) 'Concepts of special educational needs', *Education Today*, 31, pp. 3–9.

WEDELL, K. and LINDSAY, G.A. (1980) Early identification procedures: what have we learned?' *Remedial Education*, 15, pp. 130–5.

WINTERINGHAM, D.P., MORRIS, S. and WINN, M.B. (1983) *Daily Measurement: A Guide to Assessing the daily Progress of Children with Learning Difficulties*. Coventry LEA Publication.

Assessing the Advantages of Team Teaching in Remedial Education: The Remedial Teacher's Role

Neil Ferguson
Lecturer in Education, University of Aberdeen
and
Muriel Adams,
Remedial Teacher, Portlethen Primary School

Introduction

Only three or four years ago remedial education would have meant extra attention for low ability children in reading, spelling and, less frequently, mathematics. Had anyone asked what was special about this provision, most schools could have pointed to those individuals and small groups who were regularly withdrawn from ordinary classrooms to practise their 'basic skills' with a teacher who was familar with the child's learning difficulties and was able to give him a good deal of individual attention and encouragement. Remedial sessions for these children identified as slow learners would generally be teacher directed, highly structured, fairly intensive and characterized by a good deal of formal and informal assessment and a considerable emphasis on the repetition and practice of skills already acquired by a very large majority of the remedial pupil's classmates. But there are now a growing number of remedial teachers who see themselves as specialists in teaching and learning with a responsibility for helping children at all levels to improve their understanding of the subject matter of the school curriculum. This new role for remedial teachers has grown out of recent experiments in which schools have made provison for class teachers and remedial teachers to work in the same classroom at the same time. 'Team teaching' as it has been called has been introduced into some secondary schools in the Grampian Region and is growing in popularity. Remedial teachers enjoy team teaching and welcome the opportunity it provides to work with able pupils ('you can forget what bright children are like'). Yet the definition of

This article originally appeared in *Remedial Education* (1982) 17, 1

remedial education which is implied by all this and the less distinctive rôle which has been adopted by the new breed of remedial teacher raises many questions about the best way of providing for the needs of the schools' least able pupils.

The Aims of the Study

This paper concentrates on just one aspect of many topics which were examined in a recent Aberdeen University department of education (1980) evaluation of remedial education in the Grampian region. This aspect could perhaps be described as the rôle of the remedial teacher in the ordinary classroom but in the present study this has come to mean finding the answers to three fairly straightforward questions:

1 How do remedial teachers describe what they do when they are working with a subject specialist?
2 What part do remedial teachers play in the planning of courses and the preparation of lessons?
3 How satisfied are remedial teachers and class teachers with the remedial teacher's contribution to team teaching sessions?

The final section of the chapter discusses some of the advantages and disadvantages of team teaching methods. The answers to the three questions which have been asked cannot settle current controversies about traditional methods and team teaching but they do provide a good deal of information which is relevant to the debate.

The Investigation

Six secondary schools were asked if they would be willing for some of their teachers and pupils to give their opinions of the school's team teaching arrangements. All of the schools agreed but were apprehensive about our plans to interview pupils and needed to be reassured that no mention of remedial education would be made or as one principal remedial teacher put it 'Don't blow the remedial teachers' cover'. All six schools, it was found, did some team teaching in English and home economics, five had remedial teachers in maths, history and geography lessons, four of the schools had some team teaching in their science, religious education and technical subjects courses, two schools taught modern studies this way, one did integrated studies, one child care, one music and one art.

Forty-eight class teachers were interviewed in school. They described the way that remedial teachers operate for team teaching lessons. Fifty-four pupils described the roles played by both members of the teaching team. The remedial teachers had already been interviewed about other aspects of remedial education and forty-one gave their opinions about team teaching in a questionnaire. But the questions emphasized the same things: the rôles which remedial teachers play and their opinions about team teaching as a strategy for the provision of extra help for children with learning difficulties.

What do Remedial Teachers do?

Table 1 shows how a sample of thirty-six teachers divided their time between traditional remedial teaching, team teaching and other activities. One school taught integrated studies in which a team of subject specialists together with remedial teachers, developed themes (for example, barriers or communication) which formed the basis for work with around a hundred pupils who are taught together in the same room at the same time. The children are organized in small working groups which can then draw upon the resources of the entire teaching team. This has been included under the heading 'team teaching' but it is a different kind of teaching than would normally be undertaken by a history teacher, for example, who has a remedial teacher for only one of the four periods of history which he teaches to a particular class in any given week. Two schools allow time spent with remedial teaching staff as an optional subject. Thus while most children opt for biology, modern studies and so forth, some choose to go to the remedial education department for extra help in wide variety of subjects or for what has been called basic skills option. This does not fit easily into any other category and (see Table 1, column 6) has been classified separately.

Remedial teachers seem to give the impression that subject specialists work their way through the syllabus with what might appear to be an extraordinarily restricted range of methods and a heavy reliance on work sheets and a prescribed text. Lessons begin when the class teacher talks to the whole class for perhaps quarter of an hour and then distributes work sheets containing exercises which test the pupils' understanding of the points which have been made. In this setting, remedial teachers believe that their task is to listen while the subject specialist talks to the whole class and then circulate among the children responding to the needs of those who are in difficulties. There are remarkably few variations in what seems to have become a widely accepted role for remedial teachers.

Only five of the forty-one remedial teachers, jointly prepared and taught lessons with a subject specialist. Eighteen teachers said that they had never addressed the whole class and of the twenty-three who did take the class on occasions, some qualified their answer with comments which showed that they did not necessarily have a more demanding or a less passive classroom role than those who did. One teacher said that she spoke to the whole class 'when the subject teacher is disinclined to make much effort or wishes to do something else'. Another commented, 'If by chance I have helped out when the subject teacher has been called away and he/she returns

Table 1 *How a sample of thirty-six remedial teachers divide their time between team teaching, withdrawal and other activities in six secondary schools*

School	No. of remedial teachers	Proportion of time spent in team teaching	Proportion of time spent with pupils withdrawn from classroom	Free time/ preparation time/ Departmental meetings	Basic skills option	Other teaching
1	7	38.8	34.8	25.8	—	0.7
2	5	20.2	38.6	19.0	22.3	—
3	4	46.2	33.0	18.7	4.4	—
4	8	41.9	24.1	33.0	—	—
5	5	61.1	8.9	27.4	—	2.7
6	7	54.0	13.8	29.7	—	2.5

he/she might say "Just carry on". Then she takes over again when I'm finished.' Other comments were 'when he needs to Xerox'; 'while the teacher is busy with end of term reports'; 'when the teacher has a lot of marking to do'; 'when the class teacher has been "spirited off" somewhere', or 'the subject teacher marks the papers while the remedial teacher works through the answers'.

There is little doubt in the minds of most subject specialists that remedial teachers are not intended to share teaching in the way that the phrase 'team teaching' seems to imply. Our sample of forty-eight class teachers were asked whether they ever sat and listened while the remedial teacher taught the class. Five class teachers were not currently involved in any team teaching but thirty of the forty-three said that the remedial teacher had never taught the whole class while the class teacher was in the classroom. The thirteen who had listened to a remedial teacher teaching were asked whether this was a lesson or a brief explanation of a particular point. Only five teachers said that their team teaching colleague had ever taken one of their lessons while they were there.

How do Remedial Teachers Prepare for a Team Teaching Lesson?

It is possible for a remedial teacher to go into a classroom without a very clear idea of the content of the lesson which is about to be taught. But once the remedial teacher has listened to a lesson and the instructions for completing the written work he or she can then answer questions and provide additional explanations of the main teaching points for children who need extra help of this kind. Occasionally, the system breaks down and class teachers (especially maths teachers it seems) can be very scathing about remedial teachers who have failed to understand some point in their lesson, but home economics teachers too express surprise at their remedial teaching colleagues' failure to master what they believe are elementary practical skills.

The sample of forty-one remedial teachers were asked 'How do you prepare for a team teaching lesson? (If it varies with the subject teacher please give details)'. Two teachers did not answer this question and two gave answers (for example 'cooperation with the class teacher') which were so vague that they could not be interpreted. Of the thirty-seven remedial teachers who gave information about their preparation, sixteen seem to indicate that there was at least one subject in which they did no preparation other than finding out the topic which was about to be taught. A remedial teacher complained 'Often I do not know in advance what the subject teacher is teaching the class. I never see these teachers in the staffroom'. One teacher who was satisfied with her preparation explained, 'It is not always possible to predict exactly what topic will be being studied. I usually check on a Friday either with a pupil or with the teacher just what stage they have reached since I saw the class on the Monday.' One teacher suggested that it is sometimes better not to know. 'In science I have a copy of the syllabus and can study the lesson in advance. I see the class in every science period (five per week). Preparation for other subjects is negligible. Lack of knowledge of the subject can be used to advantage as I see the lesson from the pupil's point of view and can understand their problems.' More typical perhaps are those teachers who accept the arrangements unquestioningly, 'Little preparation for maths as teacher prefers taking lesson herself', or who regret that they do not do more, 'my present very tightly scheduled duties simply restrict such deliberations to a few moments at the end of sessions or a fleeting few words at natural breaks in the day'.

Most of the time remedial teachers do have opportunities to prepare for lessons. Twenty-three teachers who described their preparation procedures mention reading through the work sheets or studying the work sheets. Twelve of these teachers add that they have been involved in preparing some of the work sheets or that they sometimes modify existing work sheets or write simpler versions of them for remedial pupils.

Preparation varies from subject to subject and a teacher may do no preparation for maths but may study work sheets and enter into regular discussions before team teaching in geography or history for example. Table 2 summarizes the number of teachers who mention one of the various ways of preparing for team lessons in their description of their preparation practices.

Satisfaction with the Remedial Teacher's Contribution

Nearly all remedial teachers are cast in the rôle of teachers' aides or more accurately are 'the classroom's faithful retainers' because most accept their role and recognize the importance of the class teachers' specialized knowledge. 'There is no way I could teach a better lesson than the maths or

Table 2   Remedial teachers' preparation for team teaching lessons

Preparation practice	No. of teachers giving at least one mention
Study work sheets, work cards, work books	23
No preparation for some lessons	16
Regular discussion with class teacher	12
Devising and revising work sheets	12
Read the textbook	6
Prepare lesson to give to class	5
Study the syllabus only	2
Read the lesson notes	1
Prepare remedial pupils for lesson in advance	1

science specialist.' 'There is no danger that I can mislead pupils by wrong emphases at presentation.' The pupils are aware of the relationship and almost all of them (forty-nine out of fifty-four) describe the class teacher as 'the real teacher' or 'the proper teacher', 'the English teacher' and so forth. The remedial teacher is 'the helper'. Whether remedial teachers' preparation for team teaching lessons is adequate or not depends on how the team teaching task is interpreted and class teachers and remedial teachers on occasions implied that remedial teachers did not need to prepare a great deal. Yet eighteen remedial teachers were dissatisfied with their preparation. When the forty-three subject specialists who were currently team teaching were asked for an opinion about the adequacy of the remedial teachers' preparation nineteen said that it was not adequate, seven said that they did not know and only seventeen were satisfied.

The general picture which emerges of the remedial teachers in the classroom is one of passive acceptance and contentment with an undemanding role. Most accept that it is the class teacher's responsibility to undertake the planning and preparation of lessons and courses and the class teachers, in turn, jealously guard their right to maintain control of the progress of each lesson. One class teacher described remedial teachers as 'rather ingratiating — embarrassed by their position. They have an urge to justify their existence'. Another commented testily 'she (the remedial teacher) is inclined to want to take over the whole class. She seems to have this need to have a whole class. Suddenly she's in the middle directing the class if I go out for a minute'. Most class teachers who never allow the remedial teacher to teach a particular point or part of a lesson (and some that do allow this) comment on the remedial teachers' lack of experience with the content of their subject specialism, 'Remedial teachers are reluctant to do this. They do not know the subject well enough'. 'I am a specialist in English. The remedial teacher may be a maths specialist. It is an unfair burden to expect her to teach all subjects.'

The pupils usually describe the remedial teacher in the role of teacher's assistant and then express their general satisfaction with having a second adult in the room ('You don't have to wait so long when there are two teachers'). Their comments, however, often confirm that the remedial teacher's role is not an easy one. 'She does not help you quite so much in maths. She is there learning I think.' 'There is more time for teaching if one is checking.' 'I don't know the other one. She just sits and listens.' 'He is the English teacher — he has taught people English before.' 'The other teacher does not come to the front.' 'She just comes to stand in her spare time.'

Traditional Remedial Education or Team Teaching?

Team teaching is usually assessed against a background of criticisms of traditional remedial education in which individuals and small groups are withdrawn from the classroom for the provision of extra help in the basic subjects. The practice is thought to stigmatize children, isolate them and breed discontinuities in their classroom work. It is also suggested (see Clark, 1979) that remedial teaching sessions are often too narrow and specific and so different from other teaching that improvements observed by remedial teachers may not be reflected in children's regular classroom work. There may even be some deterioration because class teachers choose to believe that they can shed some of the responsibility for their least able pupils who are receiving remedial help. Nevertheless when we asked class teachers and remedial teachers to compare the benefits of team teaching with those of traditional remedial education only eight teachers in each group believed team teaching to be the more effective strategy with remedial pupils. Twice as many remedial teachers (sixteen) and more than twice as many class teachers (nineteen) felt that extra help given outside the ordinary classroom was of more benefit to the least able children. Sixteen class teachers and seventeen remedial teachers either did not know, felt that the benefits were about the same or felt that either approaches or differing combinations of the two approaches were likely to succeed with different remedial pupils. There was no feeling that it would be sensible to abandon 'the withdrawal strategy' entirely and replace it with team teaching.

In 1967, Chazan reviewed the effects of the remedial teaching of reading and all of the studies he reviewed were of children who were withdrawn from ordinary classrooms for the provision of extra help. His conclusion was that remedial education does not alter the overall rate of children's progress but merely brings about improvements rather earlier than they might otherwise have been recorded. The studies reviewed (for example Collins, 1961; Lovell *et al.*, 1962 and 1963) seem to suggest that remedial pupils do not, as a rule, maintain their initial rate of improvement and are eventually caught up by control groups of children who have not been given extra remedial help. Cashdan and Pumfrey (1969) confirm Chazan's conclusions, adding that there is no evidence either to show that children receiving remedial help acquire healthier or more positive attitudes to reading than their matched controls.

The finding that remedial education brings about improvements which cannot be sustained is probably what might be expected by those who are concerned about the discontinuities and differences in style and content which emerge when remedial teaching and the work of the ordinary classroom are compared. It was recognized that new initiatives and proposals for change were needed which would take account of the need to make provision for classroom teachers and remedial teachers to work more closely together, formulating common approaches and ensuring that care is taken to integrate the remedial programme with the ongoing work of the school. One way to ensure this is to make provision for both to work in the same classroom at the same time. This is a potentially useful way of integrating remedial education with the school curriculum, eliminating some of the stigmatizing effects and helping both class teachers and remedial teachers to improve their understanding of each other's problems and special skills. If a pupil is failing in maths, for example, there is perhaps no better way for the remedial teacher to appreciate his difficulties than by attending his maths lesson and giving him the extra help he needs. This help need not confine itself to English and mathematics but may be found to be just as worthwhile in science or geography or home economics. It means that extra help for slow learning pupils is no longer interpreted narrowly as a repetition of past failures or restricted to the basic skills. The child is more likely to be exposed to a wide range of educational experiences and to receive his remedial help in a variety of contexts while avoiding some of the undesirable effects of being taken away from his usual classroom. It is, in the spirit of the *Warnock Report's* recommendation, opting for the advantages of a greater degree of integration in the hope that being treated like everyone else will indeed mean social acceptance, more personal happiness and more progress at school.

The *Warnock Report* goes on to argue that teaching should be better adapted to the needs of those children with special needs who are a large and significant minority of the school population. But team teaching is not the only answer to questions about the nature of the changes which should be made to adapt remedial teaching to children's needs. There may be special advantages in close relationships, individual treatment and the concentrated attention of an interested adult. In the United States individualized reading had come to mean diagnostic and prescriptive reading instruction based on the pre- and post-testing of reading objectives and the provision of 'instructional sequences' selected or devised to fit individual needs. The reasons for choosing highly systematic, individualized approaches seem well founded. They are derived from work (see Brennan, 1979) on the characteristics of slow learning children whose incidental learning, it is claimed, is poor. The remedial child has particular difficulties in perceiving relationships and differences and thus in organizing material for retention and future use. It is important to understand the limitations of the relatively unstructured learning environment of the regular classroom. Remedial pupils seem to learn more effectively when difficult tasks are broken into gradients of small steps presented one at a time with frequent checks on progress and plenty of opportunities for repetition and practice. Team teaching may not be capable of creating a situation in which these needs can be met. Individual attention, even in a classroom with two teachers, is rarely planned in such a detailed way and is likely to consist of brief and infrequent encounters with those who require further explanation of a particular teaching point, who cannot locate appropriate books or materials or who require an additional description of the task which the class teacher has devised. These limitations are generally recognized and in the present study for example (see Table 1) none of the schools which had adopted team teaching had abandoned the traditional approach. Yet if withdrawing remedial children from the classroom is inevitably stigmatizing and ineffective, it might be argued that it ought not to be done. It might also be suggested that team teaching methods which do not take account of what is known about the characteristics of remedial pupils' learning should not be preferred to methods which do.

Each side condemns the other by first discussing effects which seem to be unavoidable consequences of the nature of the method chosen and secondly by criticizing the ways in which the approach has been used in schools. For example, the very act of withdrawing a child is said to damage his relationship with the rest of the group, to have adverse effects upon teacher attitudes and the child's feelings about himself. Comments about the methods, materials and content of teaching for individual and small groups who have been withdrawn from the regular classroom are, on the other hand, not arguments about inevitable consequences but criticisms of the way that remedial teaching happens to have developed. Similarly, team teaching is attacked on grounds which suggest that the ordinary classroom is, by its very nature, an unsuitable place for remedial pupils to receive the kind of help which has often been claimed to be most suitable for their needs. Whether the addition of a remedial teacher to the ordinary classroom helps to overcome these limitations or not is unlikely to be answered satisfactorily without knowing what remedial teachers do when they are asked to teach alongside a subject specialist. But our discussions with class teachers and remedial teachers in six secondary schools seem to have shown that the adoption of a team teaching policy has left a number of important issues unresolved. Are remedial teachers just teacher's aides? What account must be taken of the fact that they might have trained as primary schoolteachers or at least not be qualified in some of the subjects they are teaching? In what sense is team teaching a form of remedial education and what use does the approach make of the remedial teacher's special skills? Should not class teachers trust remedial teachers to cope with the content of their subject specialism?

Many of the comments made by class teachers as well as some of the remarks of remedial teachers (happily acknowledging a lack of specialized knowledge) ought to be challenged. It is reasonable to argue that remedial teachers were not intended to be team teachers and that it is not important for them to take on this responsibility. But there are undoubtedly difficulties in adopting the role of 'teaching's aide', 'extra pupil', 'helpful visitor' or 'faithful retainer' and at the same time retaining sufficient control and confidence to develop a distinctly different rôle. A second belief which ought to be questioned is the notion that it is possible to act as an expert in learning difficulties without making reference to curriculum content. Difficulties do not occur in a vacuum and it is not entirely convincing to claim to be an expert in learning and at the same time to admit that one is not to be trusted to teach maths, science, technical subjects and so forth to pupils who find these subjects difficult. It is doubtful if the job of listening to a lesson and then circulating within the classroom and responding to children's queries fulfils what some have seen as a need for improvements in the quality of traditional remedial teaching. An approach is yet to be found which marries the benefits of systematic, individual attention to the advantages of awareness in detail of the demands of the regular classroom. Without detailed knowledge of content and methods and effective arrangements for liaison with class teachers, remedial staff will be unable, for example, to experiment with the possibilities of preparing children with learning difficulties to tackle a future series of difficult lessons. They will not know how to follow up lessons which have proved difficult for some pupils and will not find it easy to analyze and isolate the processes, concepts or steps in thinking about science or home economics, etc. which present particular difficulties for some pupils. Finally, it is difficult to see how remedial teachers can operate within a classroom and yet provide the individual treatment, personal interest and concentrated attention which it was earlier argued is of particular benefit to remedial pupils. Helping the subject specialist to ask better questions, provide more attractive materials or get round the whole class so that everyone's written work is seen before the end of the lesson is a useful contribution which makes for better teaching. But it is still necessary to question whether improving the quality of teaching for all children is the most effective way of providing extra help for children with learning difficulties.

Acknowledgements

We gratefully acknowledge the generous support of the Grampian Region Education Authority and the help of all those teachers and pupils who provided us with our information.

The opinions expressed in this paper are our own.

References

BRENNAN, W.K. (1979) *The Curricular Needs of Slow Learners*, Schools Council.

CASHDAN, A. and PUMFREY, P.D. (1969) 'Some effects of the remedial teaching of reading'. *Educational Research.* 11, 2, pp. 138–42.

CHAZAN, M. (1967) 'The effects of remedial teaching in reading: A review of research'. *Remedial Education.* 2, 1, pp. 4–12.

CLARK, M.M. (1979) 'Why remedial? Implications of using the concept of remedial education' in GAINS, C. and McNICHOLAS, J.A. (1979) *Guidelines for the Future*, Longman.

COLLINS, J.E. (1961) *The Effects of Remedial Education*, London, Oliver and Boyd.

LOVELL, K., BYRNE, C. and RICHARDSON, B. (1963) 'A further study of the educational progress of children who have received remedial education', *British Journal of Educational Psychology*, 33, pp. 3–9.

LOVELL, K., JOHNSON, E. and PLATTS, O. (1962) 'A summary of a study of the reading ages of children who had received remedial education'. *British Journal of Educational Psychology*, pp. 66–71.

Adopting a Resources Approach

Elizabeth Jones, HMI
and
Sandra Berrick
Head of Special Resources Department,
Carterton School, Oxford

Introduction

What are the options open to an education authority trying to meet the special educational needs of children in ordinary schools? One type of provision — the 'resource room' model — is being tried out in Oxfordshire, at the Carterton Comprehensive School, purpose built and opened in September 1978. It is an experiment aimed at maximizing the integration of children in ordinary classes, given certain kinds of provision.

The Carterton project is one of a number of alternative ways, both in Britain and abroad, of (a) supporting handicapped children in ordinary schools; (b) providing greater flexibility in methods of selection, placement, and programming; and (c) increasing coordination between those working in ordinary and special education. The resources model approach is one that, having been tried extensively in Denmark, America, New Zealand and Australia, is being considered carefully in Oxfordshire as part of the county's response to the *Warnock Report*.

The Resources Model

The concept of the resource room department in ordinary schools has received considerable attention in American literature (Weiner, 1969; Clark, 1969; Glavin *et al*, 1971; Reger and Koppmann, 1971; Sabatino, 1972; Reger, 1973; Christopolos, 1973). Although a number of schools in Britain are experimenting with this form of special provision, such schemes,

This article originally appeared in *Special Education: Forward Trends* (1980) 7, 1 according to Cope and Anderson (1977) do not appear to be monitored carefully: if they are, then the findings are not written up for publication. Among the few accounts which have been published are Garnett's description (1976) of ESN(M) children in a comprehensive school, Chalk's article on 'sanctuary units' for disturbed children in ordinary primary schools (1975), and two articles by Jones (1971 and 1977) on 'adjustment units' in comprehensive schools.

The term 'resource room' is generally used to mean a room or rooms staffed by a teacher or teachers with special qualification, an ancillary helper, and specially equipped according to the child's needs. The emphasis is on programming to meet *individual* needs, rather than grouping children in categories of handicap. The guiding principle is that all children's educational needs should be met *as far as possible* within an ordinary school, and *as far as possible* within an ordinary class. The resource room programme is developed as an integral element in the total curriculum and organization of the school. Children are withdrawn from the ordinary class to the resource base only for essential small group work, individual tutoring or educational assessment; otherwise they are supported in their ordinary class by a member of staff from the resource room. The children may be receiving supplementary materials prepared by the resource staff, which enable them to remain in their normal class and follow the class's programme of work.

Carterton Comprehensive School

Carterton is a small town on the fringe of the Cotswolds (population 12,470), overshadowed by the nearby Brize Norton RAF Station which offers employment to approximately 60 per cent of the local population. Carterton School was opened in 1971 as a lower secondary school, catering for approximately 750 pupils from the immediate local catchment area. It accepted its first 11–16 age range in September 1978.

The school has four feeder primary schools with a six-form entry in the first year. It has a fairly mobile population because of the nature of the local employment. All tutor groups in years 1 and 2 are mixed ability pastoral and teaching groups, with the form tutor teaching a minimum of his timetable (25 per cent) with his form tutor group. All children, regardless of whether or not they come within the special resources department, are members of a tutor group and always register there. Humanities forms the core of the timetabled block which form tutors teach; it is taught in open-plan teaching areas with emphasis on team teaching. An interesting facet of the staff is the training many of them have had in primary education. The school accepts all ESN(M) children who live within an approximate radius of 10 miles who are physically handicapped and have been accepted through the admissions panel.

Resources Department: Facilities

The special resources department (SRD) was opened in purpose-built premises in September 1978, part of phase II building of the school, to provide for the all-range secondary intake. The block included several teaching classrooms and science laboratories and was designed to provide easy access and movement to and from subject areas. The amenities provided within the SRD include an open reception/circulation area; two teaching rooms, each capable of taking a maximum of ten pupils; a smaller teaching room which doubles up as a room available to visiting professionals such as the educational psychologist or speech therapist; an office with a telephone; a well equipped art/craft room; a modified kitchen for physically handicapped children: a bathroom and rest room/medical room. The immediate impression is one of space, light and colour. Typewriters and storage equipment have been provided as well as an array of educational materials required for such a disparate group of children using the SRD. Capitation is provided through the school's main fund, supplemented by the special education per capita allowance.

Staffing

The SRD was designed to accommodate thirty full-time children and was fully staffed from the outset — although the head of the department was appointed several years after the architect's plans had been drawn up and executed. The theoretical ratio for staffing is one teacher to ten children, and the department is expected to have its full complement of students in 1982. Staffing ratios are to be reviewed before that time. The decision to staff fully in advance was intentional; it was felt that the department should gradually build up its workload, thus enabling the main school to cope with the demands being made upon it. The staff were prepared through formal and informal discussions to incorporate the new department into their midst.

Staffing consists of three full-time teachers, two of whom have accepted a teaching commitment in the main school, offering their own specialist subject; they are thus seen as members of another subject department as well as their own. The head of the SRD is responsible to the headmaster of the school, and has a Scale 3S post. The other two staff receive a special schools' allowance. There are two full-time ancillary helpers whose primary responsibilities are to meet the physical needs of the SRD. The roles of these ancillary helpers have been extended to include those of classroom assistants and resource material providers, and also to reinforce skills demonstrated by speech therapists and physiotherapists. One of the ancillary helpers has extensive nursing experience; the other is a fully trained teacher who, with falling school rolls, opted to become an ancillary helper.

External Support

The external support available to the SRD includes a weekly commitment from the educational psychologist and, more recently, from a psychiatric social worker who has links with the local child guidance clinic. The speech therapist and physiotherapist visit monthly and leave instructions for the SRD staff, who carry out the daily programme for those children who require treatment. The principal medical officer for the area is also the medical officer to the SRD and is available for advice, consultation, assessment and forward planning in relation to primary/secondary transfer of local children.

The head of the SRD receives formal support from the headmaster with whom she has weekly discussions. She is a member of departmental meetings where such issues as curriculum planning and pastoral care are discussed and policy implemented. Additional support is offered from an admissions support team, comprising the headmaster, the principal educational psychologist (who is the psychologist to the school), the principal medical officer, and the senior adviser for special education. The team meets at least once a term to monitor admissions to the SRD, to discuss and evaluate children's progress and to determine future policy and planning.

Identifying Disability

The SRD opened with three children already known to Oxfordshire's special services department. At the end of the first year fourteen children were being programmed, three of whom had been admitted during the school year from other local schools. One of these was a severe epileptic, while others had already been in the main school. The September intake increased the number to twenty-five. The resource model had to be sufficiently flexible to meet the needs of our particular school in terms of the overall prevalence and pattern of handicap of the pupils attending it.

The school psychologist arranged for every child in the main school to be assessed by subject teachers and form tutors, using a check list eliciting *their* perception of the child's needs. The special needs listed were chronic and minor physical disorders, learning disorders (due to mental retardation, backwardness in reading and mathematical skills, and specific learning disabilities), maladjustment, giftedness, multi-cultural background and social disadvantage. The survey was intended to highlight those children who showed signs of multiple handicap. Every identified need was then checked out independently against objective criteria — for example, medical opinion, psychological testing, completion of behavioural questionnaires or evaluation by the county's specialist advisory staff. This two-way screening identified those children who had disabilities which were both handicapping and non-handicapping and other children who required more detailed assessment.

Assessment and Admission

Any children with special educational needs can be referred to the SRD. The nature or degree of the handicap is evaluated once a need has been perceived: a child does not have to fit any particular diagnostic category in order to be seen and evaluated. In fact, the present classification system in special education is seen only as part of the process of determining how much the observed disability actually handicaps a child. One child might be eligible because his abilities seem very low and he needs assistance in order to do his work. Another might be eligible because he is considered very bright but is bored, disruptive and producing no work.

Referrals to the SRD come from a variety of sources, such as the screening already described, local primary teachers, GPs, the county advisory service, parents, teaching staff or the schools' psychological service. Each referral is processed in a systematic way.

Each child is seen for full psychological testing and assessment by the educational psychologist and psychiatric social worker. Parents attend, observe their child being assessed and are considered essential to the assessment. Often, for the first time, they are made fully aware and understanding of the extent of their child's strengths and weaknesses. Test findings and implications are shared with the parents and teaching staff. Full medical information is obtained from the medical officer. The staff of the SRD spend time observing the child in his own teaching group and discuss his educational progress with his class/subject teacher. This information is collated and presented to the admissions support team for discussion. If the placement is considered appropriate, the SRD staff invite the parents and their child to meet them in the department to discuss what can be offered and to answer any queries. The SRD staff are always available to the parents for further discussion. Indeed, the SRD staff will stress that they welcome as much parental participation as possible and, to date, many parents have availed themselves of the opportunity. (SRD staff are also available at the school's regular parent-teacher meetings held throughout the year.) This ongoing contact is seen as crucial for successful integration and its informality often relaxes parents.

The SRD staff who teach a child accompany him to any lesson or provide him with material. They began by writing daily reports on each child but this became an overwhelming task as the department began to build up its clientele. The reports are now completed at least once a week. Records are kept indicating the task or goal to be met, or the programme to be followed, and the results.

The Children

As we have noted already, the SRD has built up its intake gradually. To have swamped a school with severely handicapped children at the outset, before the SRD staff had been given an opportunity to work together and test their own strengths and weaknesses, would have been tantamount to failure. To date, the range of disability presented by the 11 to 15 year old children in the SRD includes the following: the mildly mentally retarded, severely and mildly epileptic children, a leukaemic child functioning at ESN(S) level, a child with cystic fibrosis, a child disabled by polio, a child with Hirschprung's disease and others with cerebral palsy, arthritis, minimal cerebral dysfunction, partial hearing or severe learning disability. The majority of the children are aged 11 to 13 as this is the age range planned for in advance.

We recognize that some of the multiply handicapped children also have problems of emotional adjustment. Their management programme takes into account that, at certain stages of schooling, their educational needs due to maladjustment may be overriding as compared with their other disabilities. There is continuing emphasis on meeting the child's 'total person' needs, rather than on planning for some specific disability in isolation which is commonly known to affect other areas of a child's development. Identifying a child as having 'special needs' as compared to being 'ESN' or 'maladjusted', for example, has helped in providing a flexible approach.

The Roles of the SRD Staff

To provide flexibly and with expertise for each child according to ability and disability, the staff have assumed various roles.

These relate to the following functions.

(a) A child may be withdrawn from ordinary classes for specialized help in the SRD. There will be no focus on remedial reading as such but rather on perceptual-motor skills and similar basic skills, for which the department will have responsibility to draw up and implement a detailed and appropriate programme. The withdrawal may be for specialized instruction, or to reinforce learning in a particular subject, such as a newly acquired numeracy skill. It may be for emotional support and encouragement for the child who, for example, finds it very difficult to return to school after illness or prolonged treatment. The withdrawal may also be an alternative to a particular subject such as swimming in a heated indoor pool, rather than games, for a child with spina bifida.

(b) A member of the SRD staff may accompany a child into a subject class for a variety of reasons: help in a science practical lessons if a child cannot move about freely or keep up with the teaching or where the alternative would be to withdraw her completely from that subject. Not all main school staff feel entirely comfortable having another member of staff in their classroom, and this is respected, but this is a school where team teaching is an accepted practice and therefore the difficulties may be lessened. As most of the children in the SRD come from years 1 and 2, it does mean that an SRD member of staff may be monitoring several children in the same room or, as in humanities, monitoring several children in several adjoining classrooms during the same lesson.

(c) The SRD may, in consultation with the subject teacher, provide appropriate work which the subject teacher monitors in his own class. For example, materials for humanities lessons are not always appropriate — in our experience of mixed ability teaching, the level is often pitched at the 'average' child in the group and may fail to meet the needs of certain children. Increasingly, the SRD staff are providing materials for a wider group of children within a teaching group than has been recognized up till now as having special educational needs.

(d) The SRD may act as consultants on a particular child within a teaching group. On occasions, the SRD staff have gone to observe a child within his teaching group and to offer advice and suggestions as to how to bring out that child's potential within his classroom. Another development worthy of note is that the head of the SRD has been asked by several teachers to give demonstration lessons on how to teach particular class groups — not classes necessarily recognized as having special educational needs but ones which are causing concern to staff. Another member of staff is on a working party attempting to draw up an appropriate programme for 'disenchanted' non-examination fourth and fifth year pupils.

(e) The SRD staff may ensure, through the form tutor, that the child has the appropriate equipment/timetable to enable him to join in with his peer group. For example, the child in a wheelchair can be made mobile because he has a timetable that allows him to move around the school on ground floor level.

(f) The SRD can offer specialist teaching and diagnostic skills, such as the setting up of an educational programme for a child who has a specific learning disability of a dyslexic nature.

(g) The SRD staff confer jointly with parents and form/subject teachers and they initiate separate parent conferences when needed.

(h) The SRD staff initiate the full time integration of children into the form/subject room and serve as supportive resource teachers until the child has made the complete transition.

(i) The SRD staff are responsible for the final evaluation report of each referral and also for a written evaluation of the child's progress in both the classroom and the SRD.

Discussion

The Carterton experiment has thrown up many issues related to integrating the handicapped into ordinary schools. A few can be mentioned by way of illustration: the role and function of ancillary helpers both within the SRD and the main school; implementing treatment programmes directed and supervized by speech therapists and physiotherapists, with ancillary helpers acting as intermediaries between therapist and child; the career structure for special educators in ordinary schools; the relationship between the SRD and the other main school departments, particularly in claiming resources and initiating school policy; the increased effectiveness of psychological services if these were school based rather than peripatetic; the importance of staff attitudes towards the child with handicap; the impact of mixed ability teaching on the handicapped child. Some of these problems are being monitored week by week by one of the present authors (E.J.) who is a research student of the Department of Special Education, Birmingham University.

Influential factors

The following factors that can affect a programme of integration are already showing up.
(I)   Individualized programmes of work can be meaningful only if based on intensive investigation of the child's needs. This means very detailed psychological testing in addition to medical reports and parental interviews.
(II)   Specific handicaps begin to take secondary consideration if the attitudes of staff and pupils in the main school are not taken into account.
(III)   The extent to which a child can integrate into ordinary lessons cannot be known beforehand. There must be some measure of trial and error. What is important is day to day monitoring of what works well and where the child is failing, together with a willingness to plan for a child along a continuum of integration.
(IV)   A clear distinction is understood between the diagnosis of disability and handicap and their management in order that the 'total child' special needs are met. This requires identification of the disorders causing malfunctioning, such as low intelligence, reading problems, sensory deficits, maladjusted ways of coping with daily living.
    Having assessed 'need' and using the 'resource room model', equipment and personnel are used, not in relation to one or other labelled disability, but to provide a range of special skills and help for any child in need, in relation to curriculum planning, the provision of resource material, knowledge of a whole range of disabilities and their effect on learning,

consultation work with teachers and pupils in the main school and with parents, liaison with supporting and other agencies. It is this range of skills which is not confined to teaching specific groups of children such as the ESN, that creates the 'special' expertise for meeting special educational needs in ordinary schools.

References

CHALK, J. (1975) 'Sanctuary units in primary schools', *Special Education*, 2, 1, pp. 18–20.

CHRISTOPOLOS, F. (1973) 'Keeping exceptional children in regular classes'. *Exceptional Children*, 39, pp. 569–72.

CLARK, P. (1969) 'The magic of the learning centre'. *California Teachers' Assoc. Journal*, 65, pp. 16–20.

COPE, C., and ANDERSON, E. (1977) *Special Units in Ordinary Schools*, London University, Institute of Education.

GARNETT, J. (1976) "Special" children in a comprehensive', *Special Education*, 3, 1, pp. 8–11.

GLAVIN, J., QUAY, H., ANNESLEY, F., and WERRY, J. (1971) 'An experimental resource room for behaviour problem children', *Exceptional Children*, 37, pp. 131–7.

JONES, N.J. (1971) 'The Brislington Project in Bristol.' *Special Education*, 60, 2, pp. 23–6.

JONES, N.J. (1977) 'Special adjustment units in comprehensive schools', *Therapeutic Education*, 5, 2, pp. 12–19.

REGER, R., and KOPPMANN, M. (1971) 'The child oriented resource room'. *Exceptional Children*, 39, pp. 460–2.

REGER, R. (1973) 'What is a resource room program?' *Journal of Learning Disabilities*, 6, 10, pp. 15–21.

SABATINO, D. (1972) 'Resource rooms: the renaissance in special education.' *The Journal of Special Education*, 6, 4, pp. 335–47.

WEINER, L.H. (1969) 'An investigation of the effectiveness of resource rooms for children with specific learning disabilities,' *Journal of Learning Disabilities*, 2, pp. 49–55.

Helping Colleagues Cope — A Consultant Rôle for the Remedial Teacher

Colin J. Smith
University of Birmingham

A consultant role for remedial teachers is nothing new. It has been adopted by every teacher who suggests follow-up work in the ordinary class for the children to whom he has given extra help in a withdrawal group. Adapting material or providing support for poor readers through team teaching, are other aspects of remedial consultancy. However, much more of the remedial specialist's time is usually spent on assessment, diagnosis, instruction and clerical work than on giving advice to colleagues (Evans, 1980).

Training for remedial work has traditionally emphasized specialized teaching skills which help children find the key to learning. Perhaps more attention should be given to developing interpersonal skills, which will help in advising other teachers how to cope with learning difficulties (Lerner, 1976).

If prevention is better than cure, then it would seem sensible for the specialist teacher to spend more time sharing the benefits of his expertise. What can be done to encourage other staff to see the remedial teacher as a consultant, who can help increase their confidence and competence in dealing with special needs in the ordinary class?

Public Relations

Unsolicited advice is rarely welcomed and seldom followed. If his advice is to be freely sought, the consultant teacher must have a good sense of public relations. This starts with an awareness of the problems of the ordinary class teacher trying to rekindle the dying embers of academic fire amongst thirty or more pupils, often of very mixed ability (Hawisher and Calhoun, 1978). An appreciation of the difficulty anyone faces in changing to new teaching methods is another important part of an understanding and sympathetic

This article originally appeared in *Remedial Education* (1982) 17, 2

112

approach. Gray and Gerrard (1977) make some useful suggestions on developing interpersonal communication skills. Empathy, respect and warmth are probably the most important characteristics for ease of social contact. Otherwise gifted and enthusiastic teachers cannot be effective consultants if a superior or didactic manner deters colleagues from seeking their help. There are some superb practitioners whose arrival in the staff-room nonetheless produces a sudden hush or rapid dispersal!

The remedial specialist should seek to be seen as expert but equal, as someone ready to share responsiblity in solving problems. Consideration of the questions which follow should help develop this approach.

Six Questions the Consultant Should Answer

Marsh and Price (1980) suggest that certain issues most concern the teacher who may be wondering whether to seek advice from another member of staff.

1 *Will you listen; really listen?*

Communication depends to a considerable extent on the ability to listen effectively, showing an awareness of what is being said by expression, gesture and tone of response. Martin (1980) suggests a good listener should avoid finishing sentences, guessing outcomes and interrupting. Reflect back opinions by rephrasing without blame, critical comment or initially advice. A colleague with a problem needs a fair hearing rather than a pat answer.

2 *Does asking for assistance imply incompetence?*

Advice is not likely to be sought if it is thought to imply some lack of ability or sign of weakness in classroom management and organization. The consultant needs to show confidence in the mainstream teacher's capacity to adapt present skills to meet particular needs. There should be no impression that there is some special mystery or magic about remedial teaching.

3 *Will you tell the boss?*

Anxiety, that word of inefficiency which will be passed on to higher authority, may deter some teachers from seeking help. A tendency to gloat over the disciplinary misfortunes of others is an unworthy but not unknown characteristic of some members of the teaching profession. It is entirely out of place in a consultant teacher; colleagues must feel able to ask for confidential advice without fear that their difficulties will be more widely publicized.

4   Does 'help' mean extra work for me?

Concern that asking for assistance will merely add to an already heavy load is understandable. Unless suggested remedies are going to be backed by support in implementing them, there may be reluctance to bring problems forward. Support may involve providing additional help in the classroom or withdrawal of the problem pupil to provide, initially at least, some measure of relief.

5   Can anything be done, quickly?

Some problems will need investigation in depth but immediate practical advice is usually wanted at once. It is frequently possible to propose adjustments in the type and difficulty of material, work-space, time allowed for completion of tasks, or group with whom the child works (Hawisher and Calhoun, 1978). Such simple changes can often produce rapid improvements.

6   Do you really know anything which will make a difference, now?

Consultation which makes working with a particular child easier and pleasanter within the next few lessons is likely to be valued more highly than an in-depth analysis however competently undertaken. Providing a number of alternative approaches will be more likely to succeed than presenting a single solution.

Five Questions to Ask the Teacher who Seeks Advice

Asking the following questions will help the consultant teacher frame a rapid response, which should lead to a prompt improvement in classroom atmosphere and teaching performance. They should be tactfully addressed, though not necessarily in this precise form, to all teachers seeking advice about dealing with children having difficulty in learning in the ordinary class.

1   Have you told them?

Has the teacher given instructions clear enough, explicit enough and often enough to make it obvious to slow learners exactly what is required from them? It is frequently lack of clarity about what is expected from them, that leads pupils into making apparently thoughtless mistakes (Lovitt, 1977).

2 *Have you showed them?*

Has the task been demonstrated and examples worked through, not only with the whole group but individually with the pupil who is failing. Frequent recapitulation is essential for children with problems in short-term and long-term memory. A method of working may be grasped one week but forgotten or misapplied the next.

3 *Have you listened to them?*

Listening to children as they 'talk through' the steps of tackling a problem, in arithmetic for example, can often show where they are going wrong. Discussing and amending 'draft' answers can prevent 'daft' answers, by giving the teacher insight into misperceptions and misunderstandings. Readiness to invite comment and consumer participation in planning and evaluating lessons is another way of listening, that can help locate the source of problems.

4 *Have you praised them?*

The frequent use of praise is the quickest most effective route to promoting a positive atmosphere in the classroom. Praise needs to be varied and valued. It should be varied by the teacher using a range of superlatives rather than a repetitive stock phrase and valued by the pupils as a genuine reward for effort on their part. It is not easy to find occasion to praise some children and at first it may be necessary to lessen task demands in order to 'catch them being good'.

5 *Have you realized how good you are?*

Colleagues, too, need praise. Teachers should be encouraged to see their difficulties within the framework of more general success. Often examining their own more successful lessons and relationships will prompt suggestions for a different approach to problem situations. If consultation is a positive and self-enhancing experience, it is more likely to be repeated. Advice on changes should always aim at keeping interference with normal routine to a minimum.

Minimum Intervention

In accordance with the principle of Occam's razor the most parsimonious yet most effective intervention should be implemented (Heron, 1978). In other words, try the simplest way first.

In some cases, particularly with young and inexperienced teachers, the best place to start may be with a reminder of basic techniques for effective classroom management (Marland, 1975). More frequently, it is simpler to change the ways of the pupil than those of the teacher. Attention should be given in turn to the context, content and conditioning of learning and behaviour.

Focus on context requires an examination of the present 'learning environment' to see if difficulties can be accommodated by providing easier access to help and support already available in the normal classroom. Seating arrangements might be revised to decrease distraction or increase contact with the teacher. Giving monitorial jobs to promote self-image and produce more positive interactions is another modern phrasing of a traditional remedy. Sitting a child within arm's reach or out of harm's way and providing the trouble-maker with socially useful employment are scarcely original methods but nonetheless effective for that. Another long tried and frequently successful technique is to provide a more competent and mature classmate as peer tutor, teaching aide or simply minder!

Focus on content should concentrate on identifying and reducing difficulties caused by inability to cope with material which is too difficult. Task analysis and criterion referenced testing could be used to find work which the learner can do within a given subject area. Assessment of the readability of texts may point the way to the appropriate adaptation of reading and writing tasks, thus removing another source of frustration.

If changes in context and content have failed to improve the situation, then the principles of conditioning could be applied to developing a programme of behaviour modification. After careful observation of what really are effective rewards or reinforcing events for the child concerned, these may be offered as part of a 'contract' for attaining clearly specified work or behavioural goals or traded as part of a 'token economy' in return for points gained by reaching defined objectives in learning or conduct. As a last resort a form of punishment as mild as compatible with effectiveness may need to be applied to deter seriously disruptive activities.

Often before this point is reached, it may be useful to give advice relating to Heron's second line of intervention. Changing the way the class treats a troublesome child is often easier and always more positive than attempting suppression.

The peer group may frequently encourage problem behaviour by conscious or unconscious reaction to the individual concerned. The approval or amusement of contemporaries is potentially a stronger reinforcer than the deterrent effect of teacher disapproval or punishment. Advice should therefore aim to demonstrate to teachers how they might try to involve the group in helping the individual. Direct discussion with the class could be used to illustrate the benefits of attention being contingent on sensible rather than silly behaviour or to promote the integration of an unpopular child in team games and other group activities. Other teachers may prefer a more indirect approach using praise, tokens or tangible rewards to encourage fellow pupils to ignore provocative remarks and irresponsible actions on the part of the 'target' child.

As stressed earlier, the consultant teacher should show confidence in the ability and competence of the regular class teacher. There are times, however, when it will be evident that problems lie not so much with the children, as with their teacher's lack of understanding. One possible response is for the remedial teacher to provide a good model of academic and social management by becoming involved in a team teaching exercise. Another approach would be through a more formal in-service training programme within the school. In either case, success is only likely if the teacher is motivated to change, because coping with slow and reluctant learners is seen as a skilled and prestigious activity, prized and valued by the school as highly as specialist subject knowledge.

Growing Demand

As more handicapped children are helped in the ordinary school, it is likely that remedial teachers will increasingly be asked to share their knowledge of special education. This will not require a detailed definition of the aetiology of handicapping conditions. It will need an understanding of the learning problems associated with particular impairments. It is hoped that this article has helped alert teachers to the skills involved in being a successful consultant ready to provide a sympathetic, direct and practical response, which will help colleagues cope with children with learning difficulties within the mainstream classroom.

References

EVANS, S. (1980) 'The consultant role of the resource teacher', *Exceptional Children*, 46, 5.

GRAY, W.A. and GERRARD, B.A. (1977) *Learning by Doing: developing teaching skills*, Addison Wesley.

HAWISHER, M.F. and CALHOUN, M.L. (1978) *The Resource Room: an educational asset for children with special needs*, Merrill.

HERON, T.E. (1978) 'Maintaining the mainstreamed child in the regular classroom: the decision-making process', *Journal of Learning Disabilities*, 11, 4.

LERNER, J.W. (1976) *Children with Learning Disabilities*, Houghton Mifflin.

LOVITT, T.C. (1977) *In spite of my resistance . . . I've learned from children*, Merrill.

MARLAND, M. (1975) *The Craft of the Classroom*, Heinemann.

MARSH, G.E. and PRICE, B.J. (1980) *Methods for Teaching the Mildly Handicapped Adolescent*, Mosby.

MARTIN, R.J. (1980) *Teaching through Encouragement: techniques to help students learn*, Prentice Hall.

3
Pupil Assessment and Curriculum Development

Introduction

Though increasingly involved with preventing educational failure in integrated contexts, remedial education is still also concerned with identifying individual difficulties in learning and adapting the school curriculum to take account of these. This sometimes leads to accusations that remedial specialists assume that faults are always to be found within the child rather than the environment and that pupils with special needs should be offered only a limited and restricted curriculum.

The articles in the final section of this book show that such criticisms are trite and facile taking little or no account of recent developments in assessment procedures and curriculum development.

Cornwall indicates the way in which evaluation in schools has moved away from reliance on formal tests relating pupil performance to a notional norm to an informal assessment of the match between pupil progress and material to be learnt.

Raybould and Solity offer a particular application of this criterion referenced approach. Precision teaching is by no means a panacea but it is a most useful addition to the remedial teacher's armoury.

Richmond concentrates upon the assessment of difficulties in learning to read and reflects on the influence of recent concern for children with specific difficulties. He describes one response to meeting the needs of children labelled as 'dyslexic' and questions the relevance of that concept when developing a teaching programme which meets individual needs.

Williams shows that mathematics for the low attainer need not be a slow and sterile exercise in the progressive acquisition of number skills through rote learning and routine practice. He advocates a conceptual, problem solving approach and shows how it can be applied.

Hinson looks at the growing awareness of the special needs of children with learning difficulties across the whole range of the curriculum. He cites examples of positive responses in the teaching of history, geography and science and elucidates valuable guidelines for future curriculum planning.

Finally, Widlake examines the case for a radical change to make the curriculum for all pupils more relevant to the pressures of modern life and considers the implications of such innovations for remedial teachers.

Some Trends in Pupil Evaluation: The Growing Importance of the Teacher's Role

K.F. Cornwall
Principal Educational Psychologist,
Hampshire Local
Education Authority

It is becoming increasingly recognized that the most important and useful evaluation is carried out in school by teachers. Such curriculum related assessment has many advantages over more traditional norm-based procedures. A model for school assessment is proposed and some of the techniques associated with this model are discussed.

If one examines test catalogues produced ten years ago and compares them with current editions, a number of differences become clear immediately. There are fewer 'mental ability' tests and fewer attainment tests which take their norms from large populations. However, there are more diagnostic tests and there are, occasionally, tests of process and, more rarely still, criterion referenced measurements which examine the mastery of a particular set of skills. There is the promise of item banked materials and of other forms of assessment which do not rely on the normal curve of distribution of scores and all that denotes. The change that has taken place in the world of publishing is only a minor indicator of the change in evaluation procedures being practised in schools today. For most of the important techniques are not published at all but produced by teachers for use in their own classrooms. Quite simply, schools are evaluating more and they are doing so in relation to what is being taught.

The New Scheme

How has this come about so quickly? There are probably two discernible sources of influence for the change, the first, the matter of accountability and the second, the growing dissatisfaction with the old model of evaluation

This article originally appeared in *Remedial Education* (1981) 16, 4

K.F. Cornwall

and a related desire for the kind of approach which has greater relevance to the needs of pupils. The new mood at the DES is perhaps best summed up by a quotation from an article by Marjoram published at the time when he was the Head of the DES Assessment of Performance Unit (APU), 'Assessment in its fullest sense is an integral part of good teaching and sound management' (Marjoram, 1977). These two elements — assessment as part of *teaching* and as an activity concerned with *management* — were closely related to the general tenor of the DES' views on education starting from the middle of the last decade. For example, *Report on Education, No. 93* (DES, 1978) sought to explain how the APU was to proceed with its national monitoring task by stressing the importance of assessment. Assessment, the report claimed, was seen as valuable at a number of levels. It was 'important for pupils themselves to know how well they are progressing and for their parents. It is important for teachers to know that their pupils are learning effectively and that the teaching material and approaches adopted are suitable. It is important for employers, particularly those who must look for certain aptitudes in those they employ'. Moreover, the business of assessment, says the report, is a matter of 'considerable interest to central and local government'.

The scene was set therefore for assessment to become a major issue in education. The Green Paper *Education in Schools* (DES, 1977) had already claimed that the need for schools to demonstrate their accountability required 'a coherent and soundly based means of assessment for the education system as a whole for schools and for individual pupils'. And the *Primary Survey* (DES, 1978) following up the lead, stressed that while teachers should be knowledgeable in what they teach, 'it is just as necessary that they should be able to assess the performance of their pupils in terms of what they next need to be taught'. Similarly, in the *Secondary School Survey* (DES, 1979) the HMI Report expressed the view that 'regular and systematic evaluation of progress is needed if work is to be matched to pupils' capacities'. In saying this, the report took up a theme which was a variant of the accountability argument and which comes close to the concern expressed by any good educator: that there should be a match between what is being taught and what and how fast the pupil is able to learn. The fact that both reports found mismatches at primary and secondary levels was further indication of the need for continuous assessment and monitoring of pupils at these levels.

Not surprisingly the DES expressed views that were very close to those of teachers who for a long time had been looking for changes in educational assessment techniques. These were largely teachers who were dealing with children with special needs. Indeed, when the *Warnock Report* (DES, 1978) expressed the importance of 'close and continuous observation of pupils' progress by their teachers', it is likely that those in special education were the least in need of such reminders. By the time of the *Warnock Report*, special education had already set about assessing the progress of pupils in a

124

way which related what was being assessed to what was being taught. In other words, assessment had become curriculum related to a greater degree than had been seen in the 'ordinary' school. The concern with the structure of the curriculum in special education sprang directly from a desire to match teaching to needs and the concomitant of this desire was to produce and maintain effective assessment procedures.

Already, due to the influence of people like Mager, schools were examining the relationship between teaching and assessment. Mager's maxim 'If you're not sure where you are going, you are liable to end up some place else — and not even know it' (Mager, 1962) became something of a common phrase in the early 1970s. Because of this, the need for broad aims and precise objectives was being expressed in exactly that region of education where such precision had not been seen before — the world of the ESN(S) child, for example. The influence of the Hester Adrian Centre in Manchester was paramount here and the ideas generated by the research team in that area have had a profound effect on the way in which assessment is treated in schools for children with severe or moderate learning disabilities.

New v Old Approaches

The approach is to specify the aims and objectives of the education process in question and then to gear one's assessment of progress to these aims and objectives. A useful model for the purposes of illustrating this approach may be taken from Leeming *et al.* (1979). As Figure 1 indicates, the model covers aims, objectives, methods, organization, teaching style and child behaviour.

In the model, the authors make a valuable distinction between assessment and evaluation. Assessment as they see it is the means of gaining knowledge about the behaviour, abilities and attitudes of the child in order to select appropriate objectives and thus to define the entry point for a child into the curriculum. Evaluation is 'the measurement of the quantitative and qualitative discrepancy between the child's behaviour as observed and the child's behaviour as specified by objectives'. If a discrepancy exists, then modification of the objectives, organizations or techniques is necessary.

As Leeming and his colleagues claim, 'if assessment is to become part of teaching, the teacher should play a key part'. But as they note, in special education particularly the educational aspects of assessment have been secondary to other considerations. Psychologists, Leeming and his colleagues hold, must accept their share of the blame for allowing assessment to become divorced from the aims and objectives of education. The use of intelligence tests is seen by Leeming to have been of little importance to teachers. 'While intelligence tests may be of administrative value, they are of little direct use to the teacher in planning a progamme suited to the child's specific needs. The conventional intelligence test does not yield enough

Figure 1   A teaching model

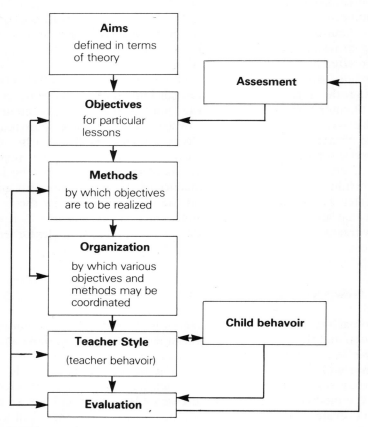

Source: Leeming *et al*

information about a child's strengths and weaknesses to provide a foundation for the design of a programme of individual teaching.'

These views on the value of the IQ are similar to many which have been
made public over the last fifteen to twenty years. Foremost among the critics
of the IQ have been practising educational psychologists themselves (Gillham, 1978). For the sake of illustration and at the risk of over-polarizing the
debate, one could say that assessment in the past was too often thought to be
about the pupil in vacuo. The notion was that it was in principle and in
practice possible to measure ability and learning potential and this usually
took the form of a global IQ test score. This view was stated in the 1920s by
Burt in a way that now looks like a caricature of the position psychologists
took up at that time. In the early 1920s, Burt had a feeling of certainty that
sufficient work had been done on intelligence to enable us to know very
much about the individual once we had obtained an IQ score for him.

Accordingly, it was 'a duty of the State, to its school services, first to find out to what order of intelligence each child belongs, then to give him the education most appropriate to his powers, and finally, before it leaves him, to place him in the particular type of occupation for which nature has marked him out' (Burt, 1925).

This view is in clear contra-distinction to that expressed by educationalists such as Leeming and by theoreticians such as Brody and Brody (1976). For these, the IQ has no value except where it can help to construct an educational programme. But as Brody and Brody say, there are better ways of doing this than by using the cumbersome IQ test. A clear and balanced view of the debate is provided by Ingenkamp (1977) who surveys the general educational assessment scene in Europe. In particular, he lists the kind of criticisms that are levelled against the Burtian approach and suggests that this direction towards assessment for selection has side-effects such as undue stress, examination anxiety, cheating, frustration and 'the falsifying of educational objectives through orientation towards competition and efficiency'. Ingenkamp cites a number of proponents of the view that the 'only assessment that is educationally justifiable is that which promotes the individual learning process'.

In this context, assessment is about a pupil's strengths and weaknesses and is concerned not to see how he compares with other pupils, but how he matches up to the curriculum being offered. The aim is *criterion-referenced* or, as some may prefer to call it, *objectives-referenced*, rather than norm-referenced. Similarly it is formative — concerned with the formation of a pupil's learning skills — rather than competitive.

The picture that emerges of the difference between the old and new approaches could allow us to make a contrasting list of the procedures. If so it would probably be something like Figure 2.

To this could be added a further dimension, the personnel employed in carrying out assessment. In the past, as Leeming has indicated, it was often the case that educational pychologists were those who administered the tests and gave the results to teachers to translate into teaching terms. Although the role of the educational psychologist is certainly a valuable one — though

Figure 2   Approaches to assessment of pupils

	Traditional	Recent
Purpose	To compare pupils with others.	To compare pupil progress with what is to be taught.
Type of assessment	Competitive — usually norm-referenced measures.	Formative — usually criterion or objectives-referenced measures.
Materials	Published tests.	School devised measures relating to the curriculum.
Frequency of assessment	At fixed intervals, for example termly, annually.	Continuous assessment.

a very different one from the traditional role — there is little doubt that with curriculum related measures, the *teacher* has begun to be the most important person in the assessment process. Even if a teacher employs only the simplest of teaching models (for example teach and then see whether learning has taken place), it would follow that a frequent assessment of results was required. If a more complicated model is adopted — like that of Leeming *et al.* — the teacher's main concern is to examine the match between child and curriculum for much of the school day. A model of assessment that might be used at all age and ability levels will address itself to this match, to analyzing mismatch and to monitoring the continuation of the match. It would also wish to evaluate outcomes in the way that Leeming's model does.

There would be four aspects of the assessment process which would need to be incorporated into an assessment plan for schools, therefore:

1 Assessing the match between pupil and curriculum;
2 Analyzing the mismatch if one occurs;
3 Monitoring progress where matching is appropriate;
4 Evaluating outcomes of a particular set of teaching objectives. Diagrammatically this would take the form in Figure 3.

'Bought' tests have their place in such a programme, but they should not be taken to be of major importance as measures of the progress being made by individuals. Indeed, it might be argued that the most relevant place of the 'bought' test, particularly of the norm-referenced nature, is to act as a periodic check on the achievement of pupils as a means of satisfying administrators and elected members that the education being provided in a school is adequate. Whether these published tests are more 'objective' than curriculum-related assessment techniques is more a matter of semantic analysis than educational reality. Many 'objective' tests fall short of the necessary criteria on counts of validity, reliability and appropriateness of norm data. Conversely, a simple check list, for example of the signs of readiness for a particular stage in school, drawn up by members of staff and related to the curriculum, has an empirical status which renders it more objective than many would believe it to be. Certainly, the methodological problems of objectives-referenced assessment have still to be solved as Ingenkamp (*op cit*) acknowledges. However, this should not detract from the relevance of such assessment techniques to the assessment and monitoring tasks that must be carried out daily in schools.

This brings us full circle to the notion with which we began, Marjoram's view that assessment in its fullest sense is 'an integral part of good teaching and sound management'. The fact that assessment is therefore mostly the duty of the classroom teacher, who will be employing his or her own assessment techniques, should not be a source of apology based upon a feeling that there is a better way of carrying out assessment and that what the teacher does is 'not proper assessment'. With curriculum-related assess-

A Model for School Assessment

Figure 3   A plan of this type permits a full and careful assessment of pupil progress which includes all sorts of assessment techniques used where they are most appropriate.

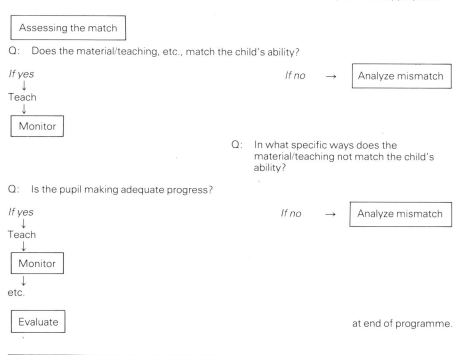

ments there is no other way, neither is there any other person but the class teacher who will have the intimate contact with the classroom situation that is required to make such assessment meaningful and effective, but to devise the techniques themselves is a major task. There is, however, no reason why we would reach for inappropriate measures, for example a graded word test to analyze mismatch, because such tests happen to be there. Now that the way ahead is reasonably clear, what is required is confidence on the part of teachers that they are the best placed professionals to carry out assessment of pupil progress. More exchange of examples of good assessment techniques is required, more LEA study groups need to be set up to produce curriculum-related measures, and so on. The work will be arduous but it will mean that, to remember Mager, in educational terms we will have an idea of where we are going, and a good set of maps to ensure that we do not end up 'some place else'.

Some Techniques Associated with the Four Aspects of the Assessment Model (Figure 3)

Assessing the match

— Check lists (for example of abilities required by the pupil to cope with the teaching material provided)

— *Ad hoc* tests of difficulty level of material (for example 'cloze' type test of sample pages of reading book to assess readability)

— Observation procedures (for example to examine pupil's response to what is provided — in terms of his behaviour, attitude, etc.)

— Published attainment tests (for example graded word test used as a broad 'screening' measure — to find out, broadly, what level of attainment the pupil is at)

Analyzing the mismatch

— Diagnostic tests (for example published tests of the reading process as well as check lists of sound/symbol associations)

— Error analysis (for example an Informal Reading Inventory approach in reading or an examination of errors in mathematics)

Monitoring

— All relevant curriculum related measures

— Published attainment tests (for example tests of attainment in reading published by NFER-Nelson)

Evaluation

— Curriculum-related measures examining the outcome of teaching programme (for example essentially objectives-related tests which will show mastery of the subject area)

References

BRODY, E.B. and BRODY, N. (1976) *Intelligence,* London, Academic Press.
BURT, C.L. (1925) 'Psychological tests for scholarship and promotion'. *The School* XIII. p. 734–42.

DEPARTMENT OF EDUCATION AND SCIENCE (1978) *Assessing the Performance of Pupils*, DES Report on Education No. 93, London, HMSO.

DEPARTMENT OF EDUCATION AND SCIENCE (1971) *Education in Schools*. (Green Paper). London, HMSO.

DEPARTMENT OF EDUCATION AND SCIENCE (1978) *Primary Education in England*. London, HMSO.

GILLHAM, W.E.C. (1978) *Reconstructing Educational Psychology*. London, Croom Helm.

INGENKAMP, K.H. (1977) *Educational Assessment — European Trend Report on Educational Research*. Slough, NFER.

LEEMING, K., SWANN, W., COUPE, J. and MITTLER, P. (1979) *Teaching Language and Communication to the Mentally Handicapped*, Schools Council Curriculum Bulletin No. 8. London, Evans/Methuen Educational.

MAGER, R.F. (1962) *Preparing Instructional Objectives*. California, Fearon Press.

MARJORAM, D.T.E. (1977) *The APU and Assessment in the Middle Years*, notes circulated by the DES Assessment of Performance Unit, Manchester.

Teaching with Precision

Ted Raybould
and John Solity
Senior Educational Psychologists,
Walsall Metropolitan Borough

For Whom is Precision Teaching Intended?

Precision teaching uses many important behavioural principles to provide a framework for the direct, systematic teaching of children with learning difficulties and the daily evaluation of progress (White and Haring, 1980; Haring *et al.*, 1978; Lovitt, 1979; Formentin and Csapo, 1980; Raybould, 1981). While it can be used with handicapped pupils in general, the techniques are most directly applicable to children who appear to be 'remedial' or 'slow learning', i.e. children with special needs. But what kind of problems does the typical slow learner present?

Mark is nine years old and, characteristically, has difficulties in most curricular areas but especially in basic educational skills. His teacher reports:

> Mark has a very short concentration span and never seems to be able to settle down to work. He has great difficulty in working on his own and is always looking around the classroom to see what other children are doing. Either that or he wanders off into a world of his own. Unless someone is standing over him all the time he won't do a stroke of work. As a result of his poor concentration Mark never finishes a piece of work.
>
> Another problem is that Mark has a very poor memory. The number of times I've taught him something one day only to find he's forgotten everything the following day.
>
> All these things aren't helped by the fact that he doesn't seem at all interested in school. The main trouble is that he is not motivated to do any work.

This article originally appeared *Special Education: Forward Trends*, (1982) 9, 2

What is Precision Teaching?

Paradoxically, as Muncey and Williams (1981) emphasized, precision teaching *is not a method of teaching as such* but *a way of trying to find out 'what teaches best'* by providing daily feedback on the effectiveness of instruction. Precision teaching provides techniques for direct and daily measurement, charting and evaluation of individual pupils' progress towards mastery of specific educational tasks.

An important assumption here is that if the pupil is not succeeding on a task, the teacher examines her own teaching as a potential source of difficulty before inferring there is something wrong with the child's ability to learn. Furthermore, children who have fallen behind educationally require teaching which is not only successful but which is also highly cost effective. Their rate of skill acquisition must be positively *accelerated* if they are to have any real chance of catching up with their peers and of taking full advantage of the school curriculum. Teachers therefore need a way of making the most of the time, teaching methods and resources which they have available to help such children.

Since precision teaching is a way of trying to find out what teaches best, the teacher can be flexible in her use of teaching approaches. Precision teaching uses behavioural principles to enable changes in the pupil's daily performance to be observed and measured. It does not *necessitate* the use of behavioural *teaching* techniques but allows for a wide range of possible intervention strategies including the more traditional approaches favoured by many teachers. Notwithstanding, precision teaching is most closely compatible with intervention based on the principles of task analysis (Howell, Kaplan and O'Connell, 1979) and direct instruction (Lovitt, 1977; Haring and Gentry, 1976; Becker and Engelmann, 1977; Becker, 1977). The emphasis is on skills taken directly from the school curriculum and on giving children regular, systematic teaching and practice in those skills.

The Methodology

The methodology of precision teaching can be described as comprising five basic components (Figure 1), each of which will be considered in turn. Descriptions of the procedure may vary in detail — Muncey and Williams (1981) identify seven steps, for instance — but the content is similar.

(1) Specifying Performance

This component is a prerequisite for precision teaching. Having decided upon what is to be taught, the teacher must formulate the teaching target in terms of a behavioural outcome. That is to say the desired behaviour of the

Figure 1

(1)	Specify desired pupil performance in observable, measurable terms.
(2)	Record the performance on a daily basis.
(3)	Chart the performance on a daily basis.
(4)	Record teaching approach in relation to pupil performance.
(5)	Analyze the data to determine whether:
	(i) progress is satisfactory or unsatisfactory;
	(ii) changes are needed in teacher behaviour or teaching approach in order to maintain or accelerate progress.

pupils who are following instruction must be both observable and measurable (i.e. countable). Traditionally, teaching targets have required that children should 'understand', 'appreciate', 'know' and so on but such terms do not permit unambiguous observation and measurement of pupils' performance.

Specifying pupil performance in objective terms has been described and discussed by various writers (for example Mager, 1962; Popham 1975; Gronlund, 1978). Increasing use is being made of this approach in the teaching of children with learning difficulties in this country (for example Ainscow and Tweddle, 1977 and 1979). Unless pupil performance can be stated in this way it will not be possible to determine whether or not the child has acquired the appropriate skill.

(2) Daily recording of performance

To make the most of available teaching time the teacher needs to get regular feedback as to the effectiveness of the teaching approach. Because of the heavy demands on the class teacher, she cannot afford to persist with ineffective teaching methods.

Consider the following example. Mary's performance on a maths task varied widely over a period of eight school days, ranging from twenty sums correct on the Tuesday to sixty on the Friday. All the sums were of the same type and same level of difficulty.

A quick look at the results in the second column of Figure 2 would seem to indicate that Mary improved gradually as the week progressed but forgot over the weekend. By Wednesday of the second week she was just beginning to make progress again. However, Mary's performance can be viewed rather differently if the *amount of time allowed* to complete the sums is known (column 3).

Looking at the number of sums completed in the time available makes it apparent that Mary did not forget over the weekend but, in fact, improved steadily. The method of expressing this improvement is in terms of the number of sums completed *per minute*. This is the most convenient way of viewing a child's progress from one day to another and is the basic unit of measurement in precision teaching.

Figure 2

Day	Number of Sums Correct	Time allowed	Rate per minute
Monday	30	20 mins.	1.5
Tuesday	20	"	1.0
Wednesday	36	"	1.8
Thursday	40	"	2.0
Friday	60	"	3.0
Monday	32	10 mins.	3.2
Tuesday	36	"	3.6
Wednesday	37	"	3.7

The Use of Probes

It is easy to assume that daily recording might be inconvenient and unduly time-consuming for the teacher. This problem is overcome in precision teaching by making the testing period extremely short, usually one, two or three minutes. This brief daily test is called a *probe* and samples the child's performance on a specific skill. It is different from a *normative* test since the results obtained from the probe do not tell the teacher how the child is performing in relation to other children. A probe is a type of criterion-referenced test, i.e. it indicates a child's proficiency on a specific curricular activity.

A probe is constructed by giving children a large number of examples of the skill being taught, for example: (a) two-digit addition with carrying; (b) a group of five sight words; (c) a group of initial consonant blends. Many examples of the skill are provided in the probe to avoid the problem of the pupil completing the probe in the time permitted. With practice, probes can be readily devised by the teacher to check the pupil's performance of most basic educational skills and a stock of ready made, re-usable probes built up. Detailed guidance on probe construction and use is provided in White and Haring (*op. cit.*, pp. 48–58, 131–4) and Formentin and Csapo (*op. cit.*, pp. 39–66). Sourcebooks containing extensive sequences of probes in basic number and reading skills have been prepared by Csapo and Neithercut (1976) and Csapo (1977).

Why Rate Measurement?

It is not sufficient for children to be merely accurate in completing tasks. Accuracy may be seen as a prerequisite stage for *fluency* building which, in turn, facilitates the stages of maintenance, generalization, and adaptation of skills. These stages have been represented by Haring and Eaton (1978) in a learning hierarchy (see Figure 3). Precision teaching, therefore, makes essential use of *rate measurement*, the principle being that we are not just

Figure 3

(1)	*Acquisition* — the child acquires the skill and begins to perform accurately
(2)	*Fluency* — the child performs accurately and *fluently*
(3)	*Maintenance* — teaching of the skill continues even though the child is performing accurately and fluently to ensure the skill is overlearnt and that accuracy and fluency are not lost
(4)	*Generalization* — when instructed the child can apply the new skill in different settings
(5)	*Adaptation* — the child can apply the new skill in different settings without further instruction

concerned with *what* a pupil can do but *how quickly* he can do it. This provides an indication of increasing proficiency.

Giving a probe for a fixed period of time makes it possible to count the number of correct and incorrect responses made by the pupil and to express these in terms of *rate per minute*. This method of monitoring performance provides a convenient and consistent unit of measurement enabling the teacher to observe changes in a child's performance from day to day. For the slow learner these changes might be highly significant but yet pass unnoticed without this fine degree of monitoring. Many of the advantages of rate measurement over simple frequency counts and percentage measures are discussed by Vargas (1977).

(3) Charting Performance

Having calculated the pupil's correct and incorrect rates, the teacher plots this data on a chart. The aim is to provide quick, graphic *knowledge of results* (i) for the benefit of the teacher herself, as an aid to interpreting changes in performance and planning subsequent action; and (ii) for the benefit of the pupil, to enhance and maintain motivation. Indeed, the intention is that pupils should be actively involved in the charting process and, where appropriate, learn to chart their own performance (Lovitt, 1973).

The Ratio Chart

A special type of chart is used in precision teaching. The horizontal axis uses equal intervals to indicate the successive school days on which the child's performance may be checked. The vertical axis, however, uses a logarithmic or *ratio* scale for plotting the child's level of performance. This type of chart may be unfamiliar to many teachers but has a number of distinct advantages over the conventional chart or graph. (A completed ratio chart is presented in Figure 6).

What the Ratio Chart Does

When data is plotted, we obtain a visual display of the *relative* increase or decrease in a pupil's performance rather than the absolute increase or decrease. Figure 5 is intended to give some impression of the different visual effect of the ratio chart compared with that of a conventional graph depicting the same data. Let us, for example, assume that two boys, John and Paul, were being taught the same task and were given specific daily probes over a period of seven days. Their raw data is as follows:

For example, Rate Correct per Minute

| John | 12 | 13 | 14 | 18 | 22 | 23 | 24 |
| Paul | 48 | 52 | 56 | 72 | 88 | 92 | 96 |

Figurè 5   *Comparison of performance shown on (A) conventional chart and (B) ratio chart*

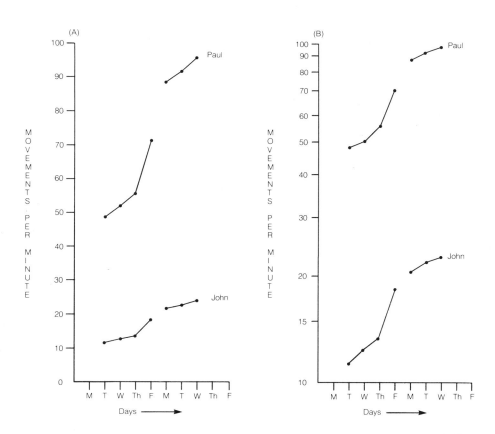

Figure 6   Completed ratio chart

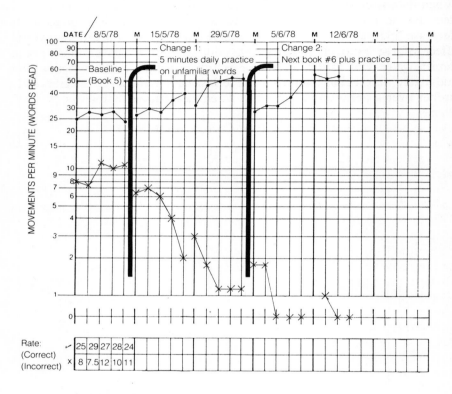

Pupil: Michael S.   *Teacher:* Mrs O.   *Adviser:* E.C.R.
Performance: Oral reading (3 minute probe)
Task: 'Pirates' reading scheme: Books 5,6.

Note in Figure 5 (A) the increasing discrepancy between the two boys in terms of absolute achievement from the first to the last day. The identical shapes of the learning curves shown on the ratio chart in Figure 5 (B), however, indicate that the two boys made the same *proportional* gains (i.e. each in relation to his own previous performance). By the Wednesday of the second week each had *doubled* his initial performance.

(4)   Recording teaching approach

This refers to the planned, systematic changes which the teacher might make in (i) her own management of the child's learning (use of praise, attention, other rewards, timing and duration of instruction, etc.); and (ii) in the nature of the teaching programme (task requirements, difficulty level, particular teaching method, published scheme employed, etc.).

The teacher keeps a detailed plan sheet and also denotes on the chart any planned (and unplanned) changes in the teaching programme so that these may be related to changes in the pupil's performance and interpreted accordingly. This makes the teaching 'experimental' in the sense used by Leach and Raybould (1977). That is to say, where the pupil's progress on a task is judged to be unsatisfactory, the teacher can systematically manipulate those features of the task, teaching approach and (if necessary) wider classroom environment, over which she has control. In this way, systematic instruction takes on some of the qualities of a single-case experimental study, exploring the functional relationship between dependent and independent variables (Skinner, 1966).

In Figure 6, systematic changes in the teaching programmes are indicated on the ratio chart by a vertical line placed between two day lines. During an initial baseline phase (week 1), the teacher listened to Michael reading aloud from his current book for three minutes each day and plotted the results on the chart. During weeks 2 and 3 Michael's oral reading was preceded by five minutes' daily practice on unfamiliar words. The result of this simple change in teaching programme was an increase in the number of words read per minute and a decrease in the number of errors. During weeks 4 and 5 Michael was given a new reading book and still allowed five minutes for practice on unfamiliar words. Again the result was an improvement in oral reading.

The significance of this simple illustration is that both teacher and child can see at a glance the degree of progress made over the time period on this specific activity. Moreover, the teacher can also see the relation of correct performance to errors and how progress relates to changes in the teaching approach or task.

(5) Analyzing the data

Careful daily inspection of a pupil's ratio chart enables the teacher to make two essential types of decision: (i) whether or not the pupil has reached the level set for mastery; (ii) whether or not the pupil is improving fast enough.

Mastery Levels

The complex but vital question of what criterion or level of performance constitutes mastery on specific educational tasks remains unanswered by educational research. The teacher is inevitably the supreme arbiter, relying on a combination of her practical experience and judgment. Precision teaching, however, provides the teacher with a number of guidelines to help determine suitable and realistic proficiency levels for different tasks. For example, comparisons could be made with the pupil's previously demonstrated rates on similar tasks or with the rates achieved on the task by a group of 'competent' peers. Moreover, a quick check on the *maintenance* of skills can be undertaken at some later date by re-administering the relevant probes and looking for similar correct and incorrect rate levels.

Rate of Improvement

It is at this stage that precision teaching provides useful guidelines for that perennial question: 'Is the child fulfilling his potential? (i.e. 'Is he improving fast enough?') Guidelines are given for deciding whether or not a pupil is showing a satisfactory rate of improvement (i.e. when the pupil is 'on target') and when ameliorative action needs to be considered. Space precludes describing the techniques involved here in any detail.

A *desired* rate of improvement in a child's performance over time (days, weeks, etc.) can be specified in advance by the teacher (for example 30 per cent). This can then be represented on the ratio chart by a straight line gradient against which the child's *actual* rate of improvement can be compared. The techniques involved may at first seem complicated to the teacher but are relatively easy to learn. They are fully described by White and Haring (*op. cit.*). Conventions for making both types of data decision (determining 'mastery' and 'rate of improvement') are outlined by Eaton (1978).

Deciding What to Do — the Principle of Parsimony

The need for highly cost effective teaching of children who exhibit learning difficulties has already been stressed. It follows, therefore, when a child is judged to be failing to make the required rate of progress, that alternative strategies should be considered in accordance with the 'principle of parsimony'. This means first choosing the simplest, most obvious, least disruptive changes likely to bring about improvement in the pupil's learning. Whilst acknowledging that a great many factors may contribute to a child's difficulties in learning, the most direct ameliorative strategies open to the teacher are (i) changing the task; (ii) changing the teaching approach; (iii) improving motivation. These methods have an *immediate* bearing on the child's likelihood of success and each will be considered briefly here.

(i) Changing the task

This can be done in two ways. The current teaching objective may need to be broken down into a series of intermediate objectives for the pupils. The task is analyzed into a sequence of prerequisite components each of which, in turn, contributes toward mastery of the terminal skill. Space precludes reference to wide literature concerning skill hierarchies and the process of *task analysis* but helpful guidelines have recently been provided by Gardner and Tweddle (1979). Another way of changing the task is to reduce the size of the task requirements whilst preserving the essential operations required (for example presenting fewer words to be learned). This is better referred to as *task slicing*.

(ii)   *Changing the teaching approach*

This might refer to changes in the teacher's management of the child or in the actual method of teaching, materials used and so on.

(iii)   *Improving motivation*

Most pupils improve their performance markedly in response to teaching programmes which are individualized to their needs, when they are given appropriate approval and feedback and especially when they help to chart their own progress. For rather more recalcitrant learners, some form of 'contingency contracting' between the teacher and pupil may be necessary. This involves certain small rewards (such as favourite activities selected by the pupil) being made contingent upon charted evidence of daily increases in correct performance and reduction of errors, for instance. More 'valued' rewards can be negotiated and made contingent upon the attainment of longer term objectives: for example, reaching mastery or criterion level on specific tasks.

The effectiveness of a variety of direct intervention strategies involving curriculum changes, different instructional techniques and behaviour modification is discussed by Lovitt (1976 and 1977) on the basis of a large number of small scale empirical studies evaluated by precision teaching methodology.

Developments in Walsall

We would like to conclude by briefly mentioning some ways in which precision teaching has been developed in Walsall during the last two years. Initially, precision teaching was introduced selectively to a number of teachers who expressed concern about individual children with difficulties in acquiring basic skills. Successful implementation of procedures led to the following developments.

(a)   Many teachers generalized the principles of precision teaching to other children experiencing difficulties in their classes.

(b) Other teachers in the schools expressed a desire to implement similar programmes.

(c) Because of the interest created within the authority generally we decided to run termly in-service training workshops in precision teaching. To date, approximately 140 teachers from special units, infant, junior, secondary and ESN(M) schools have attended. However, the vast majority of teachers attending have been teaching in ordinary schools.

Teachers in ordinary schools have implemented reading programmes and an increasing number are administering arithmetic probes, simultaneously to as many as thirty children. These developments have been achieved in the ordinary school classroom without extra staffing being made available but have required a high level of classroom organization by the teachers concerned.

A survey carried out by the authors in July 1981 indicated that in total 462 children had been on precision teaching programmes during the academic year and that approximately 400 of these children were in ordinary schools.

(d) Several schools have incorporated aspects of precision teaching into their curriculum development (for example Bond and Lewis, 1982). The schools concerned have worked in conjunction with the Schools Psychological Services and prepared finely graded sight vocabulary probes for use with the schools' reading schemes. To date this breakdown has been completed for five schemes (*Racing to Read; Pirates; One, Two, Three and Away; Ladybird; Dominoes*). Currently a detailed phonic programme is being prepared to complement the sight vocabulary probes.

(e) The principles of precision teaching are being extended to curricular areas other than reading and number, such as spelling, language and writing skills.

(f) In October 1979 the PAIRS (Parent Assisted Instruction in Reading and Spelling) project (Walsall Herald, 1982) started. This involves parents visiting the Child Guidance Centre and working with psychologists to help improve their children's reading or spelling. Parents have been introduced to precision teaching techniques and employed them successfully in working with their children. Ten illustrated booklets have been written to assist and guide parents in their work at home. These are shortly to be published. Two school-based PAIRS projects are now being run in Walsall, both involving parents in the use of probing and charting procedures.

(g) An exchange of materials and information between teachers has begun on a limited and informal basis. In the future we hope to improve this venture by printing a termly newsletter publicizing available materials and teachers' activities relating to precision teaching.

(h) Finally, and perhaps most significantly, we feel, as educational psychologists, that we are now taking part in a much more constructive dialogue with teachers in order to help children with learning difficulties.

We hope to report on some of these developments in more detail at a later date. The following summary lists the main advantages of precision teaching for teachers and pupils:

ADVANTAGES FOR TEACHERS

(i)   Efficient meants of pinpointing teacher objectives
(ii) Rapid daily feedback indicates whether teacher has been successful
(iii) Indication of whether or not the pupil is meeting expectations in terms of
      (a) rate of learning (is he improving *fast enough* on each task?) and
      (b) reaching task criteria (is he reaching a *mastery level?*)
(iv) Economic use of direct teaching and assessment time
(v)   Efficient form of record-keeping
(vi) Basis for 'contracting' between teacher and pupil

ADVANTAGES FOR PUPILS

(i)   Provides pupil with knowledge of results
(ii) Provides visual display of pupil performance
(iii) Pupil knows exactly what needs to be learned and level of mastery required.

References

AINSCOW, M. and TWEDDLE, D. (1977) 'Behavioural objectives and children with learning difficulties', *AEP Journal*, 4, 5, pp. 29–32.

AINSCOW, M. and TWEDDLE, D. (1979) *Preventing Classroom Failure — an objectives approach*. London, Wiley.

BECKER, W. (1977) 'Teaching reading and language to the disadvantaged — what we have learned from field research', *Harvard Educational Review*, 47, 4, pp. 518–43.

BECKER, W. and ENGELMANN, S. (1977) *The Oregon Direct Instruction Model: Comparative Results in Project Follow-Through — a Summary of Nine Years' Work*. University of Oregon Follow-Through Project, Eugene, Oregon.

BOND, J. and LEWIS, A. (1982) 'Daily monitoring: applications in a school for learning difficulties', *Remedial Education*, 17, 1, pp. 8–9.

CSAPO, M. (1977) *Reading Tasks*. Vancouver, Centre for Human Development and Research.

CSAPO, M. and NEITHERCUT, A. (1976) *Learning Maths Precisely*. Vancouver; Centre for Human Development and Research.

EATON, M.D. (1978) 'Data decisions and evaluation' in HARING, N.G. *et al. The Fourth R — Research in the Classroom*. Columbus, Merrill.

FORMENTIN, T. and CSAPO, M. (1980) *Precision Teaching*, Vancouver, Centre for Human Development and Research.

GARDNER, J. and TWEDDLE, D. (1979) 'Some guidelines for sequencing objectives'. *J. Association of Educational Psychologists*, 5, 2, pp. 23–30.

GRONLUND, N.E. (1978) *Stating Objectives for Classroom Instruction* (2nd edn.) New York, Macmillan.

HARING, N.G. and GENTRY, N.D. (1976) 'Direct and individualized instructional procedures' in HARING, N.G. and SCHIEFELBUSCH, R.L. (Eds.), *Teaching Special Children*. New York, McGraw Hill.

HARING, N.G., LOVITT, T.C., EATON, M.D. and HANSEN, C.L. (1978) *The Fourth R — Research in the Classroom*. Columbus, Merrill.

HARING, N.G. and EATON, M.D. (1978) 'Systematic instructional procedures: an instructional hierarchy' *in* HARING, N.G. *et. al., The Fourth R — Research in the Classroom*. Columbus, Merrill.

HOWELL, K.W., KAPLAN, J.S. and O'CONNELL, C.Y. (1979) *Evaluating Exceptional Children: a Task Analysis Approach*. Columbus, Merrill.

LEACH, D.J. and RAYBOULD, E.C. (1977) *Learning and Behaviour Difficulties in School*. London, Open Books.

LOVITT, T.C. (1973) 'Self-management projects with children with behavioural disabilities'. *Journal of Learning Disabilities*, 6, 3, pp. 138–50.

LOVITT, T.C. (1976) 'Applied behavior analysis techniques and curriculum research: implications for instruction' *in* HARING, N.G. and SCHIEFELBUSCH, R.L. (Eds.) *Teaching Special Children*. New York, McGraw Hill.

LOVITT, T.C. (1977) *In Spite of My Resistance — I've Learned from Children*. Columbus, Merrill.

LOVITT, T.C. and HARING, N.G. (Eds.) (1979) *Classroom Application of Precision Teaching*. Washington, Seattle, Special Child Publications.

MAGER, R.F. (1962) *Preparing Instructional Objectives*. Belmon, Ca, Fearon.

MUNCEY, J. and WILLIAMS, H. (1981) 'Daily evaluation in the classroom', *Special Education: Forward Trends*, 8, 3, pp. 31–4.

POPHAM, W.J. (1975) *Educational Evaluation*. New York, Prentice Hall.

RAYBOULD, E.C. (1981) 'Precision teaching: systematising instruction for children with learning difficulties' in WHELDALL, K. (Ed.) *The Behaviourist in the Classroom: Applied Behavioural Analysis in British Educational Contexts*. Birmingham, Educational Review Publications, Birmingham University.

SKINNER, B.F. (1966) 'What is the experimental analysis of behavior?' *J. Experimental Analysis of Behavior*, 9, 3, pp. 213–8.

VARGAS, J.S. (1977) *Behavioral Psychology for Teachers*. New York, Harper and Row.

WALSALL HERALD (1982) 'How to help your kids if they spel like this,' *Walsall Herald*, No. 13, March.

WHITE, O.R. and HARING, N.G. (1980) *Exceptional Teaching* (2nd edition). Columbus, Merrill.

Recent Influences on the Assessment of Reading Difficulties and the Concept of Specific Difficulties

Robin C. Richmond
General Adviser
(Special Needs)
Dudley Metropolitan Borough

This paper will consider some recent influences on the assessment of 'reading difficulties' or more appropriately 'reading needs'. The implication for both the practice of assessment and for meeting reading needs is discussed. These influences are examined in relation to those children often described as having specific reading difficulties.

The assessment of reading difficulties is undergoing a period of change as a result of a number of separate but related developments. The process of learning to read is increasingly seen as an holistic activity rather than just the acquisition of a set of subskills concerned with the visual decoding of the text. There is increasing dissatisfaction with psychometrics as helpful in teaching children to read. Related to this is the Warnock concept of special needs, now enshrined in the 1981 Education Act with the emphasis on the individual needs of children. Finally, sociological perspectives are drawing attention to the child within a system and, in particular, the curriculum itself as a cause of learning difficulties. The general effect of these developments is to emphasize the importance of the ordinary teacher in the assessment of children's responses to teaching and learning. The demand for the recognition of an identifiable group of children as dyslexic and as a consequence the provision of separate identifiable teaching provision with different and special teaching methods will be considered in the light of these developments.

The demand for these children to be taught a level of literacy that will enable full participation in the ordinary school curriculum is in line with current developments. Similarly requests for the modification of the curriculum such as more time to complete written work or alternative methods of recording work using the tape recorder and so on is a recognition that the curriculum itself can be the cause of learning difficulties by its inappropriateness to some children's needs.

Increased Understanding of the Reading Process

A major influence on the assessment of reading difficulties is a better understanding of the reading process itself. The idea that the reading process is dependent on underlying psychological processes such as is exemplified by the *Illinois Test of Psycholinguistic Abilities* (1968) is increasingly seen to be a fallacy. Hammill and Larsen (1974) reviewed thirty-eight studies of psycholinguistic training and failed to find any clear effect on reading levels. Similarly attempts to train perceptual and motor skills, other than on reading and writing tasks (Karlsen, 1966), do not appear to lead to improved literacy (Coles, 1978). Approaches to reading advocating such methods were dominated by Tansley (1967) in Britain and such approaches were enthusiastically adopted not only by remedial teachers but first schools and junior schools.

The *Aston Index* (1976) is a late-comer and likely to be the last of this genre. The test is associated with the identification of specific learning problems and includes amongst common classroom tests of general ability, vocabulary, spelling and word recognition, the assessment of such skills as visual sequential memory, auditory sequential memory and grapho-motor abilities. In particular the test is used to identify 'dyslexic' children on the dubious assumption that certain underlying component skills are vital to success in reading. Anyone who has used this test will be aware of its irrelevance in helping children to learn about reading and yet it is described as a 'classroom' test.

Further, explanations of the reading process as a disparate number of skills such as whole-word recognition, look-say, letter discrimination and phonic skills are increasingly seen as only a minor part of that process and often inaccurately understood. Traditionally, remedial teaching has concentrated almost exclusively on the training of these auditory and visual skills. As Clark (1976) says, 'This is reading more bound up with text than message'.

In passing, neither is there any evidence to believe that the brain itself plays tricks on the reader by altering the visual impression of the text. As Clay (1979) states, 'completely erroneous statements are made about words seen in reverse or the brain scrambling the signals for the eyes or squares looking like triangles. There is no evidence to support such nonsensical descriptions of how our brains work as we read'.

An impressive body of research now points to reading as an 'holistic' process; the decoding and understanding of language. The position is summarized admirably by Young and Tyre (1983). The first point about this is that 'underlying psychological processes' and 'perceptual training' with their echoes of the discredited notion of 'transfer of training' are irrelevant to the process. Successful completion of carefully structured teaching programmes in perceptual or psycholinguistic skills do not necessarily lead to improvements in reading. The second point is that the reading process is more than the sum of its parts. Reading is more than the eye and the brain discriminating between the marks on the paper. Words mean ideas and it is the recognition and response to these ideas, at all levels of reading skill, that is important for the reader to move on and grow as a reader.

Clark (1976), in her study of young fluent readers, found that the most influential factor associated with children who were fluent readers on entry to reception class was that the children asked questions of their parents about the meanings of words, sentences and so on. She concluded that successful readers extract meaning from print from the start. As such, reading should be considered in a language context. McCullough (1974) makes a similar point about the teaching of reading, 'yet in teaching reading as a skill we should always remember that it has significance only in use. Just as you can only swim in water so you can only read, in the full sense of the term, when you are surrounded by words which have meaning for you and from which you gain understanding'.

In this greater, and some would say obvious, understanding of the reading process there are profound implications for the teaching of reading. Methods should involve, as Smith (1978) would claim, learning to read by reading. This is not a tautological statement. If reading is about getting the message from the printed word then children come to the reading task with some ready made strengths. For example, spoken language, has meaning in relation to the context in which it occurs. Spoken language is part of a context, it is 'embedded' in a situation. Reading is language removed from the situation in which it occurs. Children have to learn that words can be parted from the things and events to which they apply. Hence the more reading material is removed from the everyday spoken language experiences of the children and the uses children make of language the more difficult it will be for them to read, to get the message from the print. This is not an argument in favour of 'Nippers' (Berg, 1968), a set of readers purporting to represent working class values, for the children of the lower socio-economic classes, but an argument in favour of reading material that avoids artificial and stilted language, that is about exciting and challenging events grounded in children's experiences and presented in a manner which provokes curiosity and stimulates the imagination; from the here and now to imagined possibilities.

A further strength children bring to the reading task is a familiarity with the rules of syntax derived from their experiences of spoken language. Written language follows similar rules. Given the first few words of a sentence it is relatively simple to complete the sentence. Our understanding of syntax, familiarity with the way language is put together, helps us to do this. Syntactical clues are, of course, related to the message of the text. Clay

(1979) claims that 'by far the most important challenge for the teacher is to change the way in which the child operates on print to get the message'. Without the message the syntactic possibilities would be greater and, although syntactically correct, our best guess probably absurd. It is argued therefore that there is much to be said for building on and developing children's spoken language skills into reading language skills. This is not only as reading becomes more sophisticated but as the basis for the initial acquisition of reading skills.

These developments in the understanding of the reading process and the implications for improving the teaching of reading are demanding a reappraisal of the assessment of reading difficulties. The tradition of that assessment, for remedial teachers, has focused on the perceptual, auditory and visual skills of learning to read. Although prevented from using the ITPA (1968) by other professionals and generally astute enough not to embrace the *Aston Index* (1976), remedial teachers have, for example, used the *Daniels and Diack Reading Tests* (1958) enthusiastically. However, such tests, with their almost exclusive preoccupation with visual discrimination and phonic skills are being, if not replaced by, then interpreted against, a diagnosis based on an analysis of the strategies children employ when reading.

This approach to the assessment of reading is to be found in the much respected *Neale Analysis of Reading Ability* (1958). The test booklet itself, although now dated, is like a book and the form of the items, short stories arranged according to level of difficulty, reflect an approach to assessment not unlike the informal reading inventory (Strang, 1969). This involves presenting children with reading materials of known levels of difficulty to find out if they can or cannot read them adequately. Questions follow the reading of the texts to determine understanding of what has been read. Careful observation of reading behaviour can determine levels of independent and instructional reading. Also easy texts can provide insight into strengths and harder texts insight into weaknesses.

More pertinent to recent developments in assessing reading but not unrelated to the IRI is the recording of what the handbook to the *Neale Analysis of Reading Ability* calls errors and what are appropriately described as miscues by Goodman (1976). The handbook describes six types of error that children are likely to make when reading aloud the stories which comprise the test items. These are mispronunciations, substitutions, refusals, additions, omissions and reversals. They are to be 'noted for their diagnostic value'. In practice, the recording of the type of error is often disregarded in favour of using the test to determine reading ages. Goodman (1976), amongst others, has given considerable attention to the analysis of reading and says that the so-called errors that readers make are in reality 'miscues' hence the term 'miscue analysis' to determine the strategies children are using when learning to read.

The diagnosis of strategies from performance on reading tasks also applies to non-readers and beginning readers. Clay (1979) has described an approach to the early detection of children's difficulties from careful observation of approaches to books, early responses to reading, early reading behaviour and writing. Observations are detailed to determine understanding of the message, concepts of print, visual analysis skills and sound sequences. Clay (1979) states that children 'operate on print by searching for relationships which order the complexity of print and therefore simplify it . . .' the emphasis of her diagnostic survey 'is placed on the operations and strategies that are used in reading rather than on test scores and disabilities.'

The Failure of Psychometrics

A further influence for change in assessment procedures for reading difficulties is what Gillham (1978) has called the failure of psychometrics. This is the reappraisal of the value of norm-related data, in this case, in relation to meeting the reading needs of children. This is a remarkable development since norm-related scores are directly responsible for the idea of remediation and with it remedial teaching. Schonell (1942) had drawn attention to the differences he had observed between individual children's scores on tests of scholastic ability compared with scores on tests of intellectual ability. In particular he had noted this discrepancy in relation to reading ages. Schonell (1942) described this difference as retardation, 'a condition of unrealized intellectual potential, a state of improvable scholastic deficiency and as such may characterize dull, normal or super normal pupils but is seen in its most pronounced form in bright (measured mental age) children'. The failure of special teaching to remedy this discrepancy did not appear to be of much concern as neither did the exceptions to the theory, those children with higher reading ages than mental ages.

Interestingly this idea of discrepancy arises in the case of children with specific reading difficulties and in particular dyslexia. One of the most important distinguishing features is said to be a discrepancy between measured intelligence (Miles, 1974) or general ability as evidenced in school subjects and attainment in reading and spelling. Now, this idea of discrepancy is only of importance if other criteria are absent. For example, some advocates do not include children with reading difficulties accompanied by auditory handicaps, motor or sensory impairment or environmental deprivations; the latter what Singleton (1975) has called 'the absence of disadvantage criterion'. Interesting and perhaps fanciful though this approach is to defining reading difficulties it does nothing to suggest teaching that will help children to learn to read.

Definitions, like explanations, generally do little to meet children's reading needs. This is as true for children labelled dyslexic as it is for all children experiencing reading difficulties. In these terms dyslexia can only be failure to learn to read or make progress with reading. The source of help for such children is the results of the kind of approaches to the diagnosis of individual children's difficulties on actual reading tasks as discussed earlier.

A further difficulty for psychometrics lies in the nature of norm-related data. The obvious diversity of human attainment is summarized in a mean level of performance. The behavioural sciences reduce individual instances to a representative average. The process of measuring human attainment implies that deviation from the average if not abnormal, is unusual. Hence, for example, in measuring reading attainment some children are above average and some below average. To identify children with reading difficulties as that group below the mean with the accompanying implication that they should be average is patently absurd. When the data is in the form of reading ages the problem is exacerbated by the fact that the distribution gets increasingly tailed-back as year groups get older. However the fallacy persists that for all to be well, reading ages should be the same as chronological ages. Such deceptive beliefs divert attention away from the individual reading needs of children.

Many schools will continue to use norm-referenced reading tests. The use of such tests has increased as a result of demands for accountability. Many remedial education services find the need to identify children who cannot read conflicting with local education authority demands for some measure of overall reading standards. The norm-referenced reading test is an appropriate instrument for the latter purpose but inappropriate for the former. As remedial educators are forced to administer group reading tests on behalf of local authorities the tendency is to see norm-referenced scores, be they standardized scores or reading ages, as crude estimates of the level of children's reading skills. In order to do this with standardized scores, chronological ages have to be considered but reading ages are particularly amenable to this interpretation. Daniels and Diack (1958) relate reading ages to phonic skills. The association is crude but it is possible to extend this to a wider view of the reading process. In this way reading ages can be used diagnostically. A good example of this is Ames (1980). The use of norm related reading scores in this way is in line with matching appropriate teaching to the individual reading needs of children.

Special Needs

Reference has been made to the traditional role of psychometrics in selecting children for remedial teaching in reading. But psychometrics has played a greater role in selecting children and categorizing them for segregated educational provision. For example the so-called ESN(M) children are traditionally those children with measured intelligence quotients between 50 and 75. It has long been recognized that children do not fit the categories into which psychometrics has placed them. Within such categories teachers are aware of the wide variations in pupil performance in the classroom. This change from categorizing children to focusing on individual needs was recommended by the Warnock Committee. Their report was titled *Special Educational Needs* (1978). The change in emphasis is to what an individual child can do, what he needs to learn next and under what conditions he is likely to be successful. Teachers will immediately recognize this in simple terms as the practice of teaching.

Unofficial labels such as specific learning difficulty or dyslexic in this sense are rather outdated and do nothing to meet the reading needs of children who fail to read or make progress with reading. Tansley and Panckhurst (1981), as a result of a review of research into specific learning difficulties, broaden the term to include all kinds of learning difficulties but make the point that by avoiding categorization 'the obligation of the education system to all children is affirmed'. That obligation is appropriate teaching and learning to meet the individual reading needs of all children including those with reading difficulties.

The concept of special educational needs has passed into law in the 1981 Education Act. On the pretext of encouraging integration, the 1981 Act, together with the attendant Circular 1/83 and regulations (1983), is developing as a piece of legislation for placing children in segregated provision. An advantage of the 1981 Act is that it has focused attention on the educational needs of children. In practice this is developing to the advantage of pupils with learning difficulties in ordinary schools. It is arising out of the extent to which ordinary schools believe that the law requires them to keep careful records of pupils with special needs. To quote the DES Press Notice (1983) on the 1981 Act, 'arrangements for assessing the needs of children with mild learning difficulties in ordinary schools will be a matter for LEAs. They will be expected to issue guidance to all schools in their area but the Circular sets no deadline for the issue of this guidance'. Statutory procedures will apply to the minority of children (expected to be about 2 per cent) with severe and complex difficulties whose special educational provision needs to be determined by the LEA.

If ordinary schools do feel that they are required to keep more detailed records, and this seems likely, then this process is part of the assessment procedure. More detailed record keeping by schools will direct teachers to appropriate teaching for children with learning difficulties. In this sense the 1981 Act is likely to concentrate the mind on the problem but the probability of additional or appropriate resources for children with mild learning difficulties in ordinary schools as a direct result of the 1981 Education Act is negligible.

One further point about record keeping in schools as it is likely to affect the assessments of children with learning difficulties must be made. As previously stated the LEA is expected to issue guidance to schools and in some instances this guidance has detailed the nature of the record keeping even to the point of itemized sections of the record. Some of these records for a minority of children will form the basis of the 'educational advice' to the LEA as part of a formal assessment under Section 5 of the 1981 Education Act leading to a statement of special educational needs. For those children formally assessed or for those children not formally assessed there is a danger that the local authority will be proscribing to schools what 'educational advice' is by issuing detailed guidance to schools on what 'educational record keeping' is. One example to hand of LEA guidance to schools is as much concerned with recording (and by implication assessing) psychological information, as it is educational information.

Emphasis ought to be on the recording of learning skills or response to teaching styles or the kind of plans that have been made for the education of particular pupils. Wedell and Lindsay (1980) have suggested that a predictive approach to the identification of children with difficulties should be abandoned in favour of a teaching or monitoring model. This places the teacher in a much more central role in the assessment procedure. It involves the teacher in monitoring children's methods of learning while they are engaged on real educational tasks over a period of time. There are a number of teacher-completed rating scales now available of which Lindsay (1982) and Stott (1978) are good examples. These aim to indicate present level of pupil learning or behaviour by relating what is being assessed to what is being taught. Leeming (1979) states that this is the simplest of teaching models 'to teach and see whether learning has taken place' and concludes that if assessment is to become part of teaching the teacher should play a key part.

The Curriculum

Some of the inadequacies of recording procedures are the result of disregarding the child within the context of what is provided. The proper assessment of pupils with reading difficulties must consider the school and the part it plays in determining who has a learning difficulty and who has not. There is increasing interest in the curriculum as a cause of learning difficulties. Booth (1983) as a prelude to describing a new curriculum-based approach to children's difficulties claims that traditional remedial education 'operates a casualty service for those who choke on the inappropriate educational diet on offer'. Others would claim that children only have learning difficulties when they start school!

The *Warnock Report* (1978) is responsible for the widespread belief that 20 per cent of the population have special needs. The figure has become part of the received wisdom of special education. However this authoritative statistic is the result of the importance the Warnock Committee gave to a variety of distinctly separate surveys both in time and purpose largely based on data from questionnaires. This basis for the 20 per cent belief has been heavily criticized. Lewis and Vulliamy (1980) state 'that to rely on the unexamined definitions which teachers give of their problem pupils is to beg the question ... education is surely one of those areas in which the organizational structures of schools together with teachers' expectation and pedagogies can create massive learning and behaviour problems for pupils'.

The notion that pupils with learning difficulties are those children for whom the school curriculum is inappropriate is becoming very influential. That many children are required to learn the wrong things at the wrong pace and in the wrong way is, has always been, recognized by remedial teachers. It is an important shift of emphasis away from what is a 'medical model' of learning difficulties where the assumption is that there is something wrong with the child and what is required is 'treatment' to 'cure' him; what Golby and Gulliver (1981) call the ideology of pathology, to what is sometimes called by sociologists a 'system' model (Burden, 1981). This development strikes at the very tradition of assessment itself and the science of the assessors. The 'medical model' centred as it is on deficits within the individual fits with practices of examination, assessment, diagnosis, pre-scription and so on. The sociological critique of this model leads to a consideration of cause of failure outside the children and their families; the standards of the school, the content of the teaching, the quality of the teaching, the organization of the teaching, the teacher's expectations, values and so on.

In such a model there are considerable implications for increasing the participation of all children in the educational and social life of ordinary schools. The remedial educator would move from a position of preoccupa-tion with assessing individual children to an assessment of individual children's performance in relation to the appropriateness of the content and the process of the curriculum. In particular the remedial teacher will be concerned with assessing the level of literacy demanded for participation in the subject areas of the school. Golby and Gulliver (1981) see remedial education at present as an ambulance service picking up casualties of an inappropriate curriculum. They suggest that more preventative medicine should be used. Children have difficulties when they are given something that they cannot do. Before that there is no problem. Golby and Gulliver argue that schools must adapt their curriculum to take account of individual differences. Changes of this kind are to be found in the recommendations in relation to schools in Scotland by HMI (1978). The role of the remedial specialist is to act as a consultant to other members of staff and individual children on teaching methods and resources; offer an overview of the whole curriculum especially the language content; be experts in observing and assessing children's learning difficulties; pursue cooperative working in the classroom with class teachers and subject specialists. Sewell (1982) takes a similar view emphasizing the remedial specialist's role within the curricu-lum. This includes the skills of teaching literacy, the demands of language across the curriculum, of cooperating with and supporting colleagues, of school-based in-service training and of befriending 'troublesome' pupils.

The point of all this is that assessment increasingly cannot be divorced from the curriculum as a whole. Diagnosis away from the classroom, away from the system of teaching and learning is likely to be irrelevant to meeting children's needs. Similarly the remedial specialist cannot divorce the role of assessor or diagnostician of the difficulties children experience from the role of consultant specialist teacher.

Some children's difficulties can only become apparent, sometimes later in their school careers, as the literacy demands of the curriculum increase. Amongst these children are some labelled dyslexic. The level of resources available for remedial education within a local authority may mean that such children pass early screening procedures whilst children with more severe difficulties are selected for special help by remedial educators. Many parents are the first to notice when the literacy skills of their children are inadequate to cope with the curriculum that is provided. This is particularly true as children progress from primary to secondary education. Difficulties that are not a serious or obvious handicap at a younger age can become real difficulties as children get older and are faced with the need for a higher standard of literacy skills. Often the difficulties are caused by the literacy demands of external examinations. A school can assume that capability in a subject specialism implies that children have the necessary standard of literacy demanded by the subject.

The difficulties some children can experience later in their school careers often relate to writing and spelling. This is not to ignore the very real difficulties many children experience as a result of the reading demands of school text books (Harrison, 1979). The careful individual teaching necessary for these older children often conflicts with the time demanded by the subject specialisms and although short periods of intensive teaching can help some children it is sometimes difficult to correct the habits reinforced over long periods or to overcome poor and inappropriate learning styles often the result of continued failure.

Some Case Studies

This paper has outlined some recent influences on the way children's reading difficulties are assessed. The general effect of these influences is to emphasize children's individual reading needs; to examine individual difficulties against what is known about the reading process, the categorizing of children and the demands of the curriculum. Brief reference, where appropriate, has been made to that group of children labelled as dyslexic. Children labelled dyslexic are children with reading difficulties and as such the assessment of such children is subject to the same influences that affect the assessment of all children with reading difficulties. Teaching children to read or make progress with reading is the issue. To identify what a child can do and then teach him what he needs to be able to do next, is the way forward. This is true for all children with reading difficulties including those labelled dyslexic. Dyslexia as a concept has no roots in pedagogy.

It has been argued that the variety of difficulties and the individual needs of children labelled as dyslexic are no different from the needs of any other children with reading difficulties insofar as they require a careful individual analysis of their difficulties and an individual teaching programme. The following experience of teaching provision for children with specific difficulties is an example.

Children with reading and literacy difficulties were admitted to a small teaching group. This group, the intensive learning group, was set up alongside and using the same facilities, including the teacher, resources and classroom as that of an existing remedial teaching group for children with reading difficulties. The children, aged between 7 and 13, were to be average or above average in school subjects as judged by their teachers but below average in written expression or in reading. The group met for four half days per week. The existing remedial teaching group did not conform to these criteria. They were children between 8 and 11 years of age who were experiencing reading difficulties at the level of illiteracy or beginning reading but who did not have access to remedial teaching at school.

The approach to diagnosis of the individual children's difficulties experienced in school literacy tasks and the development of individual teaching programmes was the same for children in the intensive learning group and in the remedial group. Although meeting the somewhat elitist criteria for the intensive learning group the difficulties experienced by the children were varied as the following three examples illustrate.

John

John is 8 years old and second child of parents who run a small family business. His elder sister is progressing normally and does not experience any learning difficulties. He attends a primary school where, for most children, expected high attainments are achieved. John's parents are very cooperative but concerned about his reading difficulties which became more apparent last year. Behaviour problems were arising and John was considered lazy.

Quite obvious was John's short attention span and he had developed a number of distracting techniques. He had difficulties with visual skills on reading tasks. He could not retain a sight vocabulary. He confused visually similar words and letters in context. Auditory skills constituted relative rather than absolute strengths and his phonic blending was good. Reading and spelling level were below the 6 year level (Daniels and Diack, 1958). He had a broad vocabulary and fluent spoken language skills.

John was handled sympathetically but with some firmness and his work directed by positive instructions to do certain things rather than not to do certain things. Teaching was broken down into a series of short varied learning activities. Activities were selected for motivational, attention span values as well as instruction. Use was made of word blending strengths using *Bangers and Mash* (Groves, 1975), which also have potential for maintaining interest level. A modified 'paired' reading approach was employed with the teacher directing attention to cues in the text. Free access was allowed to a variety of books, to encourage private reading and book use, for a short period during each teaching session.

Neil

Neil is 13½ years of age, the younger of two children. His teachers at his comprehensive school emphasized his willingness to participate in class discussions and his above average facility with spoken language. They also drew attention to the varied quality of his written work and an inability to express himself clearly in writing. Most noticeable was his poor spelling ability. His parents were particularly concerned that his poor spelling and writing were a handicap in the subject areas at school.

Neil had an acceptable level of fluency when reading aloud as observed on normal reading tasks in the school curriculum. This was confirmed by a *Neale Analysis* (1958) reading word accuracy age of 10.10 and a reading comprehension age of 12.7. Reading rate on the same test was 10.1. His auditory and visual memory of words was at a low level. The *Diagnostic Spelling Test* (Vincent and Claydon, 1981) produced the profile shown at figure 1.

Neil's high score on test 1 (homophones) suggested that he is able to link visual pattern and meaning, while his poor score on test 2 (common words) indicated an over-dependence on phonics coupled perhaps with faulty auditory perception. The errors which he made were:

gost	— ghost
prenses	— princess
elethants	— elephants
gyant	— giant
hostpital	— hospital
teather	— teacher

Examination of Neil's written work in school revealed errors where parts of words were missed out, for example, haply = happily and yesday = yesterday, and reversals of some letters and words, for example, b = d and was = saw. Spellings of more than one syllable presented him with considerable difficulty. His spelling age (Schonell, 1942) was 8.6. He was not aware that every word and syllable must contain a vowel.

The teaching programme attempted to reconcile the view of spelling as a visual memory skill (Peters, 1982) and the view of spelling as dependent on

Figure 1   The Diagnostic Spelling Test

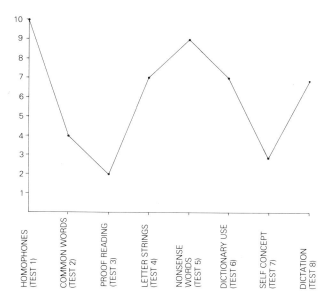

Source: Vincent, D and Claydon, J (1981) *Diagnostic Spelling Test*, NFER/Nelson

sound cues (Cotterell, 1981). Neil appeared to have difficulties in both areas. Spelling practices were based on words incorrectly spelt in school written work and a look, trace, cover, write technique was employed since this is a multi-sensory approach, but encourages a visual analysis of words. He was encouraged to build up his own word bank (Peters, 1982). Syllabification was taught by the tapping out of syllables. Attention was paid to the phoneme-grapheme relationship of words using the Edith Norrie Letter Case (Norrie, 1973). Some selected spelling rules were taught making use of Neil's reasoning ability. Remedial teaching sessions were reinforced by short 15 minute practice sessions at home using dictated sentences, hence employing words in context.

Robert

Robert is 10 years of age. He is the younger of two boys. His brother is very successful with school work. His parents were concerned with Robert's poor progress with reading and claimed that he never seemed to 'stick' at anything. His father said that he had difficulties with reading and still does. Robert is overweight but successful at sport and physical education. The school felt that Robert's lack of success with reading had resulted in an increasingly casual approach to his work. His standard of school work was very poor. He was a likeable boy who had difficulty in relating to some of his teachers. Robert liked to talk and relate anecdotes. He had a pleasant sense of humour.

Robert was reading at the 7.0 year level (*Salford Sentence Reading Test A*, Bookbinder, 1976) although his score on *Daniels and Diack Test 1* (1958), a phonic based test, was just above the 6 year level. Reading aloud was a slow and laborious process, lacking any fluency. Substitutions were added to the text without any reference to the meaning or sense of what was being read, for example, a back hat = a black hat. He also omitted many words. The use of sounds as a cue was virtually non-existent although if prompted he could identify initial sounds of some words but he could not recognize phonic patterns in the context of words. Handwriting was very poor. Letters were formed correctly but writing was uncoordinated and lacking fine motor control.

The teaching programme started by using drawings to convey messages, to tell stories. This activity was based on *Trog Books* (Butterworth, 1973). Robert's reading of texts was much improved when he was familiar with the meaning. The *Trog Books* suited Robert's humour and imagination. Further work involved Robert's mature interests in the subject areas of the curriculum at school. Subject context and message were developed using school teaching materials. Questions were posed before Robert was presented with the texts. To support this work the *Read, Write and Remember Topic Books* (Milburn, 1977) were used and also *Reading Routes Blue Box* (Leedham, 1978), since these employ sentence contexts. *Reason and Write* (Mitchelhill, 1976) was used at a later stage. These materials are helpful in teaching children to form complete sentences and in writing sentences in logical sequence leading on to writing chapters. Taped stories were used with Robert, again to emphasize the context, the message, the story, to develop fluent reading. Listening skills were developed by the use of *Concept 7–9* (Schools Council, 1972). This involves listening to sequences of instructions and remembering them. A high rate of success is built into the scheme and this was considered beneficial to Robert's needs. Handwriting was improved using the school style, which was a rather complicated loop system. Careful short, well structured, practice sessions based on school work were used.

As a matter of interest all three of these children had been labelled dyslexic following private consultations with psychologists, resulting in written, largely descriptive reports to the parents.

Young and Tyre (1983) demonstrate that for children with reading difficulties whatever the label, remedial or dyslexic, individual progress with their individual literacy needs is the issue. On this criteria the progress of children in the intensive learning group was no different from the progress of children in the remedial teaching group. This judgment is not based on any controlled comparative study but on the professional observations of the teacher, who for both groups of children followed a teaching and monitoring model to assess individual progress to which reference has previously been made (Wedell and Lindsay, 1980). This model included the use of criterion referenced tests. Individual progress was monitored against individual teaching plans. Teaching content and teaching progress were altered accordingly. Individual rates of progress and the teaching problems posed by any of the children were not unusual. This is not to say that individual children did not present demanding teaching problems. They did but these problems would not be unfamiliar to any experienced teacher of children with learning difficulties.

It has already been stated that the approach to assessing and meeting the needs of children in both the intensive learning group and the remedial teaching group was essentially the same; careful assessments on literacy tasks resulting in individual teaching programmes. That the individual progress of children was also no different in both teaching groups suggested that the separation of the two groups, on what are now considered irrelevant criteria, served no pedagogic purpose and could no longer be sustained.

Acknowledgement

I wish to thank Heather Morris for her contribution to the case studies.

References

AMES, T. (1980), *Teach Yourself to Diagnose Reading Problems*, Macmillan.

BERG, L. (1968) *Nipper Books*, Macmillan.

BOOKBINDER, G.E. (1976) *The Salford Sentence Reading Test*, Hodder and Stoughton.

BOOTH, T. (1983) 'A teaching approach to learning difficulties', *Times Educational Supplement*, 9 September.

BURDEN, R. (1981) 'Systems theory and its relevance to schools' in GILLHAM, B. (Ed.), *Problem Behaviour in Secondary Schools*, Croom Helm.

BUTTERWORTH, B. (1973) *Trog Books*, E.J. Arnold.

CLARK, M. (1976) *Young Fluent Readers*, Heinemann.

CLAY, M. (1979) *The Early Detection of Reading Difficulties: a diagnostic survey with recovery procedures*, Heinemann.

COLES, G.S. (1978) 'The learning disabilities test battery: empirical and social issues', *Harvard Educational Review*, 48, pp. 313–9.

COTTERILL, G. (1981) *Diagnosis in the Classroom*, University of Reading School of Education.

DANIELS, J.C. and DIACK, H. (1958) *The Standard Reading Tests*, Hart-Davis.

DEPARTMENT OF EDUCATION AND SCIENCE (1978) *Special Educational Needs* (Warnock Report), London, HMSO.

DEPARTMENT OF EDUCATION AND SCIENCE (1983) *New Procedures for Assessing and Meeting Special Educational Needs*, Press Notice 17/83, 31 January.

DEPARTMENT OF EDUCATION AND SCIENCE (1983) *Assessment and Statement of Special Educational Needs*, Circular 1/83, 31 January.

GILLHAM, B. (Ed.) (1978) *Reconstructing Educational Psychology*, Croom Helm.

Robin C. Richmond

GOLBY, M. and GULLIVER, J. (1979) 'Whose remedies, whose ills? A critical review of remedial education', *Journal of Curriculum Studies*, reprinted in this volume.

GOODMAN, K.S. (1967) 'Reading: a psycholinguistic guessing game', *Journal of the Reading Specialist*, College Read. Association, May.

GOODMAN, K.S. (1976) 'Miscue analysis: theory and reality in reading' in GOLLASCH, F.V. (Ed.) (1982) *Selected Writings of Goodman*, Routledge and Kegan Paul.

GROVES, P. (1975) *Bangers and Mash*, Longman.

HAMILL, D.D. and LARSEN, S.C. (1974) 'The effectiveness of psycholinguistic training,' *Exceptional Children*, 41.

HARRISON, C. (1979) 'Assessing the readability of school texts', in LUNZER, E. and GARDNER, K. (Eds.) *The Effective Use of Reading*, Heinemann.

HMSO (1981) *The Education Act 1981*.

HMSO (1983) *The Education (Special Educational Needs) Regulations 1983*.

KARLSEN, B., MADDEN, R., and GARDNER, E. (1966) *Stamford Diagnostic Reading Test Manual, level 1*, Harcourt, Brace and World.

KIRK, S.A., McCARTHY, J.J. and KIRK, W.D. (1968) *The Illnois Test of Psycholinguistic Abilities*, University of Illinois Press.

LEEDHAM, J. (1978) *Reading Routes Blue Box*, Longman.

LEEMING, K., SWANN, W., COUPE, J., and MITTLER, P. (1979) *Teaching Language and Communication to the Mentally Handicapped*, Schools Council Curriculum Bulletin No. 8.

LEWIS, L., and VULLIAMY, G. (1980) 'Warnock or Warlock? The sorcery of definitions: the limitations of the report on special education', *Educational Review*, 32, 1.

LINDSAY, G. (1982) *Infant Rating Scale*, Hodder and Stoughton.

McCULLOUGH, S. (1974) *Into New Worlds*, Hart-Davis.

MILBURN, C. (1977) *Read, Write and Remember Topic Books*, Blackie.

MILES, T.R. (1974) *The Dyslexic Child*, Priory Press.

MITCHELHILL, B. (1976) *Reason and Write Books 1–4*, Learning Materials Ltd.

NEALE, M. (1958) *The Neale Analysis of Reading Ability — manual of directions and norms*, Macmillan.

NEWTON, M. and THOMPSON, M. (1976) *The Aston Index: a classroom test for screening of language difficulties*, LDA.

NORRIE, E. (1973) *The Letter Case*, Helen Arkell.

PETERS, M.L. (1982) *The Word Bank Project: the book*, Macmillan.

SCHONELL, F.J. (1942) *Backwardness in the Basic Subjects*, Oliver and Boyd.

SCHOOLS COUNCIL (1972) *Concept 7–9*, E.J. Arnold.

SCOTTISH EDUCATION DEPARTMENT (1978) *The Education of Pupils with Learning Difficulties in Primary and Secondary Schools in Scotland: a progress report by Her Majesty's Inspectorate*, Edinburgh HMSO.

SEWELL, G. (1982) *Reshaping Remedial Education*, Croom Helm.

SINGLETON, C.H. (1975) 'The myth of specific developmental dyslexia part 1', *Remedial Education*, 10, 3.

SMITH, F. (1978) *Reading*, Cambridge University Press.

STOTT, D.H. (1978) *Helping Children with Learning Difficulties: a diagnostic approach*, Ward Lock Educational.

STRANG, R. (1969) 'Informal reading inventories' in MELNIK, A. and MERRITT, J. (Eds.) (1975) *The Reading Curriculum*, ULP.

TANSLEY, A.E. (1967) *Reading and Remedial Teaching*, Routledge and Kegan Paul.

TANSLEY, P. and PANCKHURST, J. (1981) *Children with Specific Learning Difficulties*, NFER/Nelson.

VINCENT, D. and CLAYDON, J. (1981) *Diagnostic Spelling Test*, NFER/Nelson.

WEDELL, K. and LINDSAY, G.A. (1980) 'Early identification procedures; what have we learned?', *Remedial Education*, 15, 3, pp. 130–5.

YOUNG, P. and TYRE, C. (1983) *Dyslexia or Illiteracy?*, OU Press.

Towards Success in Mathematics

Alec A. Williams
Principal Lecturer in Education,
Bishop Grosseteste College

Public concern regarding the man-in-the-street's ability to cope with everyday problems involving mathematics has yet to match the disquiet so frequently expressed regarding standards in reading. Recent reports, however, have focused upon mathematics, both as a subject in school and in relation to its application in employment and in day-to-day living. The HMI survey *Aspects of Secondary Education in England* (DES, 1979) comments that 'arithmetical competence of some of the pupils was unacceptably low ... the work with the least able 15–20 per cent giving cause for concern ... their grasp of basic principles and their ability to retain knowledge and to draw upon skill other than those immediately practised is poor'. As to adult skills, a representative of the British Confederation of Industries comments in the *Cockcroft Report*, (DES, 1982) 'It is in mathematics that the shortfall in the education of children makes itself most manifest to the employer'. Bridget Sewell (1981) suggests that an unacceptably high percentage of adults of all abilities and from all walks of life are frequently at a disadvantage in situations involving mathematics. The most striking feature of the study according to Cockcroft '... was the extent to which the need to undertake even an apparently straightforward piece of mathematics caused undue feelings of anxiety, helplessness, fear and even guilt. Many adults, normally performing relatively well, were anxious lest anything more complicated should be asked of them'.

Given both the magnitude and the complexity of the deficiencies exposed, it would be logical to expect that mathematical educators and specialists in learning difficulties would have combined to bring their joint expertise to bear on the problem. Until very recent times, few such contacts have existed to the obvious detriment of both research and literature. However the early 1980s brought the publication of the Schools Council *Low Attainers in Mathematics 5–16*, (Denvir, Stolz and Brown, 1982) the ILEA publication *Struggle*, the joint Mathematical Association/NARE

Diploma in the Teaching of Mathematics to Low Attainers in Secondary Schools, the *Cockcroft Report* itself and post Cockcroft, DES funding of major researches in the field. These initiatives could not be more timely as much of the dynamic and exciting thinking which is currently vitalizing mathematical education has a direct bearing on the needs of both children and adults with mathematical difficulties.

Throughout this paper, to avoid confusion, pupils with learning difficulties in mathematics will simply be referred to as 'low attainers'. Acceptance of this term used by the Schools Council in Working Paper No 72 and taken up by the Mathematical Association will side-step involvement with the complex semantics of special education. 'Low attainer' can be interpreted as referring to any pupil who for any reason is not succeeding in mathematics.

Aims in Teaching Mathematics

The HMI survey *Primary Education in England* (DES, 1978) draws attention to the fact that 'individual schools or teachers are making markedly individual decisions about what is to be taught (in mathematics) based on their own perceptions and choices'. Given that a similar freedom is exercised in secondary schools, the necessity for a clearly stated and accepted formulation of aims becomes apparent. Hart (1981), however, indicates that already in the middle years of schooling there exists a 'seven year difference' between the least and most able which must inevitably pose the question as to whether any single statement of aims can adequately cover so broad a range of ability and needs. Cockcroft (1982, paragraph 12) attempts to do so, offering a rationale that teaching should:

> ... enable each child to develop, within his capabilities, the mathematical skills and understanding required for adult life, for employment and for further study and training ...
> ... provide mathematics for other subjects.
> ... enable the child to appreciate and enjoy mathematics ...
> ... make pupils aware of mathematics as a means of communication.

This is an uncontentious statement, unlikely to provoke disagreement amongst teachers of pupils of any ability. For low attaining pupils, however, it can be argued not that differing aims are required but, within the general statement, that more sharply focused emphases are called for if the special needs of particular groups of pupils are to be met. Probably the most significant effect of continuing lack of success is the doubts that arise within individuals not only about themselves as achievers but even about their worthwhileness as persons. Conversely, success, particularly in a status subject such as mathematics, may have a marked effect in *promoting confidence and enhancing the self concept* of the individual. The pupil's reaction to failure may be the development of varying avoidance tactics perhaps taking the form of malingering on classroom tasks or non-attendance. Where the teacher attempts to provide success by requiring the completion of mechanistic exercises in the four basic processes, unrelated to life or reality, a likely outcome is overt rejection through boredom. Perhaps even that is preferable to the pupil developing false feelings of security through accepting and hiding behind this form of non-demanding, repetitive task which contributes neither to the achievement of Cockcroft's aspirations nor to the individual's self respect. Thus, *mathematics should seek to promote a dynamic approach to the task in hand within the context of a willingness and a capacity to face a challenge.* The HMI *Secondary Survey* (DES, 1979) regretted the extent to which mathematics tended to be teacher-controlled, making little demand on the pupil and rarely requiring a clearly formulated argument or expression of opinion. Practice, it was maintained, was nearly always regarded as sufficient in itself. Cocooned within a continuing expectation of mathematics in this form, the low attainer's will and capacity to face the realities of the outside world may well be depressed to the point of extinction. The teacher must therefore provide *activities involving decision making at many levels which present opportunities to use mathematics to make informed judgments in such situations.*

Only in a mathematics lesson is the individual presented with sums. In real life, one's mathematical skills and sensitivities must be sufficiently developed to identify and deal with problems in whatever form they present themselves. This process is likely to involve, at whatever level, the identification and collation of data and the task of seeking out the interrelationships between them. That a pupil may bring only limited learning resources to bear on such a process further emphasizes the importance of *continuing involvement in activities involving applications and problem solving at every stage of development.* Cockcroft's statement that 'the ability to solve problems is at the heart of mathematics' can thus be accepted as a primary aim and source of motivation for every low attaining pupil.

The necessity to achieve a curricular balance between content and approach is critical for the teacher of such pupils. Emotional immaturity and instability can seriously impair both the will and the ability to learn. Working with such pupils, priority must be given to *creating a climate in which pupils are encouraged to interact and to take part in the give and take of a social learning situation.* Providing, as it does, opportunities to work in pairs and groups, to examine alternatives and to converse both within and without the classroom, mathematics not only develops an effective language for communication but also facilitates the growth of personal maturity by enabling learning to take place within highly motivating social circumstances.

Instrumental and Relational Learning

Though it may be claimed that the aims as stated are no more ambitious than the pupils' needs demand, even their part-realization is likely to call for a substantial re-evaluation and revision of much existing practice. The effect of well-intended exhortations such as 'teach with understanding' appears to have relatively little effect when clarity of purpose is lacking. In such a circumstance the conscientious teacher's interpretation of such advice may well be little more than the introduction of differing forms of symbol manipulation. Skemp (1982) differentiates between *instrumental* learning whereby skills are acquired from given rules, practices and rote learning without understanding and *relational* learning whereby pupils are actively engaged in seeking relationships, building up a conceptual structure (schema) from which other relationships can evolve thereby facilitating adaptability and transfer in learning. Skemp's notion of relational understanding will form the foundation of most mathematics teaching with low attaining pupils.

Differing aspects of learning call for differing interpretations of relational theory. It is useful to distinguish between:

Formation of conceptual structures.
Acquisition of skills and processes.
Acquisition of facts and knowledge.
Formation of problem solving strategies.

Though each dimension will be considered separately, their interdependence will be readily apparent.

Formation of Conceptual Structures

Concepts cannot be taught. Their formation depends upon the abstraction and generalization of common elements from differing, but related, situations. The teacher can provide the encouragement and the circumstances within which concepts can be formed but it is the pupil who must form the concept in the light of previous knowledge, ideas, experiences and attitudes. The late Harold Fletcher conveyed the central meaning of the conceptual approach when he coined the phrase 'Have-a-go' mathematics. Such learning, dependent on activity, exploration and estimation is likely to be within the capacity of low attaining pupils providing there is a match between the developmental level of the pupil and the demand being made and further providing that the teacher clarifies and structures the situation to facilitate the pupil's appreciation of the relationships involved. Because of the highly personalized nature of concept development, a variety of teaching approaches, methods and materials will be required. The temptation to simplify learning by confining the pupil to a single approach, method or apparatus is likely to result in the formation of associations rather than concepts, thereby vastly reducing the likelihood of generalization and transfer. Thus, the exclusive use of one particular form of concrete teaching material such as Cuisinaire or Stern may facilitate the production of correct arithmetical answers but cannot in itself generate generalized thinking. The degree of conceptualization achieved in a vital area such as notation and place-value will define the limits within which the understanding of many mathematical skills and processes can develop. Conceptualization will be expected in areas as diverse as odd and even, symmetry, equivalence, ordination, classification and in relation to measures of length, distance, volume etc.

Developmental theory, particularly that associated with Piaget (1952) and his colleagues and further examined by Beard (1969), Donaldson (1978), Copeland (1974) and others, indicates that children pass through stages of intellectual growth which determine both the nature and the limits of the demands that can be made of them. For some low attaining pupils the stage of concrete operations on which a stable schema depends may not be attained until the late primary or even the early years of secondary schooling. The interpretations placed upon Piagetian theory may vary but it is undeniably the lot of many low attaining pupils to receive their basic grounding in mathematics at a stage that appears not to permit the formation of stable, permanent concepts. Perhaps surprisingly, the long-term effects of such practice has received little attention in research.

The Acquisition of Skills and Processes

Traditionally, the acquisition of skills, particularly those of an arithmetical nature, has tended to follow instrumental principles. In these circumstances, in the search for correct answers, the means become the ends with generalization and applications neither sought nor achieved.

In recent years, behavioural psychology has exerted a powerful influence on teaching strategies in many areas of special education. The progressive nature of skill acquisition in the four basic arithmetical processes would appear to lend themselves readily to the behavioural objectives model with its emphasis on clarity of objectives, rigorous task-analysis, step-by-step teaching and criterion-referenced assessment. Successful application of developmental principles, applied insightfully, can promote positive thinking on the part of both teacher and pupil. The latter is regarded as an achiever at his basal (starting) level, permitting dispensation of comparative and deficit notions — slow learning, under-achieving, remedial — as the only comparison to be made is with the pupil's own performance. Uncertainty as to curricular objectives, deplored by Brennan (1979) in his *Slow Learner Curriculum Report*, is clearly not applicable in circumstances where the objectives model is competently applied.

Lawton (1983) and others have strongly criticized the use of behavioural principles in education. Tyler (1973) laments the failure to distinguish between the learning of highly specific skills for limited job performance and the more generalized understanding, problem-solving skills and other kinds of behavioural patterns that thoughtful teachers seek to help students develop. In precision teaching, a rigorous exemplar of behavioural strategy, though it is pointed out that the method used to obtain the objective is left for the teacher to decide, both the principles and the strategy are entirely structural. Precision teaching, maintains the authors, 'is centrally concerned with the rate at which the pupil responds' (Williams, Muncey and Winteringham, 1983). Within such an approach, the likelihood of the pupil actively seeking alternatives, making explorations, experimenting with strategies and discovering relationships would appear unlikely.

The objectives model has limited diagnostic significance. The identification of the pupil's basal level by means of criterion-referenced assessment carries no implication that the preceding composite stages have been completed with understanding. An older pupil may well have reached an identified basal level many times before and experienced failure in attempts to proceed beyond it through lack of understanding at an earlier stage, particularly in relation to differing aspects of place-value. Diagnosis of skills and processes will depend upon a willingness on the part of the teacher to give sufficient examples at the breakdown stage to classify the nature of the errors made. These are frequently related less to inaccuracy than to faulty thinking regarding the early basic notational concepts and procedures. This is a major topic in itself but suffice to state that corrective procedures, to be successful, may necessitate reversion to the earliest stages of concept development, stressing relationships and understanding and making use of a variety of concrete materials.

The Acquisition of Facts and Knowledge

'A common pattern, particularly with lower ability pupils, was to show a few examples on the board at the start of a lesson and then set similar exercises for the pupils to do on their own' (HMI *Secondary Survey* DES, 1979).

Emphasis of this sort on the following of given routines, other than in relation to concepts, processes and knowledge already possessed, is unlikely to provide the foundations for future success, particularly in the case of those pupils whose short-term memorization is poor. Cockcroft (DES 1982) maintains that information is stored better 'if it is assimilated in such a way that it becomes part of a network of associated and related items which support one another'. The information involved may be related to a knowledge of multiplication tables, the number of centimetres in a metre, the value of pi or any factual aspect of mathematics. The most commonly utilized facts are those associated with the so-called number bonds (4 + 3 =

7, 9 − 1 = 8 etc), successful acquisition of which is likely to be promoted by the application of relational principles:

1   Provision of a variety of simple situations from which pupils are enabled to make up their own sums. 'Sue has four books, Tom has three. How many have they altogether?' Familiarization with this practice will largely replace the '4 + 3' of the sum book. The situations will, of necessity, be clearly defined, particularly in the early stages.

2   Having available a variety of structural and other materials to enable pupils to create concrete analogues of the situation in hand (Dienes 1973). Variability principles are a reminder that pupils differ in the manner in which they conceive relationships, thus emphasizing the necessity for a variety of materials and approaches. The pupil conditioned to accept a particular juxtaposition of rods to represent an arithmetical process using only one type of material is unlikely to make generalizations, failing the introduction of other analogue forms.

3   Providing and structuring situations in which pupils are enabled to develop appreciation of simple applications of the fundamental mathematical laws such as those governing commutativity ($3 + 4 = 4 + 3$; $3 \times 4 = 4 \times 3$) and the complementary nature of the relationships between the basic processes ($3 + 4 = 7, 7 - 3 = 4$; $3 \times 4 = 12, 12 \div 4 = 3$). Early experiments in classification with sets provides the foundation for these applications.

4   Ensuring adequacy of practice and reinforcement, not through simple repetition but through seeking opportunities for further explorations with differing materials in practical situations.

5   Considering the use of calculators. Pupils who have devised their own sums on the basis of their understanding of a given situation should have access to a variety of strategies, including the use of calculators. A prerequisite to their use with all pupils, but particularly with low attainers, will be their ability to provide an estimate or approximation of the outcome of the calculation. Their inability to do so is likely to be an indication of instrumental teaching. In such circumstances, to persist in their use may well be counter-productive, resulting in little more than mechanistic button-pressing.

The Development of Problem Solving Strategies

Within the initial statement on teaching aims, problem-solving was per-ceived as occupying a central position. Its fulfilment will involve the necessity to appreciate the relationship between skill-development and skill-using, thereby achieving a working balance between means and ends. Where this relationship has not been achieved, Cockcroft (1982) contends that teachers have tended to excuse the lack of situation-based teaching by reference to difficulties with skill-development. A veritable revolution in attitude and approach will be required if teachers such as these are to accept the implications of perceiving problem-solving as a primary aim. Present day emphasis on explorations and investigations is bringing realism and vitality to mathematics teaching. It must be assumed that low attaining pupils have a right to their share of the excitement, not solely for motivational reasons, but also because it conveys the means of achieving ends which are essential to the quality of life they have a right to expect. It follows that it is necessary both to define and to analyze the aims and means of problem-solving so as to determine those aspects where re-consideration may be necessary if the needs of the low attaining pupil are to be met.

A project which has achieved international acclaim and made a major impact in the world of mathematics is United Sciences and Mathematics in Elementary Schools (USMES) originating in Boston (Loman, 1976) Its emphasis is strongly based upon reality in that it recommends that problems should:

— have immediate, practical effect on pupils' lives;
— have no 'right' solution;
— require students to use their own ideas about what the problem is and how to solve it;
— be able to be resolved by students;
— be 'big' enough to require many phases of class activity for any effective solutions.

This model has been accepted and further developed within a British context by the Open University (1980) in its *Mathematics Across the Curriculum* course.

It can be assumed that whilst teachers of low attaining pupils would subscribe to the desirability of achieving problem-solving abilities at this level, few would consider them likely to be able to do so. If it is deemed unrealistic to expect the low attainer to develop a problem-solving capacity in USMES terms, an adaptive strategy is required that will identify and provide intermediate objectives which, whilst having curricular validity in their own right, may also encourage and lead to the wider fulfilment of the USMES aims. It can be argued that two of the criteria represent ultimate, rather than intermediate, aims:

Problems having no 'right' solution

The capacity of the individual to deal with open-ended problems is dependent on a preliminary ability to identify and process selective data from a situation to produce a 'right' answer or solution. The Advisory Council for Adult and Continuing Education (ACACE) Report indicated that many adults, even at simple levels, are unable to do so. To check change, to total amounts of money spent, to calculate the number of shopping days to Christmas and to determine speed on the basis of knowledge of time and distance call for applications of arithmetical processes with confidence, speed and accuracy. That the situations are convergent rather than divergent, susceptible to only one correct answer, in no way diminishes their significance.

'Big' problems

Wide-ranging projects in which multi-dimensional explorations are conducted by groups within a class are likely to demand acquired levels of social maturity, mathematical skill and confidence and investigational strategies beyond the competence of low-attaining pupils. Their teacher thus will seek to develop an approach, which, whilst retaining long-term aspirations towards participation in wider investigations, proceeds towards them with open-ended challenges of a more personal and limited nature.

The essentially conceptual basis of problem-solving abilities is such that there can be no ordered, step-by-step progression towards participation at higher-order levels, but three inter-related and overlapping stages can be identified. They are concerned with the ability to apply learned skills, processes and knowledge in personal 'closed' situations, in personal 'open-ended' situations and ultimately in class investigations of a multi-dimensional 'open-ended' nature.

Personal 'Closed' Problems

'Terry has £1 and wishes to buy coffees at 35p each for himself and two mates. How much more money will he need?'

The stages through which Terry must pass to bring an informed decision are as follows:

1 Identifying mathematics within a situation

Only in the classroom is the individual presented with pre-packaged sums. Nor, in real life, is there warning or indication that a problem involving mathematics is about to occur. Though in this instance Terry will have no doubt that he will need to draw upon his mathematical expertise, this may be less immediately apparent with situations involving more abstract concepts such as time, space and volume.

2   Identifying relevant elements within the problem

Only through identifying and interrelating the elements within the total situation can the relevant items be selected. Terry must identify:

The number of persons — himself, two friends
Cost of coffee per cup — 35p
Amount of money available — £1

In this instance there is no redundant information. Had Terry's problem included the cost of cakes, his weekly wage or the time of day, his conceptualization of the whole situation would have necessitated him to discard the irrelevancies. At this stage, the more realistic the problem, the greater the likelihood of effective discrimination.

3   Identifying the appropriate mathematical process(es)

In this instance, assuming a conventional approach to the problem on Terry's part, three arithmetical processes are identified:

Number of persons — $(1+2)$ — addition
Cost of coffee — $35p \times (1+2)$ — multiplication
Shortfall in money — $[35p \times (1 + 2)] - £1$ — subtraction

The ACACE Report, however, indicates that in real life conventional approaches are frequently discarded in favour of more convenient, personalized, idiosyncratic pathways. Terry might well have used a form of progressive addition to determine the cost of the coffees and 'counted-on' to determine the shortfall between £1.05p and £1.

4   Estimating the answer

The HMI *Secondary Survey* (DES, 1979) asserts that pupils 'often saw no absurdity in elementary calculations which were wrong by a factor of 10 or 100'. The necessity for initial estimations throughout the problem-solving processes, though infrequently practised, is self-apparent. A gas bill for half a million pounds due to a misplaced decimal point is likely to be identified but miscalculations of a less dramatic nature tend to occur unnoticed by low attaining pupils. Had Terry's three coffees been calculated to total £10.5 rather than £1.05 it can be assumed that this would not have passed unremarked!

5   *Working out calculations*

The difficulty of the task will determine whether working out the required calculations will be done mentally, in written form or with the use of calculator or other aid. In real life, most calculations are mental and may involve approximation or 'rounding-up'.

6   *Taking answers back to the original situation*

Terry now knows that he requires a further 5p and it remains for him to make a minor, but informed, decision:

— he can beg/borrow the 5p;
— he can buy something cheaper;
— one person can go without coffee, etc, etc.

Whilst the application of the detailed procedure to a problem of this simplicity may appear to be an over-elaboration, as problems encountered become more challenging with an increased number of stages, more variables, harder calculations and less obvious interrelationships, it will be apparent that lack of competence or confidence at any of the stages as delineated can inhibit or prevent a successful outcome. The low attaining pupil may require specific support, explanation and practice at any stage. The teacher's aim will be to provide experiences and opportunities for questioning and discussion so that confidence will grow and progression through the stages become increasingly automatic.

Personal 'Open-ended' Problems

The complex and ill-defined nature of many real-life problems should not be underestimated and an important consideration for the teacher in introducing open-ended problems is the degree of control and intervention to be exercised. Too little help may lead to frustration; too much to decreased involvement and motivation on the part of the pupil. Hopefully, on the basis of the skills and attitudes engendered at the applications stage, the decision-making implicit in open-ended problems will be regarded by the pupil as a natural progression. In case of difficulty, the teacher has the option of attempting to simplify or redefine the problem for the pupil, to consider alternative approaches, to revise or teach those skills found wanting or to concentrate on those dimensions of the problem within the pupil's ability.

Contrived problems will be avoided. Capitalizing on situations as they naturally occur is perhaps a rarely attained ideal but sensitivity to the pupils' personal interests and activities will normally enable the teacher to identify appropriate challenges. Successful personal projects have included:

Financing major purchases — alternative ways of borrowing/saving
Financing outings/journeys
Costing pet-keeping
Costing hobbies/sports/motor-cycle usage
Designing/costing pigeon loft
Designing/costing major clothing items
Planning a garden plot — layout, costing etc.
Using material with minimum waste — fabric, wood, plastics etc.
Budgeting at all levels.

Multi-dimensional Class Problem-solving Projects

Participation in class investigations exposes the pupil to all the benefits of personal problem-solving experience with the significant added advantage of working within a social context. The acronym **PROBLEMS** is neatly utilized by the Open University PME 233 course to suggest a framework within which problem-solving at class level can be approached:

Pose the problem
Refine into areas for investigation
Outline the questions to ask
Bring the right data home
Look for solutions
Establish recommendations
Make it happen
So what next?

In adopting the acronym for classes comprised of or including low attainers, adherence to the basic principles takes precedence over a rigid interpretation of the model. Sensitivity and awareness on the part of the teacher will indicate the necessity and the nature of any intervention.

Pose the problem

Collective, rather than individual, interests will determine the choice of the theme for investigations. The teacher's role is that of chairperson, clarifying issues, interpreting uncertainties, protecting minority opinions and ensuring a hearing for the introvert and socially inadequate. As it is the intention that all pupils will be actively engaged on investigational activities, the chosen theme should as far as possible be accepted by all pupils as both a stimulus and challenge. A class of 14 years old pupils in a lower ability band had variously complained that of the leisure activities open to them in the district, many were too expensive to permit participation and others were reluctant to participate in particular sporting activities on account of uncertainties regarding scoring systems. In the ensuing discussion the decision was taken to accept 'leisure' as the basic theme and to invite suggestions from individual pupils on aspects in which they were interested. The following topics emerged:

Football	Keeping score	Wimbledon
Activities needing	at cricket	Card games
little money	Darts — scoring	Cinema going
Athletics — flat racing	Snooker — scoring	Swimming records
— long jump	Badminton — scoring	Table tennis —
— high jump	Clothes and sport	league and scoring
FA Cup		

Refine into areas for investigation

Outline the questions to ask

Still in class discussion, the teacher next sought to identify the areas of main concern to the pupils within the main theme and making use of the suggested topics. To the original suggestions centring on finance and scoring, athletic and swimming times and records emerged as centres of interest. The three main areas were designated 'costs', 'scoring' and 'measuring achievement' and were subsequently further refined to permit the formation of seven groups of between three and five pupils in each. The immaturity and instability of a minority of pupils determined the necessity to keep group size to a minimum, consistent with the nature of the task to be undertaken. The 'sub areas' of the topic web represented the area of enquiries for each group (see page 174).

Within the groups the nature of the investigations was determined and individual responsibilities decided. The teacher's assistance was needed in formulating 'questions to ask' so that individual enthusiasm and initiative was harnessed in such a way that the tasks undertaken were both credible and feasible.

Bring the right data home

The main concerns were the nature of the information to be obtained, how it was to be collected and the ultimate form of presentation to facilitate the 'looking for solutions' stage.

Sources of information were sought and forms of making surveys were

THEME   MAIN AREAS   SUB-AREAS   TOPICS

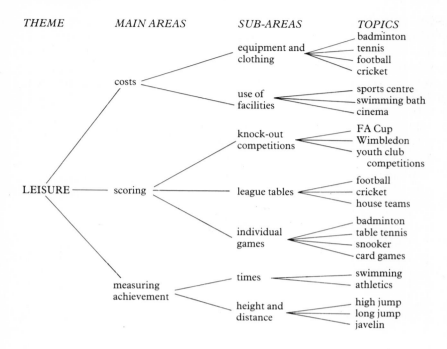

introduced. Skills involving frequency counts, tallying and various forms of measuring were introduced or revised. Amongst the groups, the weaker readers in the 'scoring in games' enquiry surprised themselves and their teacher by their ability to interpret formal rule books of games under scrutiny. Confusing variations of imperial and metric measures faced the 'height and distance' group in their search through records, necessitating familiarity with conversion tables. It was originally intended that the analysis of data would be confined to the respective groups with others involved only at the terminal reporting-back stage. With pupils insufficiently accustomed to the self-discipline implicit in enquiry methods, the teacher was probably wise to permit the collation and analysis of data occasionally to spill across group divisions as interest rapidly increased.

> *Looking for solutions*
> *and*
> *Establishing recommendations*

Only the loosest interpretation of 'solutions' was applicable at the reporting back stage. Drawing conclusions, even from a relatively ordered presentation of self-collected data tends not to come easily with low attaining pupils. The 'knock-out competition' and 'league table' groups compared the merits and demerits of their respective systems. The 'use of facilities' group devised a table of off-peak times when cinemas and baths lowered admission prices. The 'clothing and equipment' group cannibalized catalogues, etc, to produce an attractive chart indicating the price and location of bargains.

Problem-solving may involve the investigation of a narrower theme at greater depth with a greater degree of interdependence between the groups. As was the case with the 'leisure' project, however, the more immature and poorly motivated pupils are more likely to make a positive response in the pursuit of topics making an immediate personal appeal.

Making it happen

In the 'leisure' project, self-concepts and group morale were enhanced by the completion of challenging individual and group tasks and status accrued from the pupils' acceptance of the 'experts' role. The whole school gained from interesting data, attractively displayed, and from various innovations in the house sports scoring systems adopted on the recommendations from the project. For this particular class, however, it was less the products than the processes by which they were achieved that was of greater significance. A continuing necessity to communicate in mathematical terms, the obligation to develop a harmonious working relationship with a group, the abandonment of safe, skill-getting mathematics to face a challenge, the systematization implicit in presenting self-collected data and the self-respect engendered in following a difficult task through to a conclusion, went far to justify the use of the problem-solving model.

So what next?

Taking this question within the context of the **PROBLEMS** acronym, it can be argued that the pupils will henceforward be more likely to approach any form of problem involving mathematics with greater confidence. The quality of learning is enhanced when it is reflected upon and evaluated and a likely outcome of a 'leisure'-type project may well be the wish of the pupils to examine further the implications of their findings and to proceed cyclically to further problems and new solutions.

Within a broader frame of reference, 'what next' for the teacher of the child with learning difficulties in mathematics? The earlier formulation of aims drew for its substance upon the known characteristics of the pupils in relation to the nature of the society to which they must both contribute and adjust. Contemporary thinking in mathematical education embraces aspirations closely identified with those of low attaining pupils. That teaching approaches for their realization can be seen to be within the competence of the non-specialist teacher offers prospects for a future in this field that can be viewed with optimism.

Alec A. Williams

References

AINSCOW, M. and TWEDDLE, D. (1979) *Preventing Classroom Failure*, Chichester, John Wiley.

BEARD, R. (1969) *Outline of Piaget's Developmental Psychology*, London, Routledge and Kegan Paul.

BRENNAN, W.K. (1979) *Curricular Needs of Slow Learners*, Schools Council Working Paper No. 63, London, Evans/Methuen.

COPELAND, R. (1974) *How Children Learn Mathematics*, London, Macmillan.

DENVIR, B., STOLZ, C. and BROWN, M. (1982) *Low Attainers in Mathematics, 5–16*, Schools Council Working Paper No. 72, London, Methuen.

DEPARTMENT OF EDUCATION AND SCIENCE (1978) *Primary Education in England*: survey by HM Inspectors of schools, London, HMSO.

DEPARTMENT OF EDUCATION AND SCIENCE (1979) *Aspects of Secondary Education*: a survey by HM Inspectors of schools, London, HMSO.

DEPARTMENT OF EDUCATION AND SCIENCE (1982) *Mathematics Counts*, Report of the Committee of Enquiry into the teaching of mathematics in schools (Cockcroft Report), London, HMSO.

DIENES, Z. (1973) *The Six Steps in the Process of Learning Mathematics*, Windsor, NFER.

DONALDSON, M. (1978) *Children's Minds*, Glasgow, Fontana.

HART, K.M. (Ed.) (1981) *Children's Understanding of Mathematics, 11–16*, London, John Murray.

ILEA (1979) *Struggle*, details from Hackney Teachers' Centre, Digby Road, London, E9 6HX.

LAWTON, D. (1983) *Curricular Studies and Educational Planning*, London, Hodder and Stoughton.

LOMAN, E. (1976) *The USMES Guide*, Boston, Educational Development Centre Inc.

OPEN UNIVERSITY (1980) *Mathematics Across the Curriculum*, Milton Keynes, Course PME 233, Open University.

SEWELL, B. (1981) *Use of Mathematics by Adults in Daily Life*, Leicester, Advisory Council for Adult and Continuing Education.

SKEMP, R.R. (1982) *The Psychology of Learning Mathematics*, Harmondsworth, Penguin.

TYLER, R.W. (1973) 'The father of behavioural objectives criticizes them,' *Phi Delta Kappan* 55, 1, pp. 55–57.

WILLIAMS, H., MUNCEY, J. and WINTERINGHAM I. (1983) *Precision Teaching*, 3rd ed, Coventry LEA.

Teachers' Involvement in Curriculum Change

Mike Hinson
Head of Remedial Education and Advisory Department,
Sandwell Child Psychology Service

Recent Reports and Recommendations

Observers of the current educational scene can discern a gradual, yet growing awareness of the special curricular requirements of children with learning difficulties. The recommendations of national reports are gradually being translated at operational levels in schools and by local education authorities.

In the wake of the *Warnock Report* (1978) and the Education Act 1981 comes realization of the magnitude of the task to hand. The *Warnock Report* asserts that long-term educational goals for pupils with special educational needs are identical to those of all other children: firstly to enlarge children's knowledge, experience and imaginative understanding, and thus their awareness of moral values and capacity for enjoyment; secondly, to become active, responsible contributors to society, achieving as much independence as possible. These precepts are further underlined in *A View of the Curriculum* (HMI, 1980) and *The School Curriculum* (DES, 1981). In the latter document, paragraph 29 exhorts special schools, *like all other schools*, to offer curricula which effectively meet the educational needs of their children:

> They too need a written statement of their aims and, in the light of
> it, to appraise regularly the effectiveness of the programme offered
> to each pupil.

The very omission of any statement specifically concerned with pupils in the ordinary school leads one to the conclusion that its recommendations encompass *all* children, and that *all* will benefit from a broad and balanced curriculum. This being so, HM Inspectorate's checklist of eight areas of experience has equal application in the design of special curricula: aesthetic and creative; ethical; linguistic; mathematical; physical; scientific; social and political, and spiritual.

177

The *Warnock Report*, Brennan (1979), and Ainscow and Tweddle (1979) are equally critical of curriculum planning in remedial and special education. The emphasis has tended towards issues concerned with methods and materials, rather than with stating general aims and objectives. This leaves unanswered the fundamental question of, '*What* is it that we require the children to learn?'. McCall (1982) suggests four overall criteria: a clear *model* of curriculum planning is necessary; programme intentions and behavioural objectives need to be stated more specifically; the monitoring of needs should be linked with curriculum objectives, whilst record keeping procedures need to be curriculum based; finally, attempts should be made to ascertain clearly what constitute minimum levels of competence in basic skill or subject areas.

All local education authorities in England and Wales are involved in a critical appraisal of their curricula, in line with the requirements of Circulars 6/81 and 8/83. At the same time, the post-Warnock debate and enactment of the Education Act 1981 necessitates a review of arrangements for children with learning difficulties. There is evidence of three important trends within these processes, each of which is closely associated with curriculum development:

(i)   an increasing number of local education authorities are initiating programmes designed to help schools meet their responsibilities to children with special educational needs;

(ii)   this is resulting in a reappraisal of the traditional role of the remedial teacher;

(iii)   there is growing concern amongst subject specialists about the classroom problems faced by one-fifth of the school population. As a result, they are seeking informed help and support in the planning of effective curricula.

The purpose of this short chapter is to review recent developments in some of the major subject areas, in the light of these trends.

National Responses

One of the most dramatic examples of changes in classroom practice stems from a progress report published by the Scottish Education Department (1978). This regards all staff as being responsible for coping with pupils in their own classes who have learning difficulties. Joint approaches to curriculum development are suggested through the medium of team teaching shared between remedial specialists, class teachers and subject specialists. A number of areas responded to this report in a positive manner. For example, the Grampian Region Education Authority has initiated a major shift away from withdrawal groups and special classes towards team teaching as part of a comprehensive policy of education. An evaluation of the pilot scheme is fully described by Ferguson and Adams (1982).

Local education authorities in England and Wales have made a guarded, yet favourable, response to the *Warnock Report* and Education Act 1981. So far, most have been coping with the pressures resulting from the Act's bureaucratic demands and it is likely to be some time before a clearer picture emerges of progress towards its wider intentions and their consequent effect upon curriculum development. Muncey (1983) has outlined Coventry's SNAP (Special Needs Action Programme) initiative which is a good example of systematically organized local provision designed to help primary school teachers in their response to pupils' special educational needs. Similarly, a group of local education authorities in the South East have developed *One Child in Five*, a resource pack intended for use in ordinary schools. The notion that all teachers should be teachers of children with special needs is, for the majority, a radical departure from practices engendered during the past forty years. The devisers of these programmes do not underestimate the day-to-day problems which are likely to arise in the process of their implementation. Their strength lies in practical suggestions, based on sound theoretical principles, and their emphasis on strategies which involve classroom teachers in a positive way. One important factor which emerges is that no major initiative is likely to succeed unless it has the general support of the headteacher, and a special needs coordinator of sufficiently high status in the hierarchy to influence positively the ethos of the school and the remainder of the staff.

The 'Whole School' Approach

Most secondary schools in England and Wales continue to operate either special classes or withdrawal groups, or a combination of both. Remedial education tends to be concentrated on the 11–14 age range with little provision for 14–16 year olds, although many schools regard the work of lower sets in English and mathematics as fulfilling this role. *Aspects of Secondary Education in England*, (DES, 1979) shows that all types of secondary schools experience difficulties in providing for their 'less able' pupils. Curricula tend to lack coherence, whilst the programmes offered are seldom successfully pitched at a level which both 'retains interest and demands worthwhile achievement'.

Gordon and Wilcox (1983), regarding the time as ripe for change, cite joint meetings between NARE and secondary headteachers' organizations at which joint dissatisfaction was expressed regarding present provision for pupils with special educational needs. Dyson (1981) gives a realistic view of the difficulties encountered in effecting any form of change in organization and curriculum:

> If, as a remedial teacher, you wish to change what the school does to your children, a string of learned references to the latest research in the next staff meeting will not help you much. The Director of the

sixth-form still won't accept that his classes should get bigger so that yours can get smaller. The decision will go in favour not of the one with intellectual power, but of the one with political power.

If attitudes in the higher echelons do, at last, show signs of moving in favour of their charges with learning difficulties, then such opportunities should be seized upon with alacrity. Gordon and Wilcox call for the development of a 'whole school' approach based on the following principles: the amount and nature of support should be geared to pupils' individual needs; assessment of these needs should be a continuous process; withdrawal help ought to be a partnership between teacher and pupil in which true regard is given to the pupil's feelings and perceptions; resource areas and support teachers should serve the whole school.

Lewis (1984) stresses that remedial teachers must disclaim the myth that teaching pupils with special needs requires approaches, methods and techniques unavailable to, or outside the repertoire of, subject teachers. In describing the range of help that his Support Service offers to pupils and colleagues, he points out that the 'remedial department' can positively encourage subject specialists to accept a greater responsibility for those pupils who experience learning difficulties. In his school, a professional dialogue is established, thus encouraging joint development and partnership in subject planning, teaching and curriculum review. Even if, in the early stages, they do little more than adapt or modify teaching materials, subject matter will then become relevant, interesting and accessible to its recipients.

Individual secondary schools *are* showing greater concern about the effectiveness of existing curricula for Warnock's 'fifth'. Predictable, and to some extent justifiable, grumbles concerning falling roles, consequent staffing difficulties, examination pressures and meagre resources are still, too often, used as excuses for doing very little. Meanwhile, the 20 per cent become progressively frustrated, disillusioned and stroppy. Granted that there are more problems to be overcome in secondary education. Pupils who are the intended recipients of such curricular concern do not necessarily have the engaging personal qualities of younger age groups. Issues can also become clouded by inter-departmental jealousies and by aspiring empire builders.

Changing Staff Attitudes

The traditional role of the remedial department might well have caused remedial specialists to be reticent in their approaches to other departments, and vice-versa. For example, a recent survey of geography teaching, based on a sizeable sample of secondary schools, did not reveal any inter-departmental cooperation between geography specialists and staff in remedial departments.

The fundamental problem seems to be that of changing staff attitudes.

Remedial specialists are genuinely concerned about the welfare and integration of those pupils for whom they are responsible. This concern ought to become the spur for action, the motivation to act as change agents. In the present educational climate in schools, it would be unusual not to find at least one subject department anxious to cooperate. Colleagues can agree on the nature and extent of the help required. The most obvious manifestations of teachers' understanding and cooperation in curriculum planning will show in pupils' improved attitudes to lessons. Such tangible results are likely to encourage other departments to take the plunge. Such changes won't necessarily cost a great deal, nor disrupt the timetable, but they *will* take time to initiate. In the paragraphs which follow are details of some of the most recent developments along these lines.

History

History teachers are becoming increasingly concerned about the survival of their subject in schools. There is evidence that half of all pupils over the age of 14 have ceased to study the subject. Apparent lack of interest might stem from competition with newer subjects and the failure of a number of specialists to revitalize their approaches. Some reassurance has come from the present Education Secretary, Sir Keith Joseph (1984), who states that history should be included in every child's timetable up to the age of 16. He has called for a clearer view of objectives in history teaching and the elimination of 'clutter'. He uses this term to refer to those parts of the curriculum which emphasize the accumulation of unrelated facts or over-repetition of themes at the expense of a serious quest for the truth on the basis of evidence.

In similar vein, West (1980 and 1983) asserts that history for children is not a matter of collecting and storing inert information about the past. Some teachers are misled by their preoccupation with the content of history, as opposed to the processes of learning and understanding. In a four-year longitudinal study of 1500 children in the 7 to 11+ age range, West has demonstrated that primary children are capable of forming and using the essential concepts, also of practising the skills necessary to develop their sense of the past. He shows that they can consolidate and adapt the concept of evidence from the age of 7.0 years, if not before. He finds that tangible oral and pictorial evidence are most productive of their reasoning. Since test items in the study are mainly non-verbal, the real and not inconsiderable abilities of 'less able' children are revealed, even though they may have scored poorly on other, more conventional tests of ability and attainment. The classroom development of the Dudley project is based on pupils' first-hand experience of artefacts, pictures and documents. This is organized in a group situation where the teacher's role is that of enabler, adjudicator and guide.

Hallam (1982) makes a helpful contribution to the teaching of history to children with learning difficulties in his critical appraisal of various approaches. He suggests a developmental approach for pupils in the 9–14 age range.

A recent and valuable handbook for teachers entitled *Teaching History to Slow-Learning Children in Secondary School* (1982), has its origins in summer schools organized by the Department of Education, Northern Ireland (DENI) during 1979 and 1980. On these occasions, history teachers and remedial specialists came together in an attempt to define aims and objectives, survey teaching methods, and generally share experiences and expertise. Over a two-year period, many course members participated in follow-up work on these topics:

Group One	The beginning teacher and the slow-learning child
Group Two	Criteria for assessing the usefulness of history text-books
Group Three	The design and use of worksheets
Group Four	Local history studies and history trails for slow-learning children
Group Five	Survey of resources for teaching slow-learning children
Group Six	Syllabus design in history for slow-learning children.

The strength of this handbook, edited by Vivian McIver and published in association with Stranmillis College, Belfast, lies in its systematic approach to problems expressed by both history and remedial teachers. Although some items refer specifically to Northern Ireland, much of the content has relevance to teachers in other parts of the United Kingdom.

Geography

The teaching of geography to pupils with learning difficulties has become an issue of growing concern to subject specialists. Williams (1982) identifies problems associated with *graphicacy* as being some of the most evident of those experienced by pupils. The word 'graphicacy' is defined as 'the communication of spatial information that cannot be conveyed adequately by verbal or numerical means,' particularly through photographs and maps. In a recent article, Catling (1984) presents a variety of ideas that he has developed with primary school children, enabling them to become actively involved in the idea of map reading. He stresses that, when working with 'less able' pupils, it should be constantly borne in mind that developing a sound understanding of the principles, concepts, methods and uses of mapwork is as complex as the development of language and mathematical skills. The Geographical Association has produced a comprehensive handbook (Mills (Ed.), 1981) which reflects recent developments in geography teaching in primary and middle schools. Original approaches and ideas are outlined by practising teachers, including the basic structure of a syllabus for the 5–13 age group.

In response to increasing numbers of requests for help and advice, the Geographical Association has initiated an enquiry into the teaching of 'less able' pupils in the 11–14 age range. This is being undertaken by its New Techniques and Methods Working Party who published its first report in 1982. It identifies four key issues:

(i) Who are the 'less able' pupils? — the report calls for further clarification of the criteria for assessing the needs of these children. Its initial data show a range of judgments based on a variety of factors, from attainments in reading and writing to behavioural problems and socio-economic background. It is not surprising, therefore, that estimates of the proportion of less able in a particular year group vary greatly, or that the strategies for dealing with them range so widely. (No doubt this criticism could be levelled at other subject areas.)

(ii) Aspects of general living — the most common difficulties which less able pupils experience in geography lessons appear to be concerned with: low attainments in reading, writing and numeracy; ability to generalize and abstract ideas; retaining information; concentration span, and the appreciation of other people's viewpoints. The Report argues that geography could play a more significant role in pupils' personal and social development by utilizing local issues and environmental problems as part of curriculum content and making more effective use of group work, creative activities, also those which foster oracy.

(iii) Characteristics of geography — the fascination of faraway places, the 'enjoyment of land-form recognition' and the stimulus of local-based work might represent appropriate starting points. Apparently, many teachers do not attempt to carry out geographical fieldwork with these pupils, yet evidence suggests a strong relationship between achievement in mapwork and involvement by pupils in outdoor activities.

(iv) Teaching strategies — the report recommends that further work should be carried out to explore the potential of resource-based enquiry; drama and creative work; structured worksheets; role-play and simulation, and the use of audio-visual aids.

The survey was based on interviews with heads of geography departments in a number of middle and secondary schools. Following its publication and a stimulating national conference held at Trent Polytechnic, the NTM group then embarked upon the preparation of a second publication. Its intentions are to provide advice, guidance and trialed examples of teaching approaches and will be published in 1984.

For more than a decade, materials emanating from the Schools Council Curriculum Development Project *Geography for the Young School Leaver*, have provided a mainstay in geography courses for 14–16 year old, less academic pupils. When first published, it set new standards in the presentation of interesting, relevant and challenging materials. Recognizing that 'less able does not necessarily mean less interested' (Higginbottom and Renwick, 1983), the Project seeks to extend pupils' experience and insights by drawing on their own experiences as starting points for enquiry. With the assistance of local education authorities and teachers, a nationwide network of working parties and regional coordinators has been established.

Science

Science is now regarded as an essential component of 5–16 education for all children. Over the past twenty years, a number of major curriculum projects have been initiated. Although overall opportunities for children to study science have greatly improved, the main emphasis has tended to benefit those of average and above average attainment.

In a stimulating, yet contentious, book, Driver (1983) asserts that science teaching needs to relate to what is familiar to children, not just at the level of the world of events and experiences, but also in 'their worlds of ideas'. In her view, insufficient attention has, so far, been paid to what is known about the development of pupils' thinking. Her ideas are supported by the work of Shayer and Adey (1981) who reveal a significant mis-match between pupils' cognitive development and the cognitive demands of science curricula intended for the secondary age range. As the result of administering *Science Reasoning Tasks* to a large population drawn from the 9–16 age group, these researchers suggest that Piaget's picture of cognitive development requires modification and that the ages of attainment for each stage are significantly higher that those originally suggested by the Geneva school. For example, Shayer and Adey show that at 14 years only 20 per cent of children are using even early formal operations. Below the 60th percentile, it is unlikely that pupils will develop beyond concrete operational thinking during the years of compulsory schooling.

Schools Council *Science 5–13*, a major Project which adopts a developmental approach, stresses that children's scientific understanding can best be fostered through investigations based on their interests and experiences in a familiar environment. The present writer is currently involved in a survey of science materials suitable for use with children who have learning difficulties. Evidence from teachers shows that *Science 5–13* can be readily adapted to any level from nursery to top juniors. It is particularly suited to situations where children work in groups, as children with learning difficulties can then be included along with other pupils who can help and guide them. The twenty-six units do provide teachers with a great deal of reading homework! A follow-up project entitled *Learning Through Science* was published in 1983. It has adopted a similar developmental approach and provides much needed pupils' materials to supplement *Science 5–13*. *Learning Through Science* is aimed at children who have reached Stage 2 (concrete operations) or Stage 3 (thinking in abstract terms), as described by Piaget. *Science for Children with Learning Difficulties* (1983) is a unit for teachers which is complementary to the twelve work card packs. It provides examples of ways in which scientific work can be planned and modified for children with learning difficulties. Both projects have relied heavily on teachers' participation at all stages of their development.

Teachers' observations reveal that most published materials, even those which purport to be for the 'less able', require further adaptation before they can be used with pupils who have learning difficulties. Examples of purpose-adapted schemes, based on a number of series, have emerged from schools in which science teachers and remedial teachers are working together. For example, a primary school in the West Midlands has produced its own 'jam jar' approach after careful perusal of several schemes and kits, including *Science 5–13* and the *Craigie kits* (Oliver and Boyd). Empirically-based work units are intended to develop the skills of observing, explaining, communicating and experimenting. Members of staff enjoy having specific objectives to work towards, especially as they develop a confident approach, even for those with little previous scientific background. Units are used in either a class or group format, individual teachers choosing the approach most suited to the needs of children with learning difficulties.

A secondary boys' school in Merseyside has designed its scheme for 11–16 year olds around *Centre Science* (Collins), *Open Science* (Hutchinson), *Science at Work* (Addison-Wesley) and *LAMP* (Association for Science Education). Covering a similar age range, the science department in a London comprehensive school uses: *Science Horizons* (West Sussex/Globe Educational); *Learning Through Science; Centre Science*, and *Science at Work*. The head of department writes:

> I have found, as a non-remedial teacher, that most teachers' guides do not explain clearly enough the approaches to be adopted for the slow learner ... There is a lot to be gained from studying any material which could possibly help them. However, the system which works best is the one that a particular teacher feels *confident* with.

A young teacher from the Home Counties has outlined the changing role of the remedial department in the comprehensive school in which she teaches. Besides team-teaching with the lower ability mathematics and English groups, she acts in a support role for second year mixed ability lessons in physics, chemistry and biology, using a syllabus based on *Science for the Seventies* (Heinemann). She helps children with learning difficulties by: compiling glossaries which explain difficult words found in wall displays; writes questionnaires which pinpoint the salient features of chemistry video tapes; produces worksheets to facilitate the drawing of diagrams and the writing up of experiments, and advises on the effective use of such techniques as cloze procedure. She sees this new role as being mutually beneficial to both departments. In return for her advice on basic teaching techniques, she feels that she is learning much about the particular problems involved in science teaching.

Some Guidelines

This chapter has outlined efforts being made to improve the curriculum for children with learning difficulties in just three subject areas, whilst recognizing that similar initiatives are being made in other areas, such as religious education. Nevertheless, history, geography and science, in addition to English and mathematics, continue to occupy a major part of the academic curriculum. They continue to cause the majority of difficulties for low attainers. A number of factors have emerged in previous paragraphs which can be summarized as guidelines helpful in future curriculum planning:

1   The 'Whole School' Approach

Due to the historical development of remedial education, the special educational needs in many schools have been conveniently delegated to low-status departments or peripatetic teachers from local support services. This has led to a lack of emphasis in providing a realistic and varied curriculum for these pupils. It is salutory that, in one form or another, science, history and geography have traditionally been accorded large sections of the school timetable, yet have remained relatively inaccessible to at least one-fifth of the school population. Here and there, we can find encouraging local initiatives. Recent discussions with subject specialists, eager to play a part, reveal certain priority areas which need attention if further initiatives are to emerge:

(a) Pre-service and In-service Training
Heretofore, courses on special educational needs have frequently been offered as options, rather than as a compulsory element in pre-service training. Yet an awareness of children's special curricular needs ought to be instilled in teachers from the earliest stages of their training if the wider ideals of the Education Act 1981 are to be realized.

Many subject teachers are acutely aware of the gaps of their training. Many would appreciate in-service education in order to help them cope more adequately with low attainers. This places a heavy responsibility on local education authorities, headteachers and special needs coordinators if curriculum planning is to become effective.

(b) Support Services

Subject specialists will not only need to work more closely with SEN support departments within their own schools, but also become aware of the range of support offered by LEA services. It is reported that teachers are often unaware of the regular visits paid by peripatetic staff, or are unsure of their function when they do visit.

(c) Working Parties

Many subject teachers would welcome opportunities to participate in working groups concerned with curriculum development, in cooperation with remedial and support colleagues. Such groups could best be organized by inspectors, teacher-advisers or local subject associations.

2   Developmental Factors

Historically, syllabuses and lessons have been based on teachers' own, often idealized, perceptions of a particular body of knowledge. Scattered bastions of the, 'Ram it in! Ram it in! Children's heads are hollow,' philosophy of education still appear to be surviving. However, there are encouraging signs of a growing trend towards the consideration of developmental factors in curriculum planning. Recent evidence from the *Concepts in Secondary Mathematics and Science programme* (CSMS), together with a substantial literature on cognitive development in other subject areas, at both primary and secondary school levels, adequately demonstrate that school curricula can no longer be dictated by tradition. Curriculum initiatives based on cognitive growth might be more complex to devise and more trouble to implement, but in the long run they will be of greater benefit to all children, not least those with learning difficulties. Brennan's (1979) four questions concerning content are still relevant: 'Is the curriculum real?'; 'Is it relevant?'; 'Is it realistic?'; 'Is it rational?' Evidence suggests that curricula which start from situations familiar to children obviously offer considerable advantages.

3   Social and Personal Factors

There is scope for, where necessary, the reform of personal attitudes. Improvement in the interaction between teachers and their pupils, teachers and their colleagues, also teachers and parents can create a healthy atmosphere for making educational decisions. There is ample evidence from a whole variety of countrywide parental involvement and community projects that such partnerships generate mutual trust and an all-round improvement in pupils' progress.

Additionally, teachers need to come to terms with two recent developments. With regard to pupils in the 14–18 age range, it has been argued that the ramifications of the Secretary of State's programme for low achievers and TVEI might have resulted from schools' previous lack of success in providing effective curricula for the pupils concerned. Be that as it may, it *is* important that teachers do not reject these projects out of hand. At the end of the day, they might well provide courses which, although limited in scope, are of lasting practical value.

Micro-technology is certainly here to stay, yet some teachers are still unsure about its educational importance. It is true that often children's home use of computers goes little further than playing games which are a variation of *Space Invaders* and that some of the software currently in circulation is of dubious quality. If anything, these facts should become an urgent stimulus to obtain some training and 'hands on' experience in order to make effective use of this new aid to learning.

In Conclusion

During the second round of discussions in the 'Great Debate', a headteacher grumbled that schools were beginning to suffer from 'innovation fatigue'. This he defined as a 'sloppiness' brought about by too much change. There has been no noticeable slackening of pace in the intervening years. However, far from being sloppy, schools have attempted to keep pace with a rapidly changing educational scene, and have made a poisitive, professional response towards curriculum development. Even so, aims and objectives are unlikely to be attained, however clearly defined, unless teachers are prepared to act as agents of change. A growing realization of this is now permeating curriculum planning for special educational needs to the lasting benefit of all concerned.

References

BRENNAN, W.K. (1979) *Curricular Needs of Slow Learners*, Schools Council Working Paper 63, London, Evans/Methuen.

CATLING, S. (1984) 'Building less able children's map skills', *Remedial Education*, 19, 1.

CORNEY, G. and RAWLING, E. (1982) *Geography and Less Able Pupils*, Geographical Association.

DEPARTMENT OF EDUCATION AND SCIENCE (1979) *Aspects of Secondary Education in England*, London, HMSO.

DEPARTMENT OF EDUCATION AND SCIENCE (1981) *The School Curriculum*, London, HMSO.

DRIVER, R. (1983) *The Pupil as Scientist?* Open University Press.

DYSON, A. (1981) 'It's not what you do, it's the way that you do it', *Remedial Education*, 16, 3.

GEOGRAPHICAL ASSOCIATION (1982) *Teaching Geography to Less-Able 11–14 Year Olds*.

GORDON, M. and WILCOX. S. (1983) 'Integration or alienation?' *Times Educational Supplement*, 9 September.

HALLAM, R. (1982) 'History' in HINSON, M. and HUGHES, M. (Eds.) *Planning Effective Progress*. Hulton/NARE.

HER MAJESTY'S INSPECTORATE (1980) *A View of the Curriculum*, HMI Series: Matters for Discussion, 11. HMSO.

HIGGINBOTTOM, T. and RENWICK, M. (1983) 'Springboards for change'. *Times Educational Supplement*, 2 December.

JOSEPH, SIR K. (1984) 'The value of history in the curriculum,' address to Historical Association's Conference, London, reported in *Times Educational Supplement*, 17 February.

LEWIS, G. (1984) 'A supportive role at secondary level', *Remedial Education*, 19, 1.

McCALL, C. (1982) 'Some recent national reports and surveys: implications for the remedial specialist', in HINSON, M. and HUGHES, M. (Eds.) *Planning Effective Progress*, Hulton/NARE.

McIVER, V. (Ed.) (1982) *Teaching History to Slow-Learning Children in Secondary Schools*, Learning Resources Unit, Stranmillis College, Belfast.

MILLS, D. (Ed.) (1981) *Geographical Work in Primary and Middle Schools*, Geographical Association.

MUNCEY, J. (1983) 'Launching SNAP in Coventry', *Special Education: Forward Trends*, 10, 3.

SCHOOLS COUNCIL (1972 onwards) *Science 5–13*, Macdonald Educational.

SCHOOLS COUNCIL (1981) *The Practical Curriculum*, Schools Council Working Paper 70, London Methuen.

SCHOOLS COUNCIL (1983) *Learning Through Science*, Macdonald Educational.

SCOTTISH EDUCATION DEPARTMENT (1978) *The Education of Pupils with Learning Difficulties in Primary and Secondary Schools in Scotland: A Progress Report*, HMSO, Edinburgh.

SHAYER, M. and ADEY, P. (1981) *Towards a Science of Science Teaching*, Heinemann.

WARNOCK, H.M. (Chairman) (1978) *Special Educational Needs*. HMSO.

WEST, J. (1980) *Children's Awareness of the Past*, unpublished PhD thesis, University of Keele.

WEST, J. (1983) 'Boundless curiosity,' *Times Educational Supplement*, 9 December.

WILLIAMS, M. (1982) 'Geography' in HINSON, M. and HUGHES, M. (Eds.) *Planning Effective Progress*, Hulton/NARE.

Beyond the Sabre-toothed Curriculum

Paul Widlake
Consultant, Community Education Development Centre,
Coventry

There is a famous satire which relates how, long, long ago, cavemen set up a school where the main elements in the curriculum were concerned with techniques for resisting the depradations of the sabre-toothed tigers, who were present in large numbers. The school flourished and the curriculum became well organized, with departments (headed by specialists who received extra allowances of meat and lived in the best caves) for tiger development, tiger habitat, tiger tracking, weaponry (sub-divided into spear-throwing, knife and close combat, and poisons) and general studies (strategy). Students came from great distances; it became the most famous school of its kind and many others were started on the same principles. But there was a change in climate, an ice-age commenced, the tigers disappeared. Still the schools continued to teach the well-established curriculum, turning out experts on sabre-toothed tigers into an icy world where their painfully acquired skills were not really much help.

The Satire is Too Close to Modern Britain for Comfort

It is well to remind ourselves of the scale, intensity and persistence of the phenomenon of unemployment. An excellent, non-polemical, fact packed book by Giles Merritt (1981) sets the scene not just nationally but worldwide and the statistics he juggles with are truly awe inspiring. Merritt's review of various estimates of unemployment indicated that they were nearly always too optimistic — though invariably denounced as alarmist by the government of the day when they first appeared. Moreover, these figures exclude the 'discouragement' factor — those so put off by the impossibility of finding any employment that they never enter the competition at all, which may add as much as 20–30 per cent.

This article originally appeared in Remedial Education (1984) 19, 1

It does not appear that the vanished manufacturing jobs will ever be recovered — at least this is Merritt's conclusion: 'it was the speed and ferocity with which the depression gnawed at the hard industrial core of the manufacturing base that began to provoke the greatest concern, for many of those job losses implied an irreversible contraction of the country's industrial muscle'. Summing it all up, including the still unpredictable impact of what he calls the 'micro-electronics monster', he rejects the view of the jobs crisis as an avalanche which will soon stop and from which Western economies will soon be able to dig themselves out. 'A more realistic analysis', he suggests, 'is that of a glacier, which beneath its surface is gouging away at our familiar economic, social and political structure, just as savagely as the glaciers which once landscaped the earth.' There is a close analogy with the changes that rendered the sabre-toothed curriculum obsolete!

The changes may be structural and irreversible; this is a fearfully difficult message to accept. This unwanted and unwonted leisure, which has been predicted for the future, may already have arrived. The gap between prediction and fulfilment of the prophecy reduces almost to vanishing point and nobody can begin to suggest what impact the microchip will have as it becomes more widely used and as new uses are invented. The only certain thing is that it will happen quickly.

The effects on individual lives are devastating. Unemployment is closely associated with ill-health, deep distress, child cruelty; its effects move on into the next generation. Under 25s are disproportionately represented and in some districts two out of three school leavers were unable to find work in 1981; for example, Redditch New Town in the Midlands had 74 per cent school leavers unable to find work, Preston, in the North-West, 66 per cent: 'unemployment will have become one of the most widely shared conditions outside the usual human experiences such as birth, hunger, sex, death'.

Pupils in schools are, of course, vividly aware of the facts of life about unemployment. There are curricular implications of many kinds, among which are that schools will have to take the responsibility for explaining about the disappearance of work and begin to pioneer alternative forms of occupying time. They can take the lead in producing a new attitude. There is still a stigma attached to being unemployed and one very unpleasant effect which philosophers tend to overlook or omit: a chronic shortage of money with which to buy the ever increasing range of consumer goods which the improved methods of production make available.

The Case for Changing Schools

Unemployment is only one of a number of factors which are bringing about vast changes in the structure of modern Britain. Everyone will have a personal private list and mine is as follows:

Paul Widlake

Figure 1   *Some Change Agents in Contemporary Multicultural British Society*

Family Structure   'Nuclear' family (F + M + 2C) no longer the only model: Divorce rate increased nearly 400 per cent since 1971; many child-rearing situations — single parent; dual rather than single worker families; re-constituted families (involving step-brothers and sisters, step-parents/families with adopted or fostered parents); extended families.

Employment   Changes in job content and locations; slower entry; earlier retirement; fewer hours; more training; structural unemployment affecting especially school leavers.

Increased Tension   Experience of breakdowns in law and order; increased crime rate; disaffection of minority groups.

Leisure   More disposable time available even for employed people; enforced 'leisure' for unemployed.

Technology and Communications   Television and videotape machines; computers provide alternative learning systems to schools; the 'new knowledge' explosion.

Schools which continue to act as if their walls were as thick as those of a medieval castle will find that they are perceived as being just about as relevant by their pupils. They *cannot* ignore the impact of the larger society. Every event in a pupil's life may have some bearing on his or her capacity to learn. When 'normal' individuals show an inability to learn in school, yet are perfectly capable of learning in other situations, one should be driven to consider what aspects of the society are creating negative attitudes to schools and whether changes are necessary in the schools themselves. It is obvious that attempts to treat learning difficulties cannot be confined to more and more intensive work with individuals, however desirable it is to increase our understanding of, and empathy with, particular pupils. Yet this seems to be the direction of many special education programmes in ordinary schools offering, for example, intensive language 'development' based on a teacher-provided, American originated programme such as *Distar*, instead of encouraging the use of language appropriate to school learning and personal growth, such as those used by the Vauxhall teachers (1982). I want to argue in favour of these pupils being given access to as much of the content of a 'normal' curriculum as is compatible with their skills and abilities; and where there seems any doubt, to err on the side of expecting too much rather than too little.

The processes by which we label pupils may turn out to be more seminal to the causality of learning difficulties than any other activity teachers engage in, and it may completely undo the benefits of the skilled tuition which is offered.

Teachers who have specialized in treating learning difficulties sometimes appear to be fearful that their own skills will become redundant under such a regime as has been advocated. A dynamic example to the contrary is the UNESCO World Literacy Project (1973) which started from the writings of Paulo Freire (1972), the Brazilian educator who has perfected a method that 'helps illiterates to awake from their lethargy and to participate, as subjects, in the development of their countries'. Thus methods which recognize the social context of learning actually extend the scope of specialist teachers and ultimately raise their status, even though at first they may seem to pose a threat. Schools must change, then, if they are to meet special educational needs in the last two decades of twentieth century. There is an inner dynamic, as has been shown, deriving from the urgent, unmet needs of individual pupils. But there are other fundamental changes in the structure of society which affect everyone and cannot be ignored by teachers if they are to have any credibility with their pupils.

Alas, it is certain that nothing much has changed in many secondary schools since Wilf Brennan and his team (1979) surveyed 'successful' work with slow learners in curriculum areas for 265 secondary schools. There were *no* successful courses at all in history and French; only 12 per cent were teaching successfully in the humanities and social studies; only a third in English and parenthood education. By far the most successful courses were those for school leavers in special and secondary schools (though fewer than half the schools had these). The point is that these courses were chiefly orientated towards a world of work and this, as we have seen, no longer exists for most of the pupils whom I prefer to call the 'hard-to-teach'. The challenges from within and without are such that no school can continue to teach its present curriculum in an unchanged form. The new conditions apply *particularly* to the hard-to-teach; any regime which concentrates on their difficulties and ignores their reactions to the turmoil around them is unlikely to be effective, even if feasible.

Schools, being so heavily involved in certification, are bound to experience problems in devising programmes for pupils with special needs. The increasing disenchantment of some of these groups provides an unanswerable case for fresh approaches. The starting point for successful innovation, it is suggested, should be a study of the processes of change in terms of the *people* involved: the teachers, the parents, administrative team, the pupils. A great deal could be learned if the latter group really had a hearing. First, I suggest, we ought to become more accustomed to the idea of paying attention to the views of the individual within the schools; then we ought to make every effort to involve the school with the community it serves, with other branches of the formal education service, with the opportunities being provided by the Youth Training Scheme and its variants, with every organization concerned with the creation of informal education opportunities. Learning is a life-long activity which only begins with schooling and the more eagerly this notion is accepted by schools and the more obviously it is demonstrated by the presence of a wide range of learners on the one site, the more likely it is that schools will retain some appeal for the hard-to-teach.

The case for change is easily made; the difficult part is to decide what changes are necessary and feasible, and how they can be implemented. Very fundamental questions have to be raised immediately, covering the full spectrum of possibilities, such as whether every pupil should have the opportunity to gain examination success (as some heads argue, for the most humanitarian reasons) or whether it would be better to abandon external examinations except for those requiring them for entry into higher education, leaving the time free for more worthwhile, personally relevant studies (as others, with whom I would wish to be associated, argue from equally humanitarian motives). The line of argument which stems from this position may be summed up as follows:

(a)   It is necessary and desirable to obtain relevant, usable information about the learning difficulties of all pupils with special educational needs, and to arrange for individualized learning programmes for those pupils.

(b)   It is not, however, sufficient to treat the pupil on an individual basis. He/she is a member of a multicultural society and subject to the same opportunities and stresses as everyone else. This has clear implications for the selection of curriculum content and for methods.

(c)   The pupil has to learn within the organization of the school, with all the values of its hidden curriculum. These are sometimes more important in determining whether learning occurs than the overt arrangements, and must, therefore, also be considered.

I have dealt with each of these considerations in detail elsewhere (Widlake, 1983). In the remainder of this chapter, I will refer to some examples of curriculum innovations which have successfully involved older pupils and draw some implications for the new roles of teachers who wish to bring about changes in schools and their curricula to make them more relevant to the needs of the hard-to-teach.

Examples of Successful Innovations

Mini Co-operative Companies

Mini Co-operative Companies are activities developed through the Clydebank/EEC Project (Bray, 1982). They provide an experience of the working world somewhat similar to those available through the Work Experience on Employers' Premises (WEEP) provided by the Manpower Services Commission but differ from it in important respects — and also from work simulation exercises — because in a Mini Company pupils are actively responsible as directors, managers, shareholders, workers and saleforce in their own scale enterprise. They make a real product, handle real money with which raw materials are bought and wages paid, the products are sold. They are enabled, through a species of action learning to experience managerial, industrial, social and economic aspects of being at work. Moreover, the pupils have to learn to co-operate with others through a committee system and in the use of management structures, where they participate in decision-making which may affect the whole group.

The experience in Clydebank suggests that it is perfectly feasible to set up a *Mini Company* within a school environment. It may be a course lasting one term, one afternoon a week; or another mini-company has slotted into the timetable with five periods (two double, one single) straddling business studies and the art room.

The role of the teacher is seen as vital, but the *Mini Company* is a learning experience not a teaching situation and calls for a changed relationship. In the Clydebank project the terms used were:

(a) initially, the adviser is an *amateur*;
(b) he/she becomes a process helper, if necessary, a *progress chaser*;
(c) finally, he/she might become a *resource person*, available when required, but no longer initiating the process.

Community Involvement

Quintin Kynaston is a mixed comprehensive school in North London drawing pupils from St John's Wood, Paddington, Queen's Park and Camden Town. The school became a comprehensive boys' school in 1969 and a mixed school in 1976. Over four years it has been organizing the curriculum so that courses emphasize the learning process. This is partly to support mixed ability grouping, which is used in all courses for the first three years, and partly to prepare people for continuing with their studies beyond school. Describing the process, the head recounts how the first paper describing the community education centre called for facilities far too radical to be taken seriously as a proposal, but did open a debate among staff, parents and governors on the possibilities of community education expanding the educational opportunities of the Quintin Kynaston site and within the community. The staff set up a working party, which worked with a group of parent governors on the preparation of a paper to the ILEA. This focused on the integration of compulsory school and voluntary youth activities which are usually managed separately. It was argued that bringing these together would enable pupils to volunteer for activities which would complement, extend and contrast with their work in school which was inevitably seen as compulsory and unavoidable. Voluntary educational activities would cater for the 11–21 age group. They would run from the end of school until ten at night and be open to pupils from other schools. Local community groups would be involved in setting up and managing these voluntary activities. The whole process took three years. It was described as:

'*A marvellous opportunity to think through a consistent educational philosophy for 11–21 year olds.*'

A school which has taken the process some stages further is Craigroyston in Edinburgh. This is of particular interest because the processes by which the school has been developing itself into a community school have been closely monitored with the aid of a grant from the Van Leer Foundation. Documents are available which demonstrate how a school staff can engage in this difficult transition. In setting the scheme for the transition, the school identified the main problems as follows:

> With the community, school was viewed as an alien institution — not least by parents who transmitted this attitude to their children — and there was no tradition of voluntary education beyond the legal school-leaving age; most students were lacking in self-esteem and regarded themselves as outside the academic category for whom they believed schools catered; the lack of access to cultural and recreational activities meant that students were isolated within the narrow limits of their impoverished community; the absence of good adult models for many students resulted in immature and socially unacceptable behaviour; the socially vicious circle in which the students lived meant limited choices for them in regard to their future life-styles.

The Craigroyston curriculum aimed to enable every student to develop capability, confidence, co-operativeness and caringness and attempted to do this by adding a number of elements to normal Scottish education. The chosen method by which the school has set about implementing this expansion of its interest was through a series of working parties, eleven in all, each of which was given responsibility for a different part of the evolving community-school relationship. One working party looked after *Commune*, a monthly community newspaper produced and delivered to 10,000 households. Another was concerned with the learning centre, which provided hardware and software to meet the educational needs of the more able student, and students (later 'people') with learning difficulties; others dealt with out-of-door activities, life-long learning, the under fives and so on.

A very thorough work-plan was prepared and each working party kept full minutes of its meetings. They place particular emphasis on aims and objectives and noted any re-statements of objectives giving reasons for the change and details of the way in which it was effected. The minutes are refreshingly frank and record failures as well as successes. It proved more difficult than was expected to involve adults from the community in 'outdoor/residential education' and 'design for living'; but the lifelong education programme was extremely successful in recruiting adult students to day school classes. The Second Year Work Plan built on the successes and attempted to remedy the failures. The project is being evaluated by the Scottish Council for Research in Education and their document will be essential reading for anyone involved in planning a transition towards a community school.

It is, of course, possible to move towards community schooling without undertaking such massive changes. For instance, North Westminster Community School, which serves the families and communities in a large part of Marylebone and Paddington and beyond, seems to be striking an effective middle course. An eloquent interim statement of policy by the staff and governors in the summer of 1980 opens with the ringing declaration:

> North Westminster is determined to be a school of excellence and declares itself to be a 'learning school', a 'family school', and a 'community school' . . . the pupils of the school come from a rich and impressively diverse range of communities with different cultural backgrounds, ethnic origins, indigenous beliefs, occupations, social family patterns, economic positions and mother tongues. We are determined that the curriculum, the activities and the life of the school should actively reflect this richness. (Marland, 1982)

Implications for Remedial Teachers

A survey of articles in *Remedial Education* over the last five years reveals growing support for the practice of withdrawal groups, within school retreat centres, or any form of provision which retains the pupils within the mainstream.

> My experience in remedial teaching has led me to believe it is crucial for children with learning difficulty to have a classroom in the main building and not a hut on the campus. We are aiming to integrate our pupils into the mainstream so why draw attention to them by placing them in a hut away from the mainstream.' (Eliz. Falconer Hall and Georgina Mitchell. (1981) 16, 1)

> My experience as head of the remedial department in a boys' secondary school of 1100 which operates both special classes and withdrawal sessions, shows that withdrawal is most valuable as an adjunct and a support to work in special classes or in regular English classes. (Doris Kelly, (1981) 16, 2)

While the greatest care has to be exercised in integrating special and remedial education (in part because special class pupils may be legally ascertained by procedures which occur mostly outside the school, and decisions regarding remedial pupils are generally those of the school itself), nevertheless, there are examples of departments which have successfully negotiated the different roles and have succeeded in providing an adequate, safe harbour for those children requiring special care, whilst also managing to reach out into the school as a whole and to provide expertise for those whose difficulties are more within the normal range. Wilson and Broadhead (1979) described one such example in which the aims of the special educational class were essentially those of all secondary age pupils, but were stated more specifically and in terms of learning behaviours. They were to:

1 develop understanding and acceptance of their own distinguishing and disabling features;
2 be sufficiently skilful to enable them to live as normally as possible in the community;
3 have an adequate self-concept;
4 be able to seek, secure, perform and retain a job.

In this school, remedial education was seen as a service available not only to pupils but also to subject teachers by members of the Guidance Department, which provided specialist teaching, particularly to remedy deficits in basic skills of literacy and numeracy through short-term, intensive involvement. Longer-term support was also provided, so that each pupil was working at maximum capabilities, and would still receive the full benefit of the school curriculum without being educationally handicapped because of the specific difficulty. Some pupils were very able, but had specific difficulties, while others learned slowly; differences in nature, cause, manifestation and treatment were noted and prevented any neat grouping arrangements. Pupils described as under-achieving came to remedial education only when the under-achievement had its roots in educational problems within the remit of the department.

Some examples of the short-term, intensive, client-orientated programmes provided by this Guidance Department may be helpful to others wishing to follow their pattern. They would provide supportive teaching in any of the following forms:

a single lesson for each of several weeks, spent on some aspect of a subject to allow the pupil to continue successfully with work in the regular class, where otherwise this small educational deficit could have hindered progress and confidence;

specific difficulty with one skill, for example, spelling, in pupils who could otherwise pursue an academic course of study and support in notetaking; retarded skills with a whole subject area, such as mathematics — pupils were withdrawn from such classes and taught entirely by remedial teachers; attempts were made to return pupils every six months with improved number skills;

treatment of retarded communication skills was usually shared with the English department — some pupils with very severe difficulty were withdrawn from classes to spend up to half their time each week on remedial work in communication skills, arithmetic and environmental studies. The other half of the week was spent on regular classes, again with support from and discussion between the teachers involved and arrangements were made with their subject teachers to overcome the effects of segregation from their peer group.

This continuum of different abilities and needs extended to special class pupils too; a near-infinite variety was revealed: very able, backward, dull, learning disabled, under-achieving; so that individualized educational programmes were the only practical response. Not all the work was undertaken in classrooms by the remedial specialists; very many teachers throughout the school helped either directly ('on loan') or indirectly, by using individual and group methods. Thus the department was in no way separate from the rest of the school and pupils' learning difficulties were discussed with class, subject and guidance teachers, social workers, the school doctor and speech therapist, and parents.

Moving Forward from 'Remedial Education'

The above model is an excellent one for meeting special educational needs in large secondary schools. It is notable for a number of features:

(a) It is an integral part of the school — yet has a clear identity.
(b) There is constant exchange between department staff and all other school staff.
(c) Specialist tutorial skills are abundantly available.
(d) There is great flexibility of provision, covering various forms of withdrawal and special classes as required.

Teachers in such departments tend to be community-minded in the sense that they expect to know and to involve parents whenever possible. They will be experimental and adventurous in their choice of learning materials and will be well-equipped to cope with the challenges of a broader-based community school. However, what has not been much in evidence in these accounts is the capacity to enter into and influence other subject areas by the provision of appropriate materials or the adaptation of existing ones.

A survey of twenty secondary remedial departments (Bailey, 1981) provided an encouraging account of the activities and attitudes of these schools but revealed a lack of expertise in some important aspects, including a reluctance to:

1 consider the use of parents and voluntary helpers;
2 use pupil interviews, staff questionnaires and parental reports;
3 involve themselves with remedial education after the third year;
4 work alongside colleagues in the classroom;
5 give advice to other colleagues on teaching handicapped pupils, reading development in other subject areas, preparation of curriculum materials and other techniques for use in the ordinary classroom.

Now these five activities seem to me to cover almost all that requires doing in creating a learning environment for special educational needs in the coming two decades; and it appears that the specialist skills available fall well short of what is required. Remedial education, when applied with the sophistication of the above quoted models, certainly provides an excellent springboard, but the skilled teachers who can help those who are ready to leap are not being trained under present conditions. It was considerations like these which led Manchester Education Authority to disband its well-organized remedial advisory service and to create in its place a *Language, Literacy and Numeracy Support Service* with the much wider brief of supporting teachers in the classroom. The Support Service began with a year's reorientation course and has gradually evolved its own systems, resources and techniques, growing to more than sixty teachers in the process. There is a case for developing teams within comprehensive schools to evolve in much the same way, tackling aspects of curriculum development as they go along. Alderman Callow School and Community College has, in fact, set up a 'support service' which, as well as operating a 'haven' and a well-equipped remedial resources area, offers help on other curriculum matters. It prepares, among other useful materials, 'support guidelines' one of which on producing worksheets, gives excellent advice on readability, writing and design, production, presentation of worksheets to pupils and evaluation.

But yet more is required, and it is for those who know about specific educational needs to become actively involved in curriculum negotiations. Dyson (1981) reveals a worldly-wise attitude in an article entitled: 'It's not what you do, it's the way that you do it'. The rational model of change provided in texts is about as much use as a street map to someone on the Underground. Curriculum change is a political business and his way round the problem was 'to open up my concerns to anyone who would listen', to set up a Working Party to consider the curriculum of low attainers, to invite everyone and to make the point that innovation is always a joint venture, thus offering the ordinary teacher an opportunity to influence decisions in the school, perhaps for the first time in his or her career.

Dyson's working party found that the problem was not simply that what was being taught was inappropriate but that the structure of the school and curriculum actually imposed that inappropriateness on teacher and pupil alike. 'If you ask someone to teach something called "geography" to a group of pupils with special needs for an hour or so a week over two years, the chances are you will get a watered-down version of what the teacher learned as geography at college.' To stop this happening, the curriculum has to provide enough flexibility for teachers to teach what they want and for pupils to learn what they want. Two-year courses had to go, it was decided, along with assumptions about studying a subject in depth. In a final act of sophistication, this working party abolished itself before the curriculum it has established began to be taught, 'so as not to be unduly influential in its application'.

What was achieved, according to Dyson's account, was that 'in a hierarchical, fragmented high school, it is now possible to consider what is taught to the less able without reference to traditional subject areas; there is a means for biologist to talk to woodworker and mathematician to historian ... the teacher can now think of teaching what he would like to teach and for the length of time he would like to teach it ... Moreover, he has a means of influencing high-level decisions which affect what he teaches ... the pupils have a way of choosing what they learn and hence of influencing what they are taught.'

Changes have been effected at Dyson's George Stephenson High School and a way forward from 'remedial teaching' has been pioneered. Teachers with interests in special educational needs have to become actively involved in breaking down the static curriculum ... they have to look at how decisions about their pupils are made in the school, at least as much as what those decisions are; and they have to find some way of improving their position at the bottom of the hierarchy so that they can play a dynamic role in curriculum decision-making.

Specialist teachers who wish to become effective in this area of school activity must have clearly articulated ideas about methods of teaching and about curriculum content, so that they know what to fight for. Faced with an entirely new population, they have in effect to create a new pedagogy. Existing systems are either irrelevant to this age group, or have been shown not to work very effectively.

References

BAILEY, T.J. (1981) 'The secondary remedial teacher's role re-defined', *Remedial Education*, 16, 3.

BRAY, E. (1982) 'The Clydebank/EEC project', *Journal of Community Education*, 1.

BRENNAN, W. (1979) *Curricular Needs of Slow Learners*, Schools Council Working Paper 63.

DYSON, A. (1981) 'It's not what you do, it's the way that you do it', *Remedial Education*, 16, 3.

FREIRE, P. (1972) *Pedagogy of the Oppressed*. Penguin (1973), *Experimental World Literacy Project*, (UNESCO)

MARLAND, M. (1982) 'North Westminster Community School', *Journal of Community Education*, 1, 3.

MERRITT, G. (1981) *World Out of Work*, Collins.

VAUXHALL MANOR SCHOOL (1982) *Becoming Our Own Experts*, ILEA, Language Centre.

WIDLAKE, P. (1983) *How to Reach the Hard to Teach*, Open University Press.

WILSON, J.M. and BROADHEAD, G. (1979) 'Integrating special and remedial education in a Scottish secondary school', *Remedial Education*, 16, 3.

Contributors

MURIEL ADAMS	Remedial Teacher, Portlethen Primary School
MEL AINSCOW	Adviser for Special Education, Coventry
SANDRA BERRICK	Head of Special Resources Department, Carterton School, Oxford
LOUISE CLUNIES-ROSS	Deputy Education Officer, Royal National Institute for the Blind, formerly Senior Research Officer, National Foundation for Educational Research
K.F. CORNWALL	Principal Educational Psychologist, Hampshire
J.B. EDWARDS	Educational Psychologist, North Wales
NEIL FERGUSON	Lecturer in Education, University of Aberdeen
CHARLES W. GAINS	Principal Lecturer in Special Educational Needs, Edge Hill College of Higher Education
MICHAEL GOLBY	Senior Lecturer in Education, University of Exeter
RONALD GULLIFORD	Professor of Special Education, University of Birmingham
JOHN R. GULLIVER	Adviser for Primary English, Devon
MIKE HINSON	Head of Remedial Education and Advisory Department, Sandwell Child Psychology Service
ELIZABETH JONES	Her Majesty's Inspector, Department of Education and Science, formerly School Counsellor, Banbury School, Oxford

Contributors

Mike Laskier	Peripatetic Remedial Teacher, Liverpool
Jim Muncey	Senior Educational Psychologist, Coventry
Ted Raybould	Senior Educational Psychologist, Walsall
Robin C. Richmond	General Adviser (Special Needs), Dudley LEA
Colin J. Smith	Lecturer in Education, University of Birmingham
John Solity	Senior Educational Psychologist, Walsall
Paul Widlake	Consultant, Community Education Development Centre, Coventry
Alec Williams	Principal Lecturer in Education, Bishop Grosseteste College, Lincoln

Index of Authors and Sources

Ablewhite, R.C. 31, 32, 33, 38
Ainscow, M., Bond, J., Gardner, J. and Tweddle, D. 45, 47
Ainscow, M. and Muncey, J. 60, 77–91, 81, 82, 89
Ainscow, M. and Tweddle, D.A. 80, 83, 89, 134, 143, 176, 178
Akerman, T., Gillett, D. et al. 89
Ames, T. 150, 159
Anning, A. 53, 57
Association for Science Education 185

Bailey, T.J. 44, 47, 71, 76, 199, 201
Barnes, D., Britton, J. and Rosen, H. 15, 19
Beard, R. 165, 176
Becker, W.C. 83, 89, 133, 143
Becker, W.C. and Engelmann, S.E. 80, 89, 133, 143
Berg, L. 147, 159
Bijou, S.W. 84, 89
Blackburn, S. 41, 47
Blackhurst, A.E. 84, 90
Bloom, B.S. 80, 90
Boardman, D. 26, 27, 28
Board of Education (1931) *Hadow Report* 13, 19
Board of Education (1937) *Education of Backward Children* 20, 22, 26, 28
Bond, J. and Lewis, A. 142, 143
Bookbinder, G. 79, 90, 158, 159
Booth, T. 47, 152, 159
Borg, W.R. 77, 90
Bray, E. 194, 201

Brennan, W.K. 26, 28, 31, 32, 33, 34, 36, 38, 47, 100, 102, 165, 176, 187, 188, 193, 201
Brody, E.B. and Brody, N. 127, 130
Burden, R. 153, 159
Burt, C. 12, 13, 19, 30, 34, 38, 42, 126–127, 130
Bush, A.M. 52, 57
Bushell, R. 40, 48
Butterworth, B. 158, 159

Cant, M. 44, 48
Carroll, H. 41, 48
Cashdan, A. and Pumfrey, P.D. 99, 102
Catling, S. 182, 188
Centre Science 185
Chalk, J. 104, 111
Charles, C.M. 84, 90
Chazan, M. 99, 102
Chesterfield, Earl of 46, 48
Christopolos, F. 103, 111
Clamp, S. 52, 57
Clark, M.M. 31, 33, 34, 37, 38, 42, 48, 51, 57, 99, 102, 146, 147, 159
Clark, P. 103, 111
Clark, R.J. et al. 56, 57
Clay, M. 146, 147, 149, 159
Clunies-Ross, L. 60, 63–76
Clunies-Ross, L. and Wimhurst, S. 63
Cohen, J.M. and Cohen, M.J. 43, 48
Coles, G.S. 146, 159
Collins, J.E. 41, 48, 51, 57, 99, 102
Cookson, C. 41, 48
Cope, C. and Anderson, E. 104, 111

Copeland, R. 165, 176
Corney, G. and Rawlings, E. 183, 188
Cornwall, K.F. 120, 123–131
Cotterill, G. 157, 159
Cowie, E.E. 26, 28
Craigie Kits 185
Csapo, M. 135, 143
Csapo, M. and Neithercut, A. 135, 143
Cuthbert, T. 41, 48

Dearden, R.F., Hirst, P.H. and Peters, R.S. 36, 38
DENI (1982) 182
Denvir, B., Stolz, C. and Brown, M. 161, 176
D.E.S. (1962) *Newsom Report* 21, 28
D.E.S. (1967) *Plowden Report* 12, 21– 22, 25, 28
D.E.S. (1971) *Slow Learners in the Secondary School* 8, 19, 21, 28, 63, 76
D.E.S. (1972) *Educational Priority Vol. I* 12, 19
D.E.S. (1975) *Bullock Report* 9–10, 16, 19, 21–22, 28, 48
D.E.S. (1977) *Education in Schools* 124, 131
D.E.S. (1978) *Performance of Pupils* 124, 131
D.E.S. (1978) *Primary Education in England* 124, 131, 162, 176
D.E.S. (1978) *Warnock Report* 1, 4, 22, 24–25, 28, 30–38, 44–46, 48, 52, 57, 77–78, 88, 90, 100, 103, 124, 131, 145, 151–152, 159, 177–180, 189
D.E.S. (1979) *Aspects of Secondary Education* 124, 161, 163, 166, 170, 176, 179, 188
D.E.S. (1979) *Developments in the B.Ed. Degree* 23
D.E.S. (1981) *Circular 6181* 178
D.E.S. (1981) *The School Curriculum* 177, 188
D.E.S. (1982) *Cockcroft Report* 161– 163, 166, 168, 176
D.E.S. (1982) *New Teacher in School* 23, 29
D.E.S. (1983) *Circular 1/83* 151, 159
D.E.S. (1983) *Circular 8/83* 178
D.E.S. (1983) *New Procedures, Press Notice* 151, 159
Dienes, Z. 167, 176
Donaldson, M. 165, 176
Driver, R. 184, 188
Dyson, A. 179, 188, 200, 201

Eaton, M.D. 140, 143
Eaves, R.C. and McLaughlin, P. 80, 90
Edwards, J.B. 4, 30–38, 42, 48, 51, 57
Engelmann, S.E. 83, 90
Evans, R. 44, 48
Evans, S. 112, 117

Falconer Hall, E. and Mitchell, G. 197
Farrell, P.T. 81, 90
Ferguson, N. and Adams, M. 60, 92– 102, 178
Feuerstein, R. 52, 57
Formentin, T. and Casapo, M. 132, 135, 143
Freire, P. 192, 201

Gains, C.W. 5, 31, 32, 33, 35, 36, 38, 41, 48, 50–58, 51, 52, 57
Gains, C.W. and McNicholas, J. 44, 48
Galletley, I. 46, 48
Gardner, J. and Tweddle, D. 141, 143
Garnett, J. 41, 48, 104, 111
Geographical Association 182–183, 188
Georgiades, N.J. and Phillimore, L. 80, 90
Gillham, B. 149, 159
Gillham, W.E.C. 126, 131
Glavin, J., Quay, H., Annesley, F., and Werry, J. 103, 111
Golby, M. and Gulliver, J.R. 4, 7–19, 51, 57, 153, 160
Goodman, K.S. 148, 160
Gordon, M. and Wilcox, S. 179, 180, 189
Gray, W.A. and Gerrard, B.A. 113, 117
Green, L. 42, 48
Gronlund, N.E. 134, 143
Groves, P. 156, 160
Gulliford, R. 4, 20–29, 35, 38, 40, 41, 48, 52, 57
Gulliford, R. adn Widlake, P. 15, 19, 26, 29

Hall, R.V., Copeland, R. and Clarke, M. 81, 90

Hallam, R. 182, 189

Hammill, D.D. and Larsen, S.C. 146, 160

Hannon, P. and Mullins, S. 46, 48

Haring, N.G. and Eaton, M.D. 135, 144

Haring, N.G. and Gentry, N.D. 133, 143

Haring, N.G., Lovitt, T.C., Eaton, M.D. and Hansen, C.L. 83, 90, 132, 144

Harrison, C. 154, 160

Hart, K.M. 162, 176

Hawisher, M.F. and Calhoun, M.L. 112, 114, 117

Hawthorn, H. and Carter, G. 11, 19

Heron, T.E. 115, 117

Hersch, R.H. and Cohen, S.J. 84, 90

Higginbottom, T. and Renwick, M. 184, 189

Hinson, M. 120, 177–189

Hinson, M. and Hughes, M. 26, 29

H.M.I. (1980) *A View of the Curriculum* 177, 189

Howell, K.W. and Kaplan, J.S. 83, 90

Howell, K.W., Kaplan, J.S. and O'Connell, C.Y. 133, 144

I.L.E.A. (1984) *Improving Secondary Schools Hargreaves Report* 47, 48, 50, 57

I.L.E.A. (1979) *Struggle* 161, 176

Ingenkamp, K.H. 127, 131

Jones, E. and Berrick, S. 60, 103–111

Jones, N. and Jones, E. 79, 90

Jones, N.J. 104, 111

Joseph, Sir K. 181, 189

Karlsen, B., Madden, R. and Gardner, E. 146, 160

Kelly, D. 197

Kemp, R. 28, 29

Kent, M. and O'Brien, T. 43, 48

Keogh, B.K. 78, 90

Kratochwill, T.R. and Green, L.M. 83, 90

Lacey, C. and Lawton, D. 41, 48

Larsen, S.C. 83, 90

Laskier, M. 5, 39–49

Lawrence, D. 33, 38, 41, 48

Lawton, D. 16, 19, 167, 176

Leach, D.J. and Raybould, E.C. 31, 32, 35, 37, 38, 139, 144

Leedham, J. 158, 160

Leeming, K., Swann, W., Coupe, J. and Mittler, P. 81, 90, 125, 127, 128, 131, 152, 160

Lerner, J.W. 112, 117

Lewis, G. 46, 48, 180, 189

Lewis, L. and Vulliamy, G. 152, 160

Lihou, H.A. 41, 48

Lindsay, G. 152, 160

Lofthouse, A. 52, 57

Loman, E. 168, 176

Lovell, K., Byrne, C. and Richardson, B. 99, 102

Lovell, K., Johnson, E. and Platts, O. 99, 102

Lovitt, T.C. 83, 90, 114, 117, 132, 133, 136, 141, 144

Lovitt, T.C. and Haring, N.G. 144

Mager, R.F. 125, 131, 134, 144

Makins, V. 79, 90

Marjoram, D.T.E. 124, 131

Marland, M. 116, 117, 197, 201

Marra, A. 45, 49

Marsh, G.E. and Price, B.J. 113, 117

Marshall, C.P. 79, 90

Martin, R.J. 113, 117

McCall, C. 71, 76, 178, 189

McCullough, S. 147, 160

McIver, V. 182, 189

McNicholas, J.A. 31, 32, 33, 36, 37, 38, 41, 43, 44, 48, 49, 51, 52, 56, 57, 58

Merritt, G. 190, 191, 201

Milburn, C. 158, 160

Miles, T.R. 149, 160

Mills, D. 183, 189

Milofsky, C. 40, 46, 49

Mitchelhill, B. 158, 160

Moseley, D. 30, 32, 34, 35, 36, 37, 38

Moss, G. and Childs, J. 80, 90

Muncey, J. 179, 189

Muncey, J. and Williams, H. 133, 144

Naisbitt, J. 50, 58
NARE (1977) *Guidelines 1* 32, 38, 43,
  49, 51, 58
NARE (1979) *Guidelines 2* 43, 49, 51, 58
NATFHE *Handbook of Institutions* 72,
  76
Norrie, E. 157, 160
Nussel, E.J., Inglis, J.D. and
  Wiersman, W. 84, 91

O'Hagan, F. 42, 43, 49
Open Science 185
Open University *Maths Across the
  Curriculum* 161, 168, 172, 176
Owen, S.H. 43, 49

Peter, M. 45, 46, 49
Peters, M.L. 156, 157, 160
Peters, R.S. 36, 38
Petrie, I. 45, 49
Piaget, J. 165, 185
Pirandello, L. 39, 49
Popham, W.J. 134, 144
Potts, P. 44, 49
Pumfrey, P.D. 40, 49

Raybould, E.C. 132, 144
Raybould, E. and Solity, J. 53, 58, 120,
  132–144
Reger, R. 103, 111
Reger, R., adn Koppmann, M. 103, 111
Reid, M., Clunies-Ross, L., Goacher,
  B. and Vile, C. 76
Remedial Education 4, 26, 30, 40, 51, 77,
  92, 112, 123, 190
Rhine, W.R. 83, 91
Richmond, R.C. 120, 145–160
Robson, C. 81, 91
Rosenthal, R. and Jacobsen, L. 51, 58
Rutter, M., Maughan, B., Mortimore,
  P. and Ouston, J. 51, 58

Sabatino, D. 103, 111
Sampson, O.C. 30, 31, 33, 35, 36, 38,
  39, 40, 42, 49
Schonell, F. 12, 13, 19, 20, 30, 33, 34,
  38, 42, 149, 156, 160

Schools Council *Concept 7–9* 158, 160
Schools Council *Geography for the Young
  School Leaver* 26, 184
Schools Council (1981) *The Practical
  Curriculum* 189
Schools Council (1982) *Low Attainers in
  Mathematics* 161–162, 176
Schools Council (1983) *Learning
  Through Science* 184–185
Schools Council *Science 5–13* 184, 185,
  189
Science at Work 185
Scottish Education Department (1978)
  *Education of Pupils with Learning
  Difficulties* 20, 22, 29, 153, 160, 178,
  189
Sewell, B. *ACACE Report* 161, 169, 176
Sewell, G. 40, 44, 49, 153, 160
Shayer, M. and Adey, P. 184, 189
Singleton, C.H. 149, 160
Skemp, R.R. 164, 176
Skinner, B.F. 139, 144
Smith, C.J. 43, 49, 61, 112–117
Smith, F. 147, 160
Special Education: Forward Trends 26,
  45, 103, 132
Stott, D.H. 152, 160
Strang, R. 148, 160

Tansley, A. 19, 31, 32, 33, 36, 38, 146,
  160
Tansley, P. and Panckhurst, J. 151, 160
Trickey, G. and Kosky, R. 49
Tyler, R.W. 166, 176

Vargas, J.S. 136, 144
Vauxhall Manor School 192, 201

Walsall Herald 142, 144
Warnat, W.I. 55, 58
Weber, K. 52, 58
Wedell, K. 80, 91
Wedell, K. and Lindsay, G.A. 79, 91,
  152, 159
Weiner, L.H. 103, 111
West, J. 181, 189
Westwood, P. 32, 35, 38

White, O.R. and Haring, N.G. 132, 135, 140, 144
Widlake, P. 41, 49, 121, 190–201, 194, 201
Williams, A.E. 120, 161–176
Williams, H., Muncey, J. and Winteringham, I. 166, 176
Williams, M. 182, 189

Wilson, J.M. and Broadhead, G. 197, 201
Winteringham, D.P., Morris, S. and Winn, M.B. 89, 91
Wolfendale, S. 41, 49

Young, D. 65, 76
Young, P. and Tyre, C. 146, 158

Index of Subjects

accountability 123–124
adjustment 20, 24–25, 104, 108
advisory services 4, 7, 21, 28, 40, 43, 45, 47, 70–71, 78, 109–110, 112–115, 200
allocation 68–71
ambulance service 4, 11, 13–14, 17–18, 153
areas of experience 177
arithmetic 84, 115, 142, 169–172, 198
assessment 10, 13, 24, 43, 46–47, 55, 67–69, 72, 83–88, 92, 104, 106–107, 112, 120–143
assessment of reading difficulties 145–159
Aston Index 146, 148
auditory skills 146, 149, 155–159

backwardness 12, 20, 30, 35, 51, 106, 199
basic skills 7, 10, 12, 16, 23, 43, 69, 74, 92, 94, 95, 97, 108, 135, 198
behaviour modification 79, 81, 116, 133, 141
behaviour problems 89, 155, 180, 183
Biology 94, 201
Bristol Social Adjustment Guide 68

class teachers 47, 88, 92–102, 107–109, 112–117, 199
classroom management 2, 22, 25, 43, 45, 73–76, 80, 112–117, 138
communication skills 113, 198
community involvement 70, 195–199

compensatory education 10, 41
comprehension 36
computers 37, 44, 52, 188, 192
concept formation and learning 27, 120, 164–165, 181, 182
consultant role 18, 28, 43, 47, 60, 71, 109, 111, 112–117, 153
co-ordinator role 44, 78–79, 82–83, 87–88, 179
counsellors 41
criterion referenced testing 83–87, 116, 120, 123, 127, 159, 165
curriculum based assessment 125–130, 152–154
curriculum development and adaptation 7, 13–18, 26–28, 52, 60, 68, 70, 73–76, 99, 120–121, 142, 153, 177–201
curriculum, normal or mainstream 4, 10–11, 13–15, 17, 42–43, 47, 63, 71, 80, 104, 106, 145, 152

daily recording and measurement 89, 134–135, 143
Daniels and Diack Reading Tests 67, 150, 155, 158–159
diagnosis 9, 32, 40, 100, 109–110, 112, 123, 130, 154, 166
Diagnostic Spelling Test 156–157
direct instruction 133, 143
dyslexia 42, 109, 120, 145–159

Education Act, 1944 13

Education Act, 1981 1, 28, 43–44, 46–47, 52, 88, 145, 151–152, 178–179, 186
educational psychologists 7, 44, 81–83, 87, 106, 125–127, 142
emotional difficulties 33, 42, 63, 67, 89, 108, 153, 163
employment 190–195
English 66, 68, 73–75, 93, 98, 100, 179, 186, 193
Environmental studies 25–26, 198
error analysis 130, 148, 166
E.S.N.(M) 34, 104, 108, 142, 150
E.S.N.(S) 35, 108, 125
evaluation 109, 123–130, 132

Further Education 75–76

Geographical Association 182–183
Geography 25–27, 93, 100, 120, 180–184, 186, 200
giftedness 106

History 9, 25–27, 93–94, 120, 181–182, 186, 193, 201
holistic approach 146
Home Economics 93, 96, 100, 102
Humanities 15, 68–69, 72, 74–75, 104, 109, 193

Illinois Test of Psycholinguistic Abilities 146, 148
individualised treatment 12, 14, 88, 100, 104, 108–110, 120, 127, 151, 154–159, 180, 194
informal reading inventory 130, 148
instrumental learning 164–165
integrated studies 94
integration 1, 7, 44, 60, 99, 107–110, 120, 181, 197
intelligence 10, 30, 51, 110, 125–127, 149
intensive learning group 155–159

language 25, 72, 84, 142, 147, 153, 155, 163, 192
learning difficulties 1, 12, 22, 24, 26, 32, 34–35, 40, 64, 69, 74, 77–89, 102, 112, 114, 117, 120, 145, 152–159,

161, 175, 177, 182–188, 192–194, 198
less able pupils 63, 182–184
literacy 2, 9, 10, 13, 14, 15, 16, 18, 65, 69, 72–75, 145, 153–159, 198
low achievers 21, 23, 25–28, 182, 188
low attainers 161–164, 175, 186, 200

maladjustment 106, 108, 110
mastery 52–53, 86, 139–140, 142, 143
Mathematical Association 161–162
Mathematics 23, 27, 66, 68, 72–75, 92, 97, 100, 106, 120, 161–175, 177, 179, 186, 198, 201
medical model 32, 34–37, 80, 153
memory 115, 132, 166
miscue analysis 148
mixed ability teaching 23, 63, 65, 74, 109, 112
Modern Languages 73, 193
Moral Education 26
multicultural background 106, 197

National Association for Remedial Education (NARE) 2, 4, 26, 32–33, 35, 40, 43, 51, 57, 69–71
National Association of Teachers in Higher and Further Education (NATFHE) 72, 76
National Council for Special Education (NCSE) 45
National Foundation for Educational Research (NFER) 63–76, 130
Neale Analysis of Reading Ability 67, 156
norm referenced testing 12, 120, 123, 127, 135, 150
numeracy 13, 16, 36, 65, 108, 116, 142, 161–175, 198

objectives 28, 37, 60, 81, 83–88, 100, 125, 127–129, 134, 140–141, 165, 181, 188

paired reading 156
parental involvement 40, 66, 70, 107, 142, 187, 193, 199
pastoral care 106
pathology 9, 12, 32

perceptual skills 147
peripatetic teachers 28, 40, 43, 69, 78, 110, 186
phonic skills 146, 148, 150, 155
physical handicap 42, 104, 106–109
Physical Education 75
physiotherapist 106, 110
praise 115, 138
precision teaching 37, 52, 120, 132–143, 166
prescriptive teaching 43, 69, 100
prevention 18, 32, 112, 153
primary schools 13, 21, 23, 25, 60, 73, 77–89, 101, 104, 107, 124, 142, 155, 165, 187
probes 135, 142
problem solving 120, 163–175
psycholinguistics 146–148
psychometrics 10, 13, 18, 145, 149–150

rate of learning 135–136, 140, 143
ratio chart 136–138, 140
readability 17, 116, 154
reading 2, 7, 8, 10, 11, 15–17, 23, 47, 65–68, 92, 99, 106, 108, 110, 139, 142, 145–159
relational learning 164, 167
Religious Education 75
remedial centres 13, 20, 40, 41
remedial classes 20, 47, 63–76, 92, 197
remedial departments 41, 44, 52, 64, 69–73, 178–181, 197–201
remedial education, definitions 1–2, 4, 7, 8, 30–37, 40, 43, 50–52, 60
resources 20–28, 45, 60, 63, 75, 78, 83, 94, 133, 155, 179, 193
resources model, resource room model 103–111
retardation 12–13, 28, 30, 35, 51, 106, 149, 198

Salford Sentence Reading Test 158
sanctuary units 104
school leavers 193–195
school organisation 52, 60, 63–76, 92–102, 104–111, 179, 191–194
Schools Council 15, 21, 26, 151–162, 183–184, 189

schools' psychological services 70, 87, 106–107, 110, 142
Science 25–26, 68, 74, 93, 97–98, 100, 102, 105, 108, 120, 177, 189
screening 79, 106, 130
secondary schools 10, 13, 21, 23, 47, 50, 60, 63–76, 92–102, 103–111, 124, 142, 165, 179–188
segregation 79
slow learners 2, 4, 21, 25–27, 42, 51, 63–76, 92, 117, 132, 165, 182, 193
social competence 84–85
Social Studies 193
sociological perspectives 145, 153
SPAR Reading Test 65, 68, 76
special classes 8, 14, 20–21, 40, 65–68, 71, 178, 197
special education 1, 24, 32, 34, 40, 42, 44–46, 71, 78, 80, 105, 117, 125, 165, 178, 197
special needs 1, 22, 24, 43–44, 47, 74, 77–89, 108–111, 112, 132, 145, 150–152, 178–180, 186, 188, 193–194, 199–201
Special Needs Action Programme (SNAP) 77–89, 179
Special Resources Department (SRD) 105–111
special schools 1, 22, 32, 40, 44, 45, 47, 82, 87, 105, 177
specific difficulties 34, 198
specific learning disabilities 106, 108–109, 120, 199
specific reading difficulties 145–159
speech therapist 106, 110
spelling 66, 84–85, 92, 142, 146, 149, 155–157, 198
statement of special educational needs 1, 88, 152, 177
subject teachers 18, 22, 25, 47, 52, 94–102, 178–188, 198–201
support roles within school 18, 43, 69, 71, 88, 106–109, 112–117, 180, 187, 198–201
support services outside school 7, 18, 43, 46–47, 70, 82, 106, 187, 200

task analysis 83, 116, 133, 141, 165
teacher training, initial training 4, 5,

20–25, 28, 64, 71–73
teacher training, in-service training 5,
    21, 23–27, 46–47, 50, 53–57, 60, 64,
    69–73, 77–89, 117, 153
teaching styles 126, 152
team teaching 47, 52, 60, 92–102, 112,
    117, 153, 178
therapy 9, 31, 33, 43

visual skills 146, 148–149, 155–159

whole school approach 179–186
withdrawal 7, 8, 9, 15, 26, 28, 40–41,
    43, 60, 65–68, 71, 74, 99, 101, 108,
    112, 178–180, 197–199
work experience 70, 194
writing 47, 60, 84, 147, 155–158